TODAY'S
SPOKEN
SPANISH

THE SCRIBNER SPANISH SERIES
General Editor, JUAN R.-CASTELLANO
Duke University

TODAY'S SPOKEN SPANISH

Rodger A. Farley
United States Naval Academy

Laura Argüelles de Farley

CHARLES SCRIBNER'S SONS · NEW YORK

PREFACE

This text is designed primarily for third-semester college classes, but can be adapted to first-year college work. Its aim is to give impetus to the development of the audio-lingual skills, to the greatest extent possible within the limitations of the classroom. The rationale of this aim is founded on the assumption that language is first and foremost conversation, a public activity, and that the most natural way to attain the command of a language is by conversing in it. The dialogs, the exercises, all in Spanish and all oral, and the language study section, **Lengua**, provide an intense training in and a modern *description* of *a* Spanish *spoken* in contemporary time.

By "a" Spanish, we mean that the language to be studied is restricted to a single, large region—Central Spain—and therefore is homogeneous in vocabulary, idioms, and syntax. By "description," we mean that the comments on syntax are the observations of popular speech, unprejudiced by traditional rules and formulas. By "spoken," we mean that the Spanish presented is casual speech. The thirty-five dialogs, which were written by the authoress, a native of Madrid, provide the backbone for the daily class activity. The examples used to illustrate structural and lexical items also are based on native conversational speech, never on the prose of literary figures of this or any century.

Each dialog, with its accompanying vocabulary, oral exercises, and references to **Lengua**, is a unit and should not be divided, except in the case of first-year classes. The program for each recitation entails:

1. A dialog that should be presented orally as a skit, one or more times.
2. References to **Lengua**, the language study section, concerning structural and lexical items appearing in the dialog.
3. Oral exercises in Spanish, with books closed. *No translations.* At the discretion of the teacher, any of the oral exercises may be assigned as written work.

v

The cultural information contained in this book concerns contemporary activities, habits, foods, institutions, and traditions of the Spanish people. Also, one should not forget that an important aspect of culture is speech. The Spanish used in this text is, for the most part, young people's speech, a casual lexicon set in the most common syntactical patterns.

The dialogs are freely translated through **Diálogo 17**. Thereafter, only difficult passages and those containing some new words are translated. If a word appears for the first time in an untranslated passage or in an exercise, it is put in the **vocabulario adicional.**

We do not claim that this book covers all grammatical features, or any one feature in all its aspects. We have tried to be selective for the purpose of providing the limited knowledge of Spanish syntax and lexicon that we can reasonably expect the young college student to absorb and find conversationally useful.

It is sincerely hoped that the unit-lesson, devoted almost entirely to the development of the audio-lingual skills, will achieve in an efficient and pleasurable way the goal of learning to speak and understand Spanish.

Finally, we wish to acknowledge our indebtedness to Dr. Victor R. B. Oelschläger, Dr. Lincoln Canfield, Dr. Sherman H. Eoff, and Dr. Heberto Lacayo, who read the text in its early stage and made corrections and offered helpful suggestions. We also wish to thank Srta. Enriqueta Argüelles Triviño, a native of Madrid who still resides there, for her complete double check of the Spanish. The writing of this text also profited by discussions with Dr. Guy Riccio, and by the consultation of articles by Dr. William Bull, Dr. Dwight Bolinger, Mr. Gordon Fish, and others. We are particularly grateful to Dr. Juan R.-Castellano for his critical readings of the type-script, for his professional and practical guidance, and especially for his friendly encouragement throughout the entire text project.

R.A.F.
L.A.F.

FOREWORD

To the Teacher

We suggest this class procedure and program:

Procedure—

1. Speak Spanish as much as possible, and utilize signals, gestures, or drawings to get your idea across without resorting to English. Try to imagine yourself a Spanish-speaking native who knows little or no English.

It will be noted that the instructions given for the exercises are in Spanish, and that the terms used are not in the lesson's vocabulary. This means that the student must get the meaning of the instruction from the example. If he fails to understand, call on a student who indicates that he does understand, and then return to the first student after the pattern of the exercise has been made clear.

2. When the individual recites, he should speak forcefully. Do not hesitate to prompt the student and to require him to repeat when he falters. *Insist on an acceptable pronunciation.*

3. A few props can do much to help create the environment of the dialogs, and thus make the acting out of the rôles more natural.

Program—

Order of activities:

1. Read rapidly the entire dialog to the class.
2. Students present the dialog as a skit. Two or more groups should put on the skits.
3. Oral exercises. Students' books are closed.
4. Remarks on grammar of the day, *only* if necessary.
5. Read the dialog for the next lesson, the students reading in unison after you. Assign the various rôles.

You will note that the examples given in the oral exercises always involve a **profesor** and an **alumno**. This is not a slight of the fairer sex but merely a concession to expediency. You should make these terms agree with the true situation.

To the Student

1. If you earnestly wish to converse fluently in Spanish, do not develop the bad habit of translating mentally. To help you avoid this common student habit, you will find free translations of the dialogs through **Diálogo 17**, and from there on, only the more difficult speeches. The simple exercises, totally in Spanish, attempt to oblige you to respond in Spanish to a stimulus in Spanish. A conscientious and sustained effort to avoid letting English unnecessarily wedge itself in between the Spanish stimuli and the Spanish responses, plus the acting out of the various rôles of the dialogs, will aid you immeasurably to speak Spanish correctly and fluently.

2. Do your work when assigned. Continuous learning in "bite" size amounts is the *only* way to master a foreign language.

3. The vocabulary for which you are held responsible consists not only of the words in the dialogs and those given in the **modismos y vocabulario adicional** but also those appearing in the reference paragraphs of **Lengua.**

CONTENTS

CONTENTS

xi

TODAY'S
SPOKEN
SPANISH

DIÁLOGO 1

En casa de Pilar

Personajes: Pilar, Mari (su hermana), y sus padres

PADRE.—Hija, este año es tu primer año en la Universidad.

Daughter, this year is your first (*freshman*) year at the university.

PILAR.—Así es, papá, y espero terminar la carrera en cinco años.

That's right, Dad, and I hope to finish my college work in five years.

PADRE.—Cinco años de universidad para ser Licenciada en Filosofía y Letras.

Five years of university to get your Master's degree in Liberal Arts.

MADRE.—Vas a aprender muchas cosas interesantes.

You are going to learn many interesting things.

MARI.—Y vas a tener muchas experiencias interesantes.

And you are going to have many interesting experiences.

PILAR.—Espero que sí.

I hope so.

MADRE.—¿Cómo se llama tu amiga?

What is your girl friend's name?

PILAR.—Se llama Elisa Ruiz Iriarte.

Her name is Elisa Ruiz Iriarte.

PADRE.—¿Dónde vive?

Where does she live?

MARI.—¿No vive en la Calle de Serrano?

Doesn't she live on Serrano street?

PILAR.—Sí.

Yes.

MADRE.—¿Vive con sus padres?

Does she live with her parents?

PILAR.—Sí, y con un hermano que va al Instituto.

Yes, and with a brother who goes to the *Instituto.**

* Public secondary school, attended between the ages of 10 and 18.

1

Una casa de pisos en la Calle de Serrano

MADRE.—¿Dónde trabaja su padre?	Where does her father work?
PILAR.—En una compañía de seguros. La familia de Elisa es muy simpática.	In an insurance company. Elisa's family is very nice.
MARI.—Elisa es simpática, pero habla mucho.	Elisa is nice, but she talks a lot.
PADRE.—Hija, ¿qué mujer no habla mucho?	Daughter, what woman doesn't talk a lot?

LENGUA (Ver 1–8.)*

* The language study section, LENGUA, toward the back of the text, should be consulted. The indicated paragraphs cover certain points of language appearing in the dialog and those incorporated in the oral exercises. *The student must study this section in order to be able to do the exercises.*

DIÁLOGO 1

MODISMOS Y VOCABULARIO ADICIONAL

Así es. That's right.
Espero que sí. I hope so.
se llama his (her, your) name is
la casa de pisos apartment house

la lección lesson
quién who
voy I go, I am going

EJERCICIOS ORALES

1. Dar las siguientes palabras en forma singular y plural, usando los artículos definidos. (2–3.)

Ejemplo: EL PROFESOR:—año

    EL ALUMNO:—**el año, los años**

hija	radio	toro	ciudad
amiga	cosa	mano	maniquí
familia	calle	experiencia	año
lección	avión	padre	
especie	coche	costumbre	

2. Unir los substantivos con la preposición **de.** (7.)

Ejemplo: EL PROFESOR.—los libros—Elisa

    EL ALUMNO.—**los libros de Elisa**

una compañía—aviones	el coche—tu padre
las costumbres—Pilar	una casa—pisos
la amiga—la hermana	unas casas—pisos
los padres—tu amigo	la religión—la madre
una compañía—seguros	los libros—Elisa

3. Unir "Elisa habla a" con las palabras dadas. (8.)

Ejemplo: EL PROFESOR.—el policía

    EL ALUMNO.—**Elisa habla al policía.**

el amigo	el padre	los profesores
la amiga	la madre	la profesora
los padres	el profesor	los amigos
las amigas	las profesoras	el policía

3

4. Cambiar a la forma negativa. (6.)

Ejemplo: EL PROFESOR.—Va a la Universidad.
EL ALUMNO.—**No va a la Universidad.**

Va al Instituto.
Vive con sus padres.
Vive en la Calle de Serrano.
Su padre trabaja.
El hermano de Elisa habla mucho.
La familia de Elisa es simpática.
Su hermana trabaja.

Vas a aprender.
Vas a aprender muchas cosas.
Voy a terminar la carrera.
Su hermano trabaja.
La familia es simpática.
Voy a terminar la carrera en cinco años.
Espero terminar la carrera en cinco años.
Va a la Universidad.

5. Expresar como preguntas. (5. La entonación es muy importante.)

Ejemplo: EL PROFESOR.—Elisa habla mucho.
EL ALUMNO.— **¿Habla mucho Elisa?** o **¿Elisa habla mucho?**

Elisa trabaja.
La madre trabaja.
La madre de Elisa trabaja.
Su amiga habla mucho.
La amiga de Pilar habla mucho.
Elisa va a la Universidad.

Elisa vive en la calle de Serrano.
La familia vive en una casa de pisos.
Su hermano va al Instituto.
Los padres son simpáticos.
Elisa habla mucho.

PREGUNTAS SOBRE EL DIÁLOGO

1. ¿A dónde va Pilar este año? 2. ¿Es su primer año en la Universidad? 3. ¿Cuándo va a terminar la carrera? 4. ¿Qué va a aprender Pilar? 5. ¿Qué va a tener? 6. ¿Cómo se llama la amiga de Pilar? 7. ¿Dónde vive Elisa? 8. ¿Vive Elisa con sus padres? 9. ¿Trabaja el padre de Elisa? 10. ¿Dónde trabaja? 11. ¿Tiene Elisa hermanos? 12. ¿Va el hermano a la Universidad? 13. ¿Es simpática Elisa? 14. ¿Es simpática la familia de Elisa? 15. ¿Quién habla mucho?

4

DIÁLOGO 2

El desayuno en casa de Elisa

Personajes: Juan, Elisa (su hermana), su madre

JUAN.—¿Está el desayuno?

Is breakfast ready?

MAMÁ.—Está en la mesa. Hay pan tostado y chocolate.

It's on the table. There's toast and cocoa.

ELISA. (*Entra.*)—Buenos días, mamá. ¿Cómo estás hoy?

(*She enters.*) Good morning, Mama. How are you today?

MAMÁ.—No muy bien.

Not very well.

ELISA.—¿Llamo al médico?

Shall I call the doctor?

MAMÁ.—No es necesario. Anda, el desayuno está en la mesa.

It's not necessary. Come on, breakfast is on the table.

ELISA.—¡Ay! Una mancha de chocolate en mi falda de lana.

Ay! A spot of cocoa on my wool skirt.

MAMÁ.—¡Qué lástima! La llevamos al tinte hoy.

What a shame! We'll take it to the cleaners today.

ELISA.—No importa. No es grande.

It doesn't matter. It isn't big.

MAMÁ. (*A Elisa.*)—¿No terminas el chocolate?

Aren't you going to finish the cocoa?

JUAN.—Si no comes, no engordas.

If you don't eat, you won't get fat.

ELISA.—¡Mejor!

All the better!

MAMÁ.—Juanito, ¿estudias tus lecciones todos los días?

Juanito, do you study your lessons every day?

5

JUAN.—Sí, mamá, y escribo los ejercicios.	Yes, Mama, and I write the homework.
ELISA.—Es tarde. No termino el desayuno. Espero encontrar a Pilar en la parada del trolebús.	It's late. I'm not finishing my breakfast. I hope to meet Pilar at the trolley bus stop.
MAMÁ.—¿Dónde vive tu amiga?	Where does your friend live?
ELISA.—En la Calle de Velázquez. Bueno, adiós.	On Velazquez Street. Well, good-by.
MAMÁ.—Adiós, hija.	Good-by, dear.
ELISA.—¡Ah! Hoy no como en casa.	Oh! I'm not eating lunch at home today.

LENGUA (Ver 9–11.)

MODISMOS Y VOCABULARIO ADICIONAL

Anda. Come on.
Adiós. Good-by.
¡Qué lástima! What a shame!
¡Mejor! All the better!
Hay clase hoy. There is school today.

abrir to open	el **huevo** egg
el **autobús** bus	la **leche** milk
beber to drink	**leer** to read
el **café** coffee	la **mantequilla** butter
hay there is, there are	la **mermelada** preserves
	el **tranvía** streetcar

EJERCICIOS ORALES

1. Hacer concordar la forma verbal con el sujeto dado. (10.)

   Ejemplo: EL PROFESOR.—Llamar al médico. **yo**
   EL ALUMNO.—**Yo llamo al médico.**

   Llamar al médico. **tú, ella, usted, Elisa, nosotros, tú y yo, vosotros, tú y ella, ellos, Juan y Elisa, yo**
   No comer en casa. **yo, tú, el médico, nosotros, Juan y yo, vosotros, Mari y tú, ellas, ustedes**

6

La parada del trolebús

2. Repetir el verbo, dando el pronombre adecuado. (10.)

    Ejemplo: EL PROFESOR.—Comen.

           EL ALUMNO.—**Ellas comen.**

Llamo.	Bebe.	Abres.	Aprendes.	Abrís.
Estudias.	Coméis.	Engordas.	Aprenden.	Escribe.
Habláis.	Reciben.	Esperamos.	Leemos.	Comemos.
Como.	Vivimos.	Llevan.		

3. Expresar como preguntas. (5. La entonación es muy importante.)

Hay pan.	Hay pan y chocolate.
No hay mantequilla.	No hay mermelada.
Hay huevos.	No hay chocolate.
No hay huevos.	Hay café.
No hay café.	No hay pan tostado.

7

4. Contestar afirmativamente las siguientes preguntas.

Ejemplo: EL PROFESOR.—¿Hay pan?
         EL ALUMNO.—**Sí, hay pan.**

¿Hay pan y chocolate?	¿Hay huevos?
¿Hay café?	¿Hay leche?
¿Hay mermelada?	¿Hay café con leche?
¿Hay mantequilla?	¿Hay clase hoy?
¿Hay pan?	¿Hay pan tostado?

5. Unir los substantivos con la preposición **de**. (7, 11.)

Ejemplo: EL PROFESOR.—las costumbres—el amigo
         EL ALUMNO.—**las costumbres del amigo**

los padres—el amigo	los padres—la amiga
los libros—la hermana	los libros—el hermano
la parada—el trolebús	la parada—el tranvía
la parada—el autobús	la experiencia—el policía
la madre—los amigos	el café—el desayuno
la compañía—el padre	las cosas—el médico
las faldas—las hermanas	las costumbres—el amigo

PREGUNTAS SOBRE EL DIÁLOGO

1. ¿Está el desayuno? 2. ¿Dónde está el desayuno? 3. ¿Hay pan tostado? 4. ¿Hay chocolate? 5. ¿Cómo está la madre de Elisa? 6. ¿Es necesario llamar al médico? 7. ¿Es la falda de Elisa de nylon? 8. ¿Es grande la mancha? 9. ¿La llevan al tinte? 10. ¿Termina Elisa el chocolate? 11. ¿Estudia Juan todos los días? 12. ¿Qué escribe Juan? 13. ¿A dónde va Elisa? 14. ¿Cómo se llama la amiga de Elisa? 15. ¿Dónde vive Pilar? 16. ¿Come Elisa en casa hoy?

DIÁLOGO 3

Antes de entrar en la clase

Personajes: Elisa, Pilar, Ricardo, y Lorenzo

ELISA.—Ésta es la clase de Historia.

This is the history class (*room*).

PILAR.—Vamos a esperar en la puerta.

Let's wait at the door.

ELISA.—No veo muchos alumnos.

I don't see many students.

PILAR.—Mira a esos dos chicos que van por el pasillo.

Look at those two fellows going down the hall.

ELISA.—Parecen interesantes.

They look interesting.

PILAR.—Veo al chico de gris con frecuencia. Vive cerca de casa.

I see the fellow in the gray suit frequently. He lives near home.

RICARDO.—Chico, las clases van a ser difíciles.

Boy, the classes are going to be tough.

LORENZO.—Hay siete asignaturas en el primer año.

There are seven subjects in the freshman (*the first*) year.

RICARDO.—Literatura y Arte son interesantes.

Literature and art are interesting.

LORENZO.—Espero ser profesor de Arte en el futuro.

I hope to become an art teacher in the future.

RICARDO.—Pues en el presente, yo espero encontrar chicas guapas entre las compañeras.

Well in the present, I hope to meet some good-looking girls among the (*female*) classmates.

9

LORENZO.—Yo también, porque si no, va a ser muy aburrido.

I also (hope so), because if I don't, it is going to be very boring.

RICARDO.—Hablas de chicas guapas; pues, mira a dos estupendas.

You speak of good-looking girls; well, look at a couple of beauties.

LORENZO.—¿Dónde?

Where?

RICARDO.—Cerca de la puerta de la clase de Historia.

Near the door of the history class.

LORENZO.—Vamos a hablar con ellas.

Let's go talk with them.

PILAR.—¡Se acercan a nosotras!

They're coming over to us!

LENGUA (Ver 12–14.)

Un aula en la Facultad de Filosofía y Letras

DIÁLOGO 3

MODISMOS Y VOCABULARIO ADICIONAL

Vamos a/infinitivo   Let's/verb
ir a/infinitivo   to be going/infinitive
ir a casa   to go home
cerca de   near

con frecuencia   frequently
de gris   in gray, i.e., dressed in gray, in the gray suit

alemán   German
el **centro**   downtown
cuánto(s)   how much (many)
la **enfermera**   nurse

francés   French
el **hombre**   man
inglés   English
el **piso**   apartment, floor

Present indicative of **ser** (to be), **ver** (to see), **ir** (to go):

ser: **soy, eres, es, somos, sois, son**
ver: **veo, ves, ve, vemos, veis, ven**
ir: **voy, vas, va, vamos, vais, van**

EJERCICIOS ORALES

1. Contestar negativamente. (12.)

   Ejemplo: EL PROFESOR.—¿Es usted profesor?
   EL ALUMNO.—**No, no soy profesor.**

   ¿Es usted médico?
   ¿Es Lorenzo profesor de idiomas?
   ¿Es usted amigo de Pilar?
   ¿Es usted pintor?
   ¿Él es hermano de Elisa?
   ¿Es francés el pintor?

   ¿Es carpintero su padre?
   ¿Es alemana su madre?
   ¿Es inglesa la enfermera?
   ¿Es usted amigo del médico?
   ¿Es ella americana?
   ¿Es usted profesor?

2. Cambiar las oraciones, siguiendo el ejemplo. (13.)

   EL PROFESOR.—El libro es interesante.
   EL ALUMNO.—**Es un libro interesante.**

   Los libros son interesantes.
   La novela es aburrida.
   Las novelas son aburridas.
   El pintor es alemán.
   La enfermera es española.
   La profesora es simpática.

   El piso es grande.
   La familia es simpática.
   El médico es famoso.
   Las chicas son encantadoras.
   Los niños son llorones.
   El libro es interesante.

11

3. Contestar, siguiendo el ejemplo. (14.)

EL PROFESOR.—¿A quién mira usted? **el hermano de Elisa**
EL ALUMNO.—**Miro al hermano de Elisa.**

¿A quién mira usted? **el profesor**
¿A quiénes miran ustedes? **el pintor y la enfermera**
¿A quién miran ellos? **el hombre de gris**
¿A quién mira Elisa? **el americano**
¿A quién mira Lorenzo? **la chica cerca de la puerta**
¿A quiénes mira Ricardo? **las dos chicas cerca de la puerta**
¿A quién ve Pilar todos los días? **el chico de gris**
¿A quién ve usted? **el amigo de Juan**
¿A quién mira usted? **el hermano de Elisa**

4. El verbo *ir*. Seguir el ejemplo:

EL PROFESOR.—Él va a la Universidad. ¿Y usted?
EL ALUMNO.—**Yo también voy a la Universidad.**

Yo voy a casa. ¿Y usted?
Ellos van al centro? ¿Y ustedes?
Pili va a ser enfermera. ¿Y su hermana?
Yo voy a ser médico. ¿Y tú?
Nosotros vamos a la clase de Arte. ¿Y vosotros?
Los profesores van a comer. ¿Y los alumnos?
Juan va. ¿Y yo?
Él va a la Universidad. ¿Y usted?

PREGUNTAS SOBRE EL DIÁLOGO

1. ¿Dónde esperan Elisa y Pilar? 2. ¿Ven ellas muchos alumnos? 3. ¿A quiénes miran? 4. ¿Por dónde van los chicos? 5. ¿Cómo parecen los chicos? 6. ¿A quién ve Pilar con frecuencia? 7. ¿Dónde vive el chico de gris? 8. ¿Qué va a ser difícil? 9. ¿Cuántas asignaturas hay en el primer año? 10. ¿Qué asignaturas son interesantes? 11. ¿Qué espera ser Lorenzo? 12. ¿Qué espera encontrar Ricardo? 13. ¿Qué ven los dos chicos? 14. ¿Cómo son las dos chicas? 15. ¿Dónde esperan las dos chicas? 16. ¿Con quiénes van a hablar los dos chicos?

DIÁLOGO 4

El encuentro

Personajes: Ricardo, Pilar, Lorenzo, Elisa

RICARDO.—Perdón. ¿Es aquí la clase de Historia?

Pardon me. Is the history class (*held*) here?

PILAR.—Sí. Es la clase de primer año.

Yes. It's the first year class.

LORENZO.—Es la clase que buscamos.

That's the class we are looking for.

RICARDO.—Estudiamos primer año.

We're freshmen.

ELISA.—Nosotras también.

So are we.

RICARDO.—Entonces vamos a ser compañeros. Me llamo Ricardo Pacheco Durán.

Then we are going to be classmates. My name is Ricardo Pacheco Duran.

LORENZO.—Lorenzo Ortiz Álvarez. ¿Cómo os llamáis?

Lorenzo Ortiz Alvarez. What are your names?

ELISA.—Elisa Ruiz Iriarte.

Elisa Ruiz Iriarte.

PILAR.—Pilar Martínez Aparicio.

Pilar Martinez Aparicio.

TODOS.—Mucho gusto.

(*All.*) Very glad to know you.

LORENZO.—No tenemos el horario y no sabemos a qué hora son las clases.

We don't have the schedule and we don't know when the classes are.

PILAR.—Yo lo tengo. La clase de Historia es a las nueve.

I have it. The history class is at nine o'clock.

RICARDO.—¿Tienes un lápiz, por favor? Voy a copiar el horario.

Do you have a pencil, please? I'm going to copy the schedule.

13

LORENZO.—Aquí tienes mi pluma.

Here's my pen.

RICARDO.—Gracias. ¿Qué tal es el profesor?

Thanks. What's the teacher like?

ELISA.—Viene de la Universidad de Salamanca y dicen que hace estudiar.

He comes from the University of Salamanca and they say that he makes you work.

PILAR.—¿Qué hora es?

What time is it?

RICARDO.—Son las nueve menos diez.

It is ten of nine.

ELISA.—¿Entramos en la clase?

Shall we go in class?

PILAR.—Bueno, es casi la hora.

Well, it's almost time.

LORENZO.—¿Tenéis algo que hacer después de la clase?
(*Pilar da un codazo a Elisa.*)

Do you have anything to do after class? (*Pilar nudges Elisa.*)

ELISA.—Tenemos que comprar los libros.

We have to buy our books.

RICARDO.—Podemos ir juntos.

We can go together.

LENGUA (Ver 15–18.)

La Ciudad Universitaria desde la Facultad de Filosofía y Letras

DIÁLOGO 4

MODISMOS Y VOCABULARIO ADICIONAL

estudiar primer año   to be a freshman
¿Cómo os llamáis?   What are your names? (familiar, plural)
¿Cómo se llama usted?   What is your name? (formal, singular)
Me llamo . . .   My name is . . .
Mucho gusto.   Very glad to know you.
por favor   please
Aquí tienes . . .   Here is . . .
¿Qué tal es . . .?   What is . . . like?
substantivo/que/infinitivo   substantive/infinitive
tener que/infinitivo   to have to/verb, must/verb
dar un codazo   to nudge
todos los días   every day

preguntar   to ask, to inquire
la verdad   truth
si   whether, if

The present indicative of **tener** (to have), **decir** (to say, to tell), **venir** (to come):

tener: **tengo, tienes, tiene, tenemos, tenéis, tienen**
decir: **digo, dices, dice, decimos, decís, dicen**
venir: **vengo, vienes, viene, venimos, venís, vienen**

EJERCICIOS ORALES

1. Escribir el número en la pizarra después de hacer la pregunta. (17.)

   Ejemplo: EL PROFESOR.—¿A qué hora es la clase?   **9**
   EL ALUMNO.—**La clase es a las nueve.**

   ¿A qué hora es la clase?   **8, 10, 11, 1, 2, 3, 9**
   ¿A qué hora vienen ellos?   **4:30, 6:15, 7:20, 12:45, 5:30**

2. Dibujar la esfera de un reloj en la pizarra y, cambiando las manecillas, preguntar "¿Qué hora es?" (18.)

3. Los verbos **venir, decir,** y **tener.** Hacer concordar la forma verbal con el sujeto dado.

   Ejemplo: EL PROFESOR.—Venir todos los días.   **yo**
   EL ALUMNO.—**Yo vengo todos los días.**

   Venir todos los días.   **ella, nosotros, tú, tú y Pilar, el profesor, Lorenzo, Pilar y yo, yo**

   Decir la verdad.   **ella, ellas, el profesor, yo, nosotros, Juan y yo, los amigos de Elisa, tú**

   Tener que preguntar al profesor.   **él, vosotros, yo, los amigos de Lorenzo, ustedes, Elisa, tú y yo**

15

4. Preguntar el nombre al compañero, dando primero el nombre propio.

Ejemplo: JOHN BROWN.—Me llamo John Brown. ¿Cómo se llama usted?
      MARY JONES.—Me llamo Mary Jones. (*A otro alumno.*)
              Me llamo Mary Jones. ¿Cómo se llama usted?
      OTRO ALUMNO.—Me llamo . . . etc.

5. Contestar afirmativamente.

Ejemplo: EL PROFESOR.—¿Es la clase que buscan ustedes?
      EL ALUMNO.—**Sí, es la clase que buscamos.**
¿Es el libro que compra usted?
¿Es la calle que buscas?
¿Son las lecciones que vas a estudiar?
¿Es la falda que busca ella?
¿Es el chico que ves con frecuencia?
¿Es el horario que vais a copiar?
¿Son los libros que tiene usted que comprar?
¿Es la clase que buscan ustedes?

PREGUNTAS SOBRE EL DIÁLOGO

1. ¿Qué clase buscan los chicos? 2. ¿Qué año estudian los chicos? 3. ¿Qué año estudian las dos chicas? 4. ¿Quiénes van a ser compañeros? 5. ¿Cómo se llama el amigo de Ricardo? 6. ¿Cómo se llama la amiga de Elisa? 7. ¿Tienen los chicos el horario? 8. ¿Quién tiene el horario? 9. ¿A qué hora es la clase de Historia? 10. ¿Tiene Ricardo un lápiz? 11. ¿Qué va a copiar Ricardo? 12. ¿Qué tal es el profesor? 13. ¿De dónde viene el profesor? 14. ¿Qué hora es? 15. ¿Qué pregunta Lorenzo a las chicas? 16. ¿Qué tienen que comprar las chicas después de la clase?

DIÁLOGO 5

¡No hay clase!

Personajes: Pilar, Ricardo, Elisa, Lorenzo, el bedel*

ELISA.—Es un aula grande y hay muy poca gente. ¡Qué raro! ¿Verdad?

This is a large classroom, and there are very few people. That's strange! Isn't it?

PILAR.—Y ahora, ¿qué pasa? Salen todos.

And what's up now? Everybody is leaving.

RICARDO.—No sé. Salgo a preguntar. (*Sale.*)

I don't know. I'll go out and ask. (*He goes out.*)

ELISA.—Hace un día hermoso.

It's a beautiful day.

LORENZO.—Demasiado hermoso para estar en clase.

Too beautiful to be in class.

RICARDO.—(*Entrando.*) ¡La gran noticia! ¡No hay clase! Ni mañana tampoco.

(*Entering.*) The great news! There's no class! Nor tomorrow either.

ELISA.—¿Por qué?

Why?

RICARDO.—El profesor no está en Madrid.

The teacher isn't in Madrid.

PILAR.—¡Viva! ¿Qué hacemos?

Hurrah! What'll we do?

ELISA.—Tenemos una hora libre para dar un paseo.

We have a free hour to take a stroll.

LORENZO.—Eso es algo que yo nunca hago.

That's something I never do.

* A sort of uniformed handy man. There are usually several in every university building.

RICARDO.—Sobre todo cuando hay un bar cerca.

Especially when there is a (*snack*) bar nearby.

LORENZO.—No sé si es un buen bar pero hay uno en la Facultad.

I don't know whether it is a good bar, but there is one in the building (*i.e., the Liberal Arts building*).

RICARDO.—¿Podéis venir con nosotros?

Can you come with us?

ELISA Y PILAR.—Encantadas.

We'd love to.

PILAR.—¿Por dónde vamos al bar?

How do we get to the bar?

LORENZO.—No sé. Voy a preguntar. (*Al bedel.*) Perdón. ¿Puede usted indicarme dónde está el bar?

I don't know. I'll ask. (*To the beadle.*) Pardon me. Can you tell me where the bar is?

BEDEL.—El nuevo bar está en el piso bajo. Tienen que bajar por aquí. Es la única escalera.

The new bar is on the ground floor. You have to go down here (this way). It's the only stairway.

LORENZO.—Muchas gracias.

Thank you very much.

BEDEL.—De nada.

You're welcome.

RICARDO.—Vamos. Yo invito.

Let's go. I'm treating.

ELISA.—¡Pobre chico!

Poor fellow!

LENGUA (Ver 19–21.)

MODISMOS Y VOCABULARIO ADICIONAL

¿**Qué pasa?** What's up?
Hace un día hermoso. It's a beautiful day.
¡**Viva!** Hurrah!
dar un paseo to take a stroll

sobre todo especially
el **piso bajo** ground floor
De nada. You're welcome.
Vamos. Let's go.

el **autor** author
la **bailarina** dancer
la **canción** song
  divertido amusing
  emocionante thrilling
la **escuela** school

inteligente intelligent
el **inventor** inventor
largo long
moderno modern
la **película** film
popular popular

18

En el bar de la Facultad de Filosofía y Letras

Present indicative of **hacer** (to make, to do), **poder** (I*, to be able, can), **saber** (to know, to know how), **salir** (to go out, to leave):

hacer: **hago, haces, hace, hacemos, hacéis, hacen**
poder: **puedo, puedes, puede, podemos, podéis, pueden**
saber: **sé, sabes, sabe, sabemos, sabéis, saben**
salir: **salgo, sales, sale, salimos, salís, salen**

EJERCICIOS ORALES

1. (20.) *Ejemplo:* EL PROFESOR.—Las chicas son altas.
              EL ALUMNO.—**Son chicas altas.**

La clase es aburrida.
Los libros son interesantes.
El niño es encantador.
Las novelas son españolas.
La novela es larga y emocionante.
La película es interesante y emocionante.

El ejercicio es fácil.
Los ejercicios son difíciles.
Las niñas son encantadoras.
La chica es alta.
Las chicas son altas.
Las películas son largas y aburridas.

* Stem-vowel changes in verbs are denoted by I, II, and III. Check the **Addendum**, section 4.

19

2. (20.) *Ejemplo:* EL PROFESOR.—¡Qué mala idea! **día**
   EL ALUMNO.—**¡Qué mal día!**

¡Qué buenos ejercicios!	escuela, profesor, ejercicio, costumbres, médico
Algunas faldas.	huevos, universidad, médicos, día, cosas, libro
Ninguna compañía.	profesor, amiga, autobús, alumna, madre, alumno
La famosa Universidad de Salamanca.	autor Cervantes, hermanos Wright, bailarinas Rockettes, médico Salk, inventor Edison
¡Qué mal pintor!	café, costumbres, alumnos, idea, día

3. (20.) *Ejemplo:* EL PROFESOR.—El empleado público es honrado.
   EL ALUMNO.—**Es un empleado público honrado.**

La canción moderna es popular.	Las novelas modernas son aburridas.
Las novelas españolas son famosas.	La película francesa es emocionante.
El inventor americano es célebre.	Los jefes militares son rivales.
El profesor de idiomas es inteligente.	El empleado público es honrado.

4. Los verbos **hacer, saber,** y **salir.**

Ejemplo: EL PROFESOR.—Salir hoy.
   EL ALUMNO.—**Yo salgo hoy. Tú sales hoy. Él sale hoy. Nosotros salimos hoy. Vosotros salís hoy. Ellos salen hoy.**

Poder salir hoy.	No saber qué pasa.
¿Qué hacer ahora?	Salir hoy.

PREGUNTAS SOBRE EL DIÁLOGO

1. ¿Quiénes salen de la clase? 2. ¿Sabe Ricardo qué pasa? 3. ¿Qué hace Ricardo? 4. ¿Qué tal día hace? 5. Cuando Ricardo entra, ¿qué dice? 6. ¿Por qué no hay clase? 7. ¿Cuántas horas libres tienen? 8. ¿Van a dar un paseo? 9. ¿Quién nunca da paseos? 10. ¿A dónde van los chicos? 11. ¿Pueden ir las chicas? 12. ¿Qué pregunta Lorenzo al bedel? 13. ¿Dónde está el bar? 14. Cuando Lorenzo dice "gracias", ¿qué dice el bedel? 15. ¿Quién invita?

DIÁLOGO 6

En el bar

Personajes: Ricardo, Pilar, Lorenzo, Elisa

RICARDO.—¡Qué suerte encontrar una mesa vacía!

What luck to find an empty table!

PILAR.—Parece que hay más gente aquí que en las clases.

There seem to be more people here than in class.

LORENZO.—Es mucho más divertido estar aquí que asistir a clase.

It's much more fun to be here than to attend class.

RICARDO.—Hay un cine cerca con una película inglesa emocionante.

There is a movie house nearby with a thrilling English picture.

LORENZO.—Eso sí que es más divertido.

That's really more fun.

ELISA.—Pero no sabemos si vamos a tener libres otras dos horas.

But we don't know whether we are going to have free two more (*other*) hours.

PILAR.—No conoces a los profesores de Latín y Literatura, ¿verdad?

You don't know the teachers of Latin and literature, do you?

RICARDO.—Dicen que nunca faltan a clase.

They say that they never miss class.

LORENZO.—Pues vamos a tomar algo ya que tenemos sólo una hora libre.

Well, let's have something since we have only one free hour.

RICARDO.—¿Qué vais a tomar?

What are you going to have?

Un cine en una calle de Madrid

ELISA.—Coca-Cola, nada más.

A Coke. Nothing else.

PILAR.—Un batido de fresa.

A strawberry shake.

LORENZO.—Nosotros, cerveza. ¿Verdad, Ricardo?

We'll have beer. Right, Ricardo?

RICARDO.—Por supuesto. Nunca bebo nada sin alcohol.

Of course. I never drink anything without alcohol.

ELISA.—¿No bebes agua nunca?

Don't you ever drink water?

RICARDO.—Sí, cuando tomo aspirina.

Yes, when I take aspirin.

22

DIÁLOGO 6

PILAR.—¡Qué chistoso!

How funny!

LORENZO.—¿No viene nadie a ayudarme a traer las cosas?

Isn't anyone coming to help me bring the stuff?

RICARDO.—Yo voy. (*Se van.*)

I'll go. (*They go off.*)

ELISA.—La vida universitaria parece divertida.

University life seems to be fun.

PILAR.—¡Y qué suerte tener unos compañeros tan simpáticos! ¿Qué toca la radio?

And what luck to have such nice (*male*) classmates! What's the radio playing?

ELISA.—Es una canción moderna popular.

It's a popular modern song.

PILAR.—Pues no la conozco.

Well, I don't know it.

ELISA.—Es bonita. Yo sé la letra si la quieres.

It's pretty. I know the words if you want them.

LENGUA (Ver 22–24.)

MODISMOS Y VOCABULARIO ADICIONAL

parece que hay   there seem to be
es divertido   it is fun
asistir a   to attend
eso sí que es   that is really, that indeed is
nada más   nothing else, that's all
por supuesto   of course

allí there	**italiano** Italian
la **contestación** answer	**leer** to read
contestar to answer	el **nombre** name
el **dinero** money	**para** for, in order to
enviar to send	el **restorán** restaurant
España Spain	el **terreno** terrain

Present indicative of **conocer** (to know) and **dar** (to give):

conocer: **conozco, conoces, conoce, conocemos, conocéis, conocen**
dar: **doy, das, da, damos, dais, dan**

23

EJERCICIOS ORALES

1. (22.)   *Ejemplo:* EL PROFESOR.—Él no habla español.
                    EL ALUMNO.—**Pero usted habla español, ¿verdad?**
                    EL PROFESOR.—Sí.

Ella no habla inglés.
Ellos no van a dar más.
Los otros profesores no trabajan hoy.
Mis amigos no saben leer italiano.
Elisa no bebe cerveza.

El jefe no viene mañana.
Ellos no van a dar más dinero.
Pilar no sabe la lección.
Nosotros no conocemos Madrid.
Él no habla español.

2. **Saber, conocer.** (23.) Contestar negativamente.

Ejemplo: EL PROFESOR.—Usted sabe la lección, ¿verdad?
              EL ALUMNO.—**No, no sé la lección.**

Él sabe leer, ¿verdad?
Ustedes saben su nombre, ¿no?
Usted conoce la ciudad, ¿no es cierto?
Los niños saben contestar bien, ¿verdad?
Usted sabe las señas de Elisa, ¿no?
Usted conoce al profesor de idiomas, ¿verdad?
Los jefes militares conocen el terreno, ¿no es cierto?
Ellas conocen al autor, ¿no?
Usted sabe la lección, ¿verdad?

3. Según el sentido, colocar "conozco" o "sé" delante de la oración. (23.)

Ejemplo: EL PROFESOR.—la contestación
              EL ALUMNO.—**Sé la contestación.**

al hermano de Elisa
hablar español bien
la letra de la canción
al profesor de Historia
un buen restorán

la lección para hoy
a los padres del médico
España y Portugal
escribir inglés
la contestación

DIÁLOGO 6

4. Expresar en la forma negativa doble las siguientes oraciones. (24.)

Ejemplo: EL PROFESOR.—Él siempre compra algo.
     EL ALUMNO.—**Él nunca compra nada.**

Hay algo en la mesa.
Siempre dan algo a los pobres.
Yo veo a alguien.
Conocemos algún buen restorán.
Siempre envío algo a mi madre o a mi padre.
Voy a dar el dinero a alguien.
¿Ustedes tienen algo que decir?
Tenemos una hora libre.
Yo siempre hablo con alguien allí.
Él siempre compra algo.

PREGUNTAS SOBRE EL DIÁLOGO

1. ¿Hay una mesa vacía en el bar? 2. ¿Hay mucha gente allí? 3. ¿Es mucho más divertido asistir a clase? 4. ¿Qué hay cerca? 5. ¿Cómo es la película inglesa? 6. ¿Saben si van a tener libres otras dos horas? 7. ¿Quiénes nunca faltan a clase? 8. ¿Qué va a tomar Elisa? 9. ¿Qué va a tomar Pilar? 10. ¿Qué van a tomar los chicos? 11. ¿Cuándo bebe agua Ricardo? 12. ¿Quién es chistoso? 13. ¿Quién va a ayudar a Lorenzo a traer las cosas? 14. ¿Cómo parece la vida universitaria? 15. ¿Qué toca la radio? 16. ¿Conoce Elisa la canción? 17. ¿Quién sabe la letra de la canción?

DIÁLOGO 7

Cambio de planes

Personajes: Lorenzo, Ricardo, Pilar, Elisa

LORENZO.—Hola, Ricardo. ¿Cómo estás?

Hi, Ricardo. How are you?

RICARDO.—Bien, ¿y tú? Oye, ¿estás ocupado ahora?

Fine, and you? Say, are you busy now?

LORENZO.—No. ¿Por qué?

No. Why?

RICARDO.—¿Quieres venir conmigo al gimnasio?

Do you want to come with me to the gym?

LORENZO.—Sí. Buena idea. Pienso hacer algún ejercicio. Estoy en la biblioteca desde las ocho y media.

Yes. A good idea. I intend to get some exercise. I've been in the library since eight-thirty.

RICARDO.—Vamos andando. No está lejos y el día está hermoso.
(*Andan hacia al gimnasio.*)

Let's walk. It's not far and the day is beautiful.
(*They walk toward the gym.*)

LORENZO.—¡Mira! Pilar y Elisa están ahí en la parada del tranvía.

Look! Pilar and Elisa are over there at the streetcar stop.

RICARDO.—Vamos a hablar con ellas.

Let's talk with them.

LOS CHICOS.—¡Hola! ¿Qué tal?

Hi! How are you?

LAS CHICAS.—¡Hola!

Hi!

26

El tranvía de la Ciudad Universitaria

RICARDO.—¡Qué guapas estáis! ¿A dónde vais?

Aren't you all dressed up! Where are you going?

ELISA.—Al Museo del Prado.

To the Prado Museum.

PILAR.—Hay una conferencia muy interesante.

There is a very interesting lecture.

LORENZO.—¡Estupendo! Vamos con vosotras.

Swell! We'll go with you.

RICARDO.—¡Oye, oye! ¿No vienes conmigo al gimnasio?

Hey, hey! Aren't you coming with me to the gym?

LORENZO.—¿Piensas que voy contigo cuando puedo estar con las chicas?

Do you think that I'm going with you when I can be with the girls?

ELISA.—Si queréis venir con nosotras, el tranvía está ya aquí.

If you want to come with us, the streetcar is here now.

(*Todos suben al tranvía.*)

(*All get on the streetcar.*)

LENGUA (Ver 25, 26.)

MODISMOS Y VOCABULARIO ADICIONAL

pensar/infinitivo   to intend/infinitive
hacer ejercicio   to exercise, to get or do exercise
Vamos andando.   Let's walk.
¿Qué tal?   How are you?
subir a   to get on or in (a vehicle)

aburrido bored, boring	**enfermo** sick
la **carne** meat	**malo** bad, sick
contento happy	la **sopa** soup

Present indicative of **estar** (to be), **pensar** (I, to think, to intend), **querer** (I, to wish, to want, to love):

estar: **estoy, estás, está, estamos, estáis, están**
pensar: **pienso, piensas, piensa, pensamos, pensáis, piensan**
querer: **quiero, quieres, quiere, queremos, queréis, quieren**

EJERCICIOS ORALES

1. (25.)   *Ejemplo:* EL PROFESOR.—¿Dónde está Ricardo?
   EL ALUMNO.—**Ricardo está en casa.**

¿Dónde estás?   ¿Dónde está el hermano de Elisa?
¿Dónde estáis?   ¿Dónde están los padres de Juan?
¿Dónde está usted?   ¿Dónde están los libros?
¿Dónde están ustedes?   ¿Dónde está Ricardo?

2. (25.)   *Ejemplo:* EL PROFESOR.—El agua está fría, ¿verdad?
   EL ALUMNO.—**Sí, está fría.**

La cerveza está fría, ¿verdad?   El batido está frío, ¿no?
Los huevos están calientes, ¿verdad?   Las gambas están riquísimas, ¿verdad?
La sopa está caliente, ¿no?   El pan tostado está preparado, ¿verdad?
La carne está fría, ¿verdad?   El agua está fría, ¿verdad?

3. (25.)   *Ejemplo:* EL PROFESOR.—Estamos preocupados. ¿Y usted?
   EL ALUMNO.—**Yo no estoy preocupado.**

Estoy cansado. ¿Y usted?   Estoy muy contento. ¿Y usted?
Estamos cansados, ¿Y ustedes?   Estamos contentos. ¿Y ellas?
Ella está aburrida. ¿Y él?   Juan está enfermo. ¿Y sus padres?
Los profesores están aburridos. ¿Y los   Estamos preocupados. ¿Y usted?
   alumnos?

28

DIÁLOGO 7

4. Contestar, usando palabras conocidas. (25.)

¿Quién es su amigo?	¿Quiénes son las chicas?
¿Qué es su amigo?	¿Qué son las chicas?
¿Cómo es su amigo?	¿Cómo son las chicas?
¿De dónde es su amigo?	¿De dónde son las chicas?
¿Dónde está su amigo?	¿Dónde están las chicas?
¿Con quién está su amigo?	¿Con quién están las chicas?
¿Cómo está su amigo?	¿Cómo están las chicas?

PREGUNTAS SOBRE EL DIÁLOGO

1. ¿Cómo está Ricardo? 2. ¿Está ocupado Lorenzo? 3. ¿A dónde va Ricardo?
4. ¿Qué piensa hacer Lorenzo? 5. ¿Dónde está Lorenzo? 6. ¿Cómo van al gimnasio?
7. ¿Está lejos el gimnasio? 8. ¿Cómo está el día? 9. ¿Dónde están Pilar y Elisa?
10. ¿Qué van a hacer los chicos? 11. ¿Cómo están ellas? 12. ¿A dónde van ellas?
13. ¿Por qué van al Museo del Prado? 14. ¿Por qué no va Lorenzo al gimnasio?
15. ¿Cómo van al Museo?

DIÁLOGO 8

En el Museo del Prado

Personajes: Lorenzo, Elisa, Ricardo, Pilar, el Sr. Pacheco (profesor de Arte)

(*Al terminar la conferencia.*)

LORENZO.—¡Qué conferencia tan interesante!

ELISA.—El señor Pacheco conoce muy bien la pintura italiana.

LORENZO.—Bueno, ¿qué pensáis hacer ahora?

ELISA.—Yo quiero ir a la sala de los pintores flamencos.

LORENZO.—Voy contigo. Sus pinturas, para mi gusto, son las mejores.

PILAR.—Para mí, no hay pintores como los españoles.

RICARDO.—Y en particular, Goya, ¿verdad?

PILAR.—Claro que sí. A ver si en la pintura contemporánea vuestros gustos coinciden con los míos.

(*When the lecture is over.*)

What an interesting lecture!

Mr. Pacheco knows Italian painting very well.

Well, what do you intend doing now?

I want to go to the gallery of the Flemish painters.

I'll go with you. Their paintings, for my taste, are the best.

As far as I'm concerned, there are no painters like the Spanish.

And in particular, Goya. Right?

Of course. Let's see whether your tastes in contemporary painting coincide with mine.

30

El Museo del Prado

Courtesy Spanish Embassy, Washington, D.C.

LORENZO.—¡El pintor Zuloaga!	The painter Zuloaga!
ELISA.—¡Picasso!	Picasso!
RICARDO.—¡Dalí!	Dali!
PILAR.—Coincido con vosotros.	I agree with you.
ELISA.—Bueno, ¿vienes Pilar?	Well, are you coming, Pilar?
PILAR.—No, gracias. No entiendo ese entusiasmo tuyo por los pintores flamencos.	No, thanks. I don't understand that enthusiasm of yours for Flemish painters.

LORENZO.—Aquí viene el Sr. Pacheco.

Here comes Mr. Pacheco.

TODOS.—Buenas tardes, Sr. Pacheco.

Good afternoon, Mr. Pacheco.

SR. PACHECO.—¡Ah, están ustedes aún aquí! Sus compañeros acaban de salir.

Oh, you're still here! Your classmates have just left.

RICARDO.—¡Qué conferencia tan interesante la suya!

What an interesting lecture yours was!

SR. PACHECO.—Gracias. Aprecio el interés de ustedes por el Arte. El Museo del Prado es único en el mundo.

Thank you. I appreciate your interest in art. The Prado Museum is unique in the world.

RICARDO.—Su colección de pinturas es muy valiosa.

Its collection of paintings is very valuable.

SR. PACHECO.—¿Quieren ustedes venir conmigo a ver una nueva adquisición?

Would you like to come with me to see a new acquisition?

PILAR.—Con mucho gusto. ¿Dónde?

With much pleasure. Where?

SR. PACHECO.—A la sala de los pintores flamencos.

To the gallery of the Flemish painters.

LENGUA (Ver 27–31.)

MODISMOS Y VOCABULARIO ADICIONAL

al/infinitivo   when (actor)/verb
Claro que sí.   Of course, Naturally.
A ver.   Let's see.
acabar de   to have just
¿De quién?   Whose?

el **abrigo** overcoat	la **llave** key
el **apunte** note (*annotation*)	**mejor** better, best
creer to believe	**según** according to
cuál which	**señora** Mrs., lady
el **garaje** garage	el **sombrero** hat

The present indicative of **entender** (I, to understand):

entiendo, entiendes, entiende, entendemos, entendéis, entienden

DIÁLOGO 8

EJERCICIOS ORALES

1. Hacer exclamaciones de las siguientes oraciones. (27.)

   Ejemplo: EL PROFESOR.—Los niños están sucios.
   EL ALUMNO.—**¡Qué niños tan sucios!**

   La colección es valiosa.   La noche está hermosa.
   La niña es amable.   La mujer es guapa.
   Los zapatos son grandes.   Las gambas están ricas.
   La conferencia es interesante.   Los niños están sucios.

2. En lugar de la forma nominal, dar la forma pronominal. (29, 30.)

   Ejemplo: EL PROFESOR.—mi coche
   EL ALUMNO.—**el mío**

mi radio	tus pinturas	sus padres	sus fotos
mis ideas	tus hermanos	nuestro examen	su abrigo
tu libro	su sombrero	nuestras cosas	sus llaves
tu llave	nuestra casa	vuestros apuntes	mi coche

3. Hacer concordar el verbo y el pronombre posesivo con el sujeto dado. (30.)

   Ejemplo: EL PROFESOR.—*Él cree* que el reloj es *suyo.   nosotros*
   EL ALUMNO.—**Nosotros creemos que el reloj es nuestro.**

   Él sabe que el reloj no es *suyo.   vosotros, tú, ellos, el Sr. Valdés, la Sra. Cortés, usted,
   yo, nosotros, él*

4. Contestar según el ejemplo, usando la forma antepuesta del adjetivo posesivo. (29.)

   Ejemplo: EL PROFESOR.—¿Dónde está el coche del Sr. Ruiz?
   EL ALUMNO.—**Su coche está en el garaje.**

   ¿Dónde está el coche de usted?   ¿Dónde está mi coche?
   ¿Dónde está el coche de su hermano?   ¿Dónde está vuestro coche?
   ¿Dónde está el coche de ustedes?   ¿Dónde está el coche de ellos?
   ¿Dónde está el coche de los Srs. Pérez? ¿Dónde está el coche del Sr. Ruiz?

PREGUNTAS SOBRE EL DIÁLOGO

1. ¿Quién es el profesor de Arte? 2. ¿Qué conoce bien el profesor? 3. ¿A dónde quiere ir Elisa? 4. ¿Quién quiere ir con ella? 5. Para el gusto de Lorenzo, ¿cuáles son las mejores pinturas? 6. Para Pilar, ¿cuáles son los mejores pintores? 7. ¿Quién es Goya? 8. ¿Quiénes son tres de los pintores españoles contemporáneos? 9. ¿Coincide Pilar con sus amigos? 10. ¿Va Pilar con Elisa y Lorenzo? 11. ¿Quién viene hacia ellos? 12. ¿Qué aprecia el Sr. Pacheco? 13. Según el Sr. Pacheco, ¿es bueno el Museo del Prado? 14. ¿Qué va a ver el profesor? 15. ¿Quiénes van con él? 16. ¿A dónde van?

DIÁLOGO 9

En la tienda de muebles

Personajes: Pilar, Tere (hermana de Pilar), Mamá, el dependiente, Jaime (novio de Tere)

PILAR.—Si Jaime y tú os vais a casar tan pronto, ¿cuándo vais a comprar los muebles?

If you and Jaime are going to marry so soon, when are you going to buy your furniture (furnishings)?

TERE.—Pensamos ir mañana a elegirlos.

We intend to go tomorrow to pick it (them) out.

PILAR.—Me imagino que mamá quiere ir con vosotros.

I imagine that Mama wants to go along with you.

TERE.—Sí. A Jaime no le hace gracia, pero no podemos decirle que no.

Yes. It's not to Jaime's liking, but we can't say no to her.

PILAR.—Claro. Tiene que tratarla con diplomacia porque va a ser su suegra.

Of course. He must treat her with diplomacy because she is going to be his mother-in-law.

TERE.—Hasta ahora mamá y Jaime se aprecian bastante.

Up to now Mama and Jaime think a lot of each other.

PILAR.—Hasta ahora sí. Después de ir a la tienda de muebles, lo dudo.
(*En la tienda de muebles.*)

Up to now, yes. After going to the furniture store, I doubt it.
(*At the furniture store.*)

DEPEN.—Les voy a enseñar los muebles de comedor. Esta mesa y este aparador son de nogal.

I'm going to show you dining room furniture. This table and this buffet are made of walnut.

35

MAMÁ.—Estas sillas no me parecen cómodas.	These chairs don't seem comfortable to me.
DEPEN.—Puedo mostrarles otras.	I can show you others.
MAMÁ.—Vamos a ver los dormitorios.	Let's see bedroom sets.
DEPEN.—Los tenemos allí. Aquella cama, cómoda y coqueta hacen juego.	We have them over there. That bed, chest of drawers and vanity match.
MAMÁ.—¿No te parecen demasiado modernos?	Don't they seem too modern to you?
TERE.—El espejo es un poco pequeño.	The mirror is a little small.
MAMÁ.—Tenemos que verlo todo antes de decidir.	We have to see everything before we decide.
DEPEN.—Aquí tienen estos sofás y sillones para la sala. Lámparas y alfombras pueden verlas en el segundo piso.	Here are sofas and arm chairs for the living room. You can see lamps and rugs on the third floor.
MAMÁ.—Eso lo dejamos para más tarde.	We'll leave that for later.
JAIME.—Aún estoy sin decir "esta boca es mía" y yo voy a pagarlo todo.	As yet I haven't opened my mouth, and I'm going to pay for it all.

LENGUA (Ver 32–34.)

MODISMOS Y VOCABULARIO ADICIONAL

hacer gracia   to be funny
decir que no (sí)   to say no (yes)
Claro.   Of course.
hacer juego   to match, to go together
hacer un favor a   to do a favor for
el segundo piso   3d floor (*Remember that* **el piso bajo** *is the 1st floor;* **el primer piso** *generally corresponds to our 2d floor.*)

contar (I) to tell, to count	el **mapa** map		
el **cuento** story, tale	**peinar** to comb		
el **chiste** joke	el **viaje** trip		
la **historia** story, history			

36

En la Calle de Alcalá hay tiendas de muebles.

Present indicative of **vestir** (III, to dress) and **elegir** (III, to select, to elect, to choose):

vestir: **visto, vistes, viste, vestimos, vestís, visten**
elegir: **elijo*, eliges, elige, elegimos, elegís, eligen**

EJERCICIOS ORALES

1. (32–33.)   *Ejemplo:* EL PROFESOR.—¿Va usted a dejar esa silla ahí?

EL ALUMNO.—**Sí, voy a dejar esta silla aquí.**

¿Va usted a dejar esos libros ahí?
¿Va usted a dejar esas lámparas ahí?
¿Va usted a dejar ese lápiz ahí?
¿Va usted a dejar aquellas alfombras allí?
¿Va usted a dejar aquel sillón allí?
¿Va usted a dejar aquella radio allí?
¿Va usted a dejar aquellos mapas allí?
¿Va usted a dejar esa silla ahí?

* See Spelling Changes in the **Addendum.**

2. (34a.) *Ejemplo:* EL PROFESOR.—Voy a contar una historia.

                EL ALUMNO.—**¿Va a contarla ahora?**

Van a contar unos cuentos.	Va a comprar un sombrero.
Va a contar el chiste.	Van a comprar una radio.
Vamos a escribir unas cartas.	Vamos a elegir los muebles.
Van a contar el viaje.	Va a lavar el coche.
Voy a comprar estos libros.	Voy a contar una historia.

3. (34b.) *Ejemplo:* EL PROFESOR.—Yo también quiero uno.

                EL ALUMNO.—**Le van a dar otro.**

Nosotros también queremos uno.	Mis padres también quieren uno.
Ella también quiere uno.	Vosotros también queréis uno.
Ellos también quieren uno.	Elisa también quiere uno.
Ustedes también quieren uno.	Usted también quiere uno.
Ricardo también quiere uno.	Yo también quiero uno.

4. Cambiar a la forma reflexiva. (34c.)

Ejemplo: EL PROFESOR.—Yo le preparo una bebida.

            EL ALUMNO.—**Yo me preparo una bebida.**

Mi amigo me compra una pluma.	Nosotros les lavamos las manos.
Él la mira en el espejo.	Ellos me compran otro.
La madre la peina.	Ellas te miran en el espejo.
Mi padre me hace otro.	Tú le haces muchos.
La hermana los viste.	Yo le preparo una bebida.

PREGUNTAS SOBRE EL DIÁLOGO

1. ¿Quiénes se casan? 2. ¿Cuándo piensan casarse? 3. ¿Qué tienen que hacer? 4. ¿Quién quiere ir con ellos? 5. ¿A Jaime le hace gracia? 6. ¿Por qué tiene que tratarla Jaime con diplomacia? 7. ¿Quiénes se aprecian? 8. ¿A qué tienda van? 9. ¿Quién les enseña los muebles? 10. ¿Qué les enseña primero? 11. ¿De qué son la mesa y el aparador? 12. ¿A mamá le parecen cómodas las sillas? 13. ¿Qué otros muebles les enseña el dependiente? 14. ¿Cómo le parecen a mamá los muebles? 15. ¿Cómo es el espejo? 16. ¿En qué piso pueden ver lámparas y alfombras? 17. ¿Qué tienen que hacer antes de decidir? 18. ¿Quién va a pagarlo todo?

DIÁLOGO 10

El atracador

Personajes: Ricardo, Elisa, Lorenzo, Pilar

RICARDO.—Lorenzo os va a contar lo que le pasó a su vecino anoche.

Lorenzo is going to tell you what happened to his neighbor last night.

ELISA.—¿Es gracioso?

Is it funny?

RICARDO.—¡Ya lo creo! Robó una cartera sin quererlo.

You bet! He stole a wallet without wanting to.

PILAR.—¿Cómo pasó eso?

How did that happen?

LORENZO.—Salió anoche tarde y en la esquina se encontró con un hombre que le pareció sospechoso.

He went out late last night and he came across a man at the corner who seemed suspicious to him.

PILAR.—¡Qué miedo!

How frightening!

RICARDO.—Y para asustarle, se puso la mano en el bolsillo imitando una pistola.

And to scare him, he put his hand in his pocket, pretending to have a gun.

ELISA.—¡Y el otro hombre se asustó!

And the other fellow got scared!

LORENZO.—Exacto. Y tomando a mi vecino por un atracador, le tiró la cartera a él.

Right. And taking my neighbor for a holdup man, he threw his wallet at him.

RICARDO.—Y corrió como alma que lleva el diablo.

And he ran off like a scared rabbit.

PILAR.—¿Y tu vecino recogió la cartera? | And did your neighbor pick up the wallet?

LORENZO.—Sí, para poder identificar al hombre y devolvérsela. | Yes, in order to be able to identify the man and to return it to him.

ELISA.—¿Y descubrió su nombre? | And did he find out his name?

LORENZO.—No. En ese momento llegó el hombre con un policía y encontraron a mi vecino con la cartera en las manos. | No. At that moment the man arrived with a policeman and they found my neighbor with the wallet in his hands.

RICARDO.—¡Y se le llevaron a la comisaría! | And they whisked him away to the police station!

ELISA.—¡Ahí va!* ¡Qué risa! | Wow! What a laugh!

PILAR.—No se puede creer esa historia. | You (one) can't believe that story.

LORENZO.—Él nos la contó a nosotros y a un grupo de vecinos. | He told it to us and to a group of neighbors.

RICARDO.—Pero ni a nosotros ni a ellos nos pareció verdadera. | But neither we nor they thought it was true.

ELISA.—Pero tiene gracia de todas formas. | But anyway, it (the story) is funny.

LENGUA (Ver 35–39.)

MODISMOS Y VOCABULARIO ADICIONAL

¡Ya lo creo!   You bet! Yes, indeed!
encontrarse con   to come across, to meet, to bump into
¡Qué miedo!   How frightening!
correr como alma que lleva el diablo   to run off like a scared rabbit
¡Qué risa!   What a laugh!
tener gracia   to be funny
la **camisa**   shirt   el **paquete**   package
la **carta**   letter   el **trabajo**   work
   examinarse   to have an exam   **visitar**   to visit

* Pronounced **¡ay va!**

40

*La esquina de la calle
donde vive Lorenzo*

The preterit of the regular verbs **hablar**, **comer**, and **vivir**:

hablé	comí	viví
hablaste	comiste	viviste
habló	comió	vivió
hablamos	comimos	vivimos
hablasteis	comisteis	vivisteis
hablaron	comieron	vivieron

The present and preterit indicative of **oír** (to hear):

**oigo, oyes, oye, oímos, oís, oyen
oí, oíste, oyó, oímos, oísteis, oyeron**

41

EJERCICIOS ORALES

1. (35.) *Ejemplo:* EL PROFESOR.—Les contó el chiste a los alumnos.
   EL ALUMNO.—**Se lo contó.**

Le pasó la mantequilla a Elisa.	Nos enviaron los paquetes.
Le robó la cartera a mi vecino.	Me plancharon las camisas.
Te devolvieron las cartas.	Le compramos el coche al vecino.
Me pagaron el trabajo.	Nos contaron la historia a nosotros.
Se llevaron a los hombres.	Les contó el chiste a los alumnos.

2. (37.) *Ejemplo:* EL PROFESOR.—¿Dicen que es bueno?
   EL ALUMNO.—**Sí, se dice que es bueno.**

¿Van a fusilarle?	¿Oyeron todo?
¿Le encontraron?	¿Creen que es tarde?
¿Hablan español allí?	¿Pueden entrar?
¿Oyen bien ahí?	¿Dicen que es bueno?

3. (39.) *Ejemplo:* EL PROFESOR.—¿Cuándo va usted a hablarle?
   EL ALUMNO.—**Le hablé ayer.**

¿Cuándo va usted a comprarlo?	¿Cuándo van ustedes a visitarlos?
¿Cuándo van ustedes a contárselo?	¿Cuándo va a verlas su hermana?
¿Cuándo va a llegar su hermano?	¿Cuándo van ustedes a examinarse?
¿Cuándo te lo van a devolver?	¿Cuándo va usted a hablarle?

PREGUNTAS SOBRE EL DIÁLOGO

1. ¿Qué va a contar Lorenzo? 2. ¿Qué robó el vecino sin quererlo? 3. ¿Cuándo pasó eso? 4. ¿Dónde se encontró el vecino con el hombre? 5. ¿Cómo le pareció el hombre? 6. ¿Por qué se puso la mano en el bolsillo? 7. ¿Se asustó el hombre? 8. ¿Qué le tiró el hombre al vecino? 9. ¿Cómo corrió el hombre? 10. ¿Qué recogió el vecino? 11. ¿Por qué recogió la cartera? 12. ¿Descubrió su nombre? 13. ¿Quiénes llegaron en ese momento? 14. ¿A dónde se llevaron al vecino? 15. ¿A quiénes contó el vecino esta historia? 16. ¿Les pareció verdadera? 17. ¿La historia tiene gracia? 18. ¿Se puede creer esta historia?

DIÁLOGO 11

El invitado

Personajes: Pepito, Juanito, Elisa, Mamá, Papá

(*En la sala de los Srs. Ruiz.*)
PAPÁ.—Llaman a la puerta.

(*In the Ruiz's living room.*)
Someone's knocking at the door.

ELISA.—Voy a abrir.

I'll open it.

MAMÁ.—Deben de ser Juanito y Pepito.

It's probably Juanito and Pepito.

PAPÁ.—¿Pepito a la hora de comer?

Pepito, at dinner time?

MAMÁ.—Sí. Le invité ayer a comer con nosotros. (*Sale. Entran los niños.*)

Yes. I invited him yesterday to have dinner with us. (*She goes out. The boys come in.*)

PAPÁ.—Hola, Pepito. ¿Qué me cuentas?

Hello, Pepito. What's news?

PEPITO.—Buenos días, Sr. Ruíz.*

Good day, Mr. Ruiz.

PAPÁ.—¿Qué hicisteis esta mañana?

What did you do this morning?

PEPITO.—Fuimos al Instituto y en Matemáticas hicimos todos los problemas correctamente.

We went to school and in math we did all our problems correctly.

PAPÁ.—Naturalmente.

Naturally.

ELISA.—¿Fueron difíciles?

Were they difficult?

JUANITO.—Uno fue muy difícil.

One was very difficult.

* In Spain, **la comida**, generally eaten about 2 p.m., divides the morning from the afternoon. Up until **la comida**, **buenos días** is the usual salutation. **Buenas tardes** (*good afternoon*) is used after **la comida** until **la cena** (*supper*), about 9:30 p.m.

PEPITO.—Tu mamá es muy amable en invitarme a comer.

Your mother is very kind in inviting me to dinner.

JUANITO.—Bah. Nos va a dar la comida de todos los días.

Bah. She's going to give us the (usual) everyday meal.

PEPITO.—¿Sopa también?

Soup also?

JUANITO.—Seguramente. Y carne, patatas, verdura, y hasta ensalada.

Undoubtedly. And meat, potatoes, a vegetable, and even a salad.

PEPITO.—Si es carne asada, patatas fritas, y judías verdes, no me importa. Me gustan mucho.

If it's roast beef, French fries and string beans, I don't care. I like them a lot.

JUANITO.—¿Y si es guisado?

And if it's stew?

PEPITO.—Eso ya me gusta menos. Pero no importa, te digo. Me estoy muriendo de hambre.

Well, that I like less. But that doesn't make any difference, I tell you. I'm starving.

ELISA.—Lo que sé es que hay flan de postre. Eso os gusta, ¿verdad?

(What) I know (is) that there is custard for dessert. You like that, don't you?

MAMÁ.—(Entrando.) Todos a la mesa.

Everybody to the table.

PAPÁ.—¿Qué hay de comida?

What's for dinner?

MAMÁ.—Paella.

Paella.

LOS NIÑOS.—¡PAELLA!*

PAELLA!

LENGUA (Ver 40–42.)

MODISMOS Y VOCABULARIO ADICIONAL

llamar a la puerta to ring the doorbell, to knock at the door
deber de/infinitivo probably/verb
la hora de comer dinner time
no me importa I don't care
morirse de hambre to die from hunger, to starve
de postre for dessert

* Spanish dish made of rice (arroz), chicken (gallina), ham (jamón), shrimp (gambas), shellfish (mariscos), artichokes (alcachofas), peas (guisantes), onion (cebolla), green pepper (pimiento), tomato (tomate), and seasoned with garlic (ajo) and saffron (azafrán).

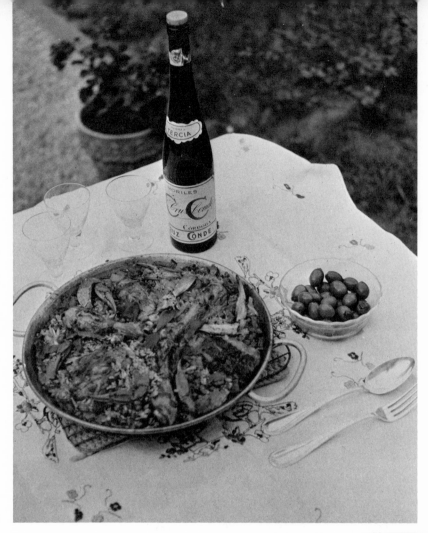

La paella

cantar to sing	el **pescado** fish (caught)
cuidadoso careful	**rápido** rapid
descuidado careless	**silencioso** silent
estupendo stupendous, wonderful	**tranquilo** quiet, tranquil
galante gallant	los **toros** bullfights
luchar to fight	**valiente** courageous
los **macarrones** macaroni	

The preterit of **hacer**, **ir**, and **ser**:

hice, hiciste, hizo, hicimos, hicisteis, hicieron
fui, fuiste, fue, fuimos, fuisteis, fueron (ser *and* ir)

45

EJERCICIOS ORALES

1. (40.) *Ejemplo:* EL PROFESOR.—Hay flan.
   EL ALUMNO.—**Me gusta el flan.**

Hay paella. Hay pescado.
Hay patatas fritas. Hay macarrones.
Hay sopa. Hay carne asada.
Hay judías verdes. Hay flan.

2. (40.) *Ejemplo:* EL PROFESOR.—¿Les gustan a ustedes las patatas fritas?
   EL ALUMNO.—**No, no nos gustan.**

¿Te gusta el pescado? ¿Os gusta el guisado?
¿Le gusta a usted este ejercicio? ¿Te gusta el guisado?
¿Le gustan a él los macarrones? ¿Le gustan a usted las verduras?
¿Le gustan a ella las verduras? ¿Les gustan a ustedes las patatas fritas?
¿Les gusta a ellos el guisado?

3. (42.) *Ejemplo:* EL PROFESOR.—fácil
   EL ALUMNO.—**fácilmente**

tranquilo   galante   lento y cuidadoso
estupendo   descuidado   rápido y fácil
silencioso   valiente   correcto

Ahora, terminar la oración con un adverbio en "mente."
Ejemplo: EL PROFESOR.—Él lo hizo _____.
   EL ALUMNO.—**Él lo hizo descuidadamente**.

Pepe entró _____. Todos comieron _____.
Esto se hace _____. Ellos lucharon _____.
Ella me habló _____. Ella sabe cantar _____.
Ellos trabajan _____. Él lo hizo _____.

4. El pretérito de **hacer, ir, y ser.** Usar siempre en la contestación "ayer."

Ejemplo: EL PROFESOR.—¿Va él al médico hoy?
   EL ALUMNO.—**No, fue ayer.**

¿Va usted al médico hoy? ¿Son los toros hoy?
¿Van ustedes al centro hoy? ¿Lo haces hoy?
¿Van ellos a la playa hoy? ¿Lo hacen ustedes hoy?
¿Es la fiesta hoy? ¿Va él al médico hoy?

DIÁLOGO 11

PREGUNTAS SOBRE EL DIÁLOGO

1. ¿Quiénes llaman a la puerta? 2. ¿Quién va a abrir? 3. ¿Quién invitó a Pepito a comer? 4. ¿Cuándo le invitó la madre? 5. ¿Qué hicieron los niños por la mañana? 6. ¿Fueron difíciles los problemas? 7. ¿Por qué es muy amable la mamá de Juanito? 8. Según Juanito, ¿qué van a comer? 9. ¿Qué le gusta a Pepito? 10. ¿Qué le gusta menos a Pepito? 11. ¿Quién se está muriendo de hambre? 12. ¿Qué es lo que sabe Elisa? 13. ¿Qué dice la mamá al entrar? 14. ¿Qué pregunta el papá? 15. ¿Qué hay de comida? 16. ¿Les gusta la paella?

Estudiantes en el jardín de la Facultad de Filosofía y Letras

DIÁLOGO 12

Los estudiantes de idiomas

Personajes: Elisa, Pilar, Ricardo, Lorenzo

PILAR.—No supe traducir el ejercicio de inglés.

I couldn't translate my English homework.

RICARDO.—Te oí preguntarle al chico que estaba a tu lado.

I heard you asking the fellow who was next to you.

48

DIÁLOGO 12

PILAR.—¿Cómo pudiste oírme? Te vi entrar en la clase y te sentaste al final.

How did you manage to hear me? I saw you enter the class and you sat in the back.

RICARDO.—Ese chico aprendió inglés en Inglaterra, ¿verdad?

That fellow learned English in England, didn't he?

PILAR.—Sí, y lo habla muy bien. Por eso me senté a su lado.

Yes, and he speaks it very well. For that reason I sat next to him.

ELISA.—Voy a preguntarle si quiere dar una clase particular.

I'm going to ask him whether he wants to give a private class.

LORENZO.—¿Por qué?

Why?

ELISA.—Anoche cuando iba a acostarme, me llamó Julita por teléfono.

Last night when I was going to bed, Julita called me by phone.

PILAR.—¿Para qué te llamaba?

What was she calling you for?

ELISA.—Quería preguntarme si podía recomendarle un buen profesor de inglés.

She wanted to ask me whether I could recommend to her a good English teacher.

RICARDO.—¿Va a aprender inglés?

Is she going to learn English?

ELISA.—Trataba de aprenderlo sola, pero llegó un momento en que no pudo seguir.

She was trying to learn it by herself, but there came a time when she couldn't go on.

LORENZO.—Es imposible aprender un idioma sin profesor.

It is impossible to learn a foreign language without a teacher.

RICARDO.—Yo quise hacerlo y perdí el tiempo.

I tried to do it and I wasted the time.

PILAR.—Se puede practicar con otro estudiante.

One can practice with another student.

LORENZO.—Claro. ¿No oíste contar el cuento del perro que, al saludar a otro perro, decía "miau"?

Naturally. Didn't you ever hear the story about the dog that, on greeting another dog, would say "meow"?

ELISA.—¿Por qué?

Why?

LORENZO.—¡Porque estudiaban idiomas, tonta!

Because they were studying foreign languages, silly!

49

LENGUA (Ver 43–45.)

MODISMOS Y VOCABULARIO ADICIONAL

por eso   for that reason
tratar de/infinitivo   to try/infinitive
la semana pasada   last week
al día siguiente   on the following day
fumar en pipa   to smoke a pipe
a menudo   often

acostarse (I)   to go to bed
comenzar (I)   to begin (*See* Spelling Changes *in the* **Addendum.**)
llegar   to arrive (*See* Spelling Changes *in the* **Addendum.**)
el **país**   country (nation)
la **televisión**   television
volver (I)   to return

The imperfect indicative of **ir, ser,** and **ver**:

ir: **iba, ibas, iba, íbamos, ibais, iban**
ser: **era, eras, era, éramos, erais, eran**
ver: **veía, veías, veía, veíamos, veíais, veían**

The imperfect indicative of all other verbs is regular.

Add to **A** verb stems: **aba, abas, aba, ábamos, abais, aban.**
Add to **E** and **I** verb stems: **ía, ías, ía, íamos, íais, ían.**

The preterit of **poder, querer,** and **saber**:

poder: **pude, pudiste, pudo, pudimos, pudisteis, pudieron**
querer: **quise, quisiste, quiso, quisimos, quisisteis, quisieron**
saber: **supe, supiste, supo, supimos, supisteis, supieron**

EJERCICIOS ORALES

1. (43a, b.)   *Ejemplo:* EL PROFESOR.—Ahora sé hablar español.
   EL ALUMNO.—**Antes (yo) no sabía hablar español.**

Ahora como muy bien.	Ahora leo mucho.
Ahora salimos con frecuencia.	Ahora van a menudo.
Ahora estudian mucho.	Ahora es muy amable.
Ahora fumo en pipa.	Ahora vemos la televisión.
Ahora bebemos café.	Ahora sé hablar español.

DIÁLOGO 12

2. En la contestación, dar siempre una hora más tarde que la indicada por el profesor. (43d.)

Ejemplo: EL PROFESOR.—Yo volví a las dos. ¿Qué hora era cuando volvió usted?
EL ALUMNO.—**Eran las tres.**

Yo llegué a la una y media.—¿Qué hora era cuando llegó usted?
Yo me acosté a las once.—¿Qué hora era cuando se acostó usted?
Yo salí a las tres.—¿Qué hora era cuando salió usted?
Yo me levanté a las seis.—¿Qué hora era cuando se levantó usted?
Yo comí a las doce.—¿Qué hora era cuando comió usted?
Yo fui a la clase a las diez.—¿Qué hora era cuando fue usted?
Yo comencé a las siete.—¿Qué hora era cuando comenzó usted?
Yo volví a las dos.—¿Qué hora era cuando volvió usted?

3. El pretérito de **poder, querer, conocer,** y **saber.** (44.)

Ejemplo: EL PROFESOR.—No poder terminar el trabajo.   él
EL ALUMNO.—**Él no pudo terminar el trabajo.**

No poder terminar el trabajo.   **yo, nosotros, ella, tú, vosotros, él, ellos**
No querer ir.   **Pepe, ustedes, nosotros, yo, tú, vosotros**
Conocerla la semana pasada.   **yo, tú, mi hermana, Juan y yo, ellos, Elisa y tú**
Saberlo al día siguiente.   **nosotros, mis padres, su madre, tú, vosotros, yo**

PREGUNTAS SOBRE EL DIÁLOGO

1. ¿Qué es lo que no supo traducir Pilar? 2. ¿Dónde estaba el chico al que preguntó Pilar? 3. ¿Quién la oyó preguntar al chico? 4. ¿Quién vio a Ricardo entrar en la clase? 5. ¿Dónde se sentó Ricardo? 6. ¿En qué país aprendió inglés el chico? 7. ¿Cómo habla inglés el chico? 8. ¿Por qué se sentó Pilar al lado del chico? 9. ¿Qué quiere Elisa preguntarle al chico? 10. ¿Qué iba a hacer Elisa cuando Julita llamó por teléfono? 11. ¿Cuándo la llamó? 12. ¿Para qué la llamaba? 13. ¿Qué trataba de hacer sola Julita? 14. ¿Pudo aprender inglés sola? 15. Según Lorenzo, ¿es posible aprender un idioma sin profesor? 16. ¿Qué perdió Ricardo cuando quiso hacerlo? 17. ¿Con quién se puede practicar? 18. ¿Por qué se decían "miau" los dos perros cuando se saludaban?

DIÁLOGO 13

El accidente

Personajes: Pilar, Elisa, el taxista, la enfermera, el médico

PILAR.—¿Te gusta mi sombrero nuevo?

Do you like my new hat?

ELISA.—Sí, es muy bonito, pero lo tienes mal puesto.

Yes, it is very pretty, but you have it on crooked.

PILAR.—¿De verdad? ¿Dónde hay un espejo?

Really? Where is there a mirror?

ELISA.—En el escaparate de esa tienda ahí enfrente.

In the window of that shop there across the street.

(*Pilar empieza a cruzar la calle.*)

(*Pilar begins to cross the street.*)

ELISA.—No se debe cruzar por aquí. ¡Cuidado! ¡Viene un coche! ¡Ay!

You (*one*) shouldn't cross here. Careful! Here comes a car. Ayyy!

(*Pilar se cae. El coche por poco la pilla.*)

(*Pilar falls. The car almost runs over her.*)

TAXISTA.—¡Señorita, señorita!

Lady, lady!

ELISA.—Pilar, ¿puedes levantarte?

Pilar, can you get up?

PILAR.—No lo sé. Creo que tengo varios huesos rotos. (*Se levanta.*)

I don't know. I think I have several bones broken. (*She gets up.*)

52

No se debe cruzar la calle por aquí.

TAXISTA.—Señorita, lo siento. No tuve la culpa. Vino usted corriendo sin mirar.

Miss, I'm sorry. It wasn't my fault. You came running without looking.

ELISA.—Estás cubierta de polvo.

You're covered with dust.

PILAR.—Ay, tengo esta pierna dolorida.

Ow, this leg hurts.

TAXISTA.—¿La llevo a la Casa de Socorro, señorita?

Shall I take you to the First Aid Station, Miss?

ELISA.—Sí, sí, por favor. Vamos.

Yes, yes, please. Come on.

PILAR.—¡Lo avergonzada que estoy!
(*En la Casa de Socorro.*)

How embarrassed I am!
(*At the First Aid Station.*)

53

LA ENFERMERA.—Mientras el médico la reconoce a usted, Srta. Martínez, su amiga puede darme la información que necesito. Ahora viene el doctor Tamames.

(*La enfermera y Elisa salen.*)

MÉDICO.—Bueno, bueno. ¿Qué fue eso?

PILAR.—¡Lo tonta que fui! El coche se me echó encima sin verlo.

MÉDICO.—¿Qué le duele?

PILAR.—La pierna derecha.

MÉDICO.—(*La reconoce.*) Tiene el tobillo dislocado. Se lo voy a vendar.
(*Lo venda.*)
Ya está. Lo importante ahora es no moverse.

PILAR.—Lo más importante es limpiar mi sombrero y mi vestido.

While the doctor examines you, Miss Martinez, your friend can give me the information that I need. Here comes Dr. Tamames now.

(*The nurse and Elisa go out.*)

Well, well. How did that happen?

How stupid I was! The car was on top of me before I knew it (*without my seeing it*).

Where does it hurt (*what pains you?*)

My right leg.

(*He examines it.*) Your ankle is sprained. I'm going to bandage it for you.
(*He bandages it.*)
There you are. What is important now is not to move about.

The most important thing is to clean my hat and dress.

LENGUA (Ver 46, 47.)

MODISMOS Y VOCABULARIO ADICIONAL

tener _____ mal puesto   to have _____ on crooked
¿De verdad?   Really?
por poco/verbo   almost/verb
tener la culpa   to be to blame, to be one's fault
cubierto de   covered with
¿Qué_____ pasa a _____?   What's the matter with _____?
a la medida   to (one's) measurement

absurdo absurd		sentir (II) to feel, to regret	
cerrar (I) to close		trágico tragic	
doler (I) to pain		vestir (III) to dress	
empezar (I) to begin			

54

DIÁLOGO 13

Present indicative of **poner** (to put, to place):

pongo, pones, pone, ponemos, ponéis, ponen

Preterit of **tener, venir,** and **poner**:

tener: **tuve, tuviste, tuvo, tuvimos, tuvisteis, tuvieron**
venir: **vine, viniste, vino, vinimos, vinisteis, vinieron**
poner: **puse, pusiste, puso, pusimos, pusisteis, pusieron**

EJERCICIOS ORALES

1. Dar el participio pasivo (*past participle*) de los verbos. (46.)

estar, poder, decir, ser, salir, hacer, oir, querer, ver, ir, dar, poner, conocer, cubrir, saber, entender, abrir, tener, vestir, romper, venir, elegir, escribir

2. Expresar el resultado de la acción. (46.)

Ejemplo: EL PROFESOR.—Los hicieron a la medida.
        EL ALUMNO.—**Están hechos a la medida.**

Abrieron la puerta.	Escribimos las cartas.
Cerramos las ventanas.	Las pusieron en la mesa.
Nos cubrieron de polvo.	Me cansaron.
Rompí el reloj.	Se casaron.
Ella se vistió.	Los hicieron a la medida.

3. (47a.) *Ejemplo:* EL PROFESOR.—Esto es interesante.
        EL ALUMNO.—**Lo más interesante queda por venir.**

Esto es trágico.	Esto es emocionante.	Esto es absurdo.
Esto es gracioso.	Esto es malo.	Esto es interesante.
Esto es difícil.	Esto es bueno.	

4. Dar la forma exclamativa a las oraciones. (47b.)

Ejemplo: EL PROFESOR.—El sombrero está muy mal puesto.
        EL ALUMNO.—**¡Lo mal puesto que está!**

Estamos muy cansados.	Ella es muy amable.
Tú andas muy de prisa.	Ellos son muy simpáticos.
Estoy muy enfermo.	Ellos trabajan mucho.
Habla muy bien.	Su madre es muy guapa.
Estamos muy preocupados.	El sombrero está muy mal puesto.

PREGUNTAS SOBRE EL DIÁLOGO

1. ¿A Elisa le gusta el sombrero de Pilar? 2. ¿Cómo es el sombrero? 3. ¿Cómo lo tiene puesto? 4. ¿Dónde hay un espejo? 5. ¿Se debe cruzar la calle por donde va Pilar? 6. ¿Qué le dice Elisa cuando ve venir un coche? 7. ¿Pilla el coche a Pilar? 8. ¿Se cae Pilar? 9. ¿Por qué dice Pilar que no sabe si puede levantarse? 10. ¿Quién tuvo la culpa del accidente? 11. ¿Vio Pilar el coche cuando ella cruzaba la calle? 12. ¿Qué le duele? 13. ¿A dónde la lleva el taxista? 14. ¿Qué va a hacer Elisa mientras Pilar está con el médico? 15. ¿Cómo se llama el médico? 16. ¿Qué hace el médico? 17. ¿Qué le pasa a Pilar? 18. ¿Qué va a hacer el médico? 19. ¿Qué es lo más importante?

DIÁLOGO 14

Después del accidente

Personajes: Pilar, Mamá, Papá, Doncella (*maid*), Elisa, Ricardo, Lorenzo

PILAR.—Me está doliendo esta pierna. Anoche no dormí nada del dolor.

This leg is hurting. Last night I didn't sleep a wink because of the pain.

MAMÁ.—Estuve telefoneando al médico esta mañana para pedir hora, pero siempre estaba comunicando.

I called and called the doctor this morning to make an appointment, but his phone was always busy.

PAPÁ.—(*Entrando.*) ¿Qué tal, Pilar? ¿Sigues cojeando?

(*Entering.*) How are you, Pilar? Are you still limping?

PILAR.—Sí, me está molestando.

Yes. It is bothering me.

PAPÁ.—Es lo que te estoy diciendo siempre. Hay que ir mirando los coches y pensando en lo que haces, no en las musarañas.

I'm always telling you that you have to be on the lookout for cars and be thinking about what you are doing, not be daydreaming.

PILAR.—Tienes razón. Me está costando caro.

You're right. I'm really paying for it.

PAPÁ.—Hablando, hablando sin saber por dónde ibas. ¡Ay, qué mujeres éstas!

Gabbing, gabbing, without knowing where you were going. Ay, what women these are nowadays!

57

Hay que ir mirando los coches. *Courtesy of Spanish National Tourist Office.*

MAMÁ.—Ella no tuvo la culpa. El taxista es quien no estaba mirando lo que estaba haciendo.

She wasn't at fault. The taxi driver was the one who wasn't watching what he was doing.

PAPÁ.—¡Ay, estas mujeres! (*Sale.*)

Ay, these women! (*He goes out.*)

DONCELLA.—(*Entrando.*) Señora, los amigos de la señorita Pilar están aquí.

(*Entering.*) Madam, Miss Pilar's friends are here.

MAMÁ.—Que pasen.
(*Entran Elisa, Ricardo, y Lorenzo.*)

Have them come in.
(*Elisa, Ricardo, and Lorenzo enter.*)

58

DIÁLOGO 14

LOS TRES.—Buenas tardes, señora. ¿Cómo está usted?	Good afternoon, Mrs. Martinez. How are you?
MAMÁ.—Bien, gracias. ¿Cómo están ustedes?	Very well, thank you? How are you?
ELISA.—¿Qué tal estás, Pilar?	How are you, Pilar?
PILAR.—Estoy mejorando lentamente.	I'm slowly getting better.
LORENZO.—Es una buena excusa para estar faltando a clase.	That's a good excuse for missing class.
PILAR.—¿Cuál es la excusa? Lo que digo es la pura verdad.	What's the excuse? What I say is really the truth.
RICARDO.—No sé entonces lo que te van a parecer nuestros planes.	I don't know then what you are going to think of our plans.
PILAR.—¿Cuáles son vuestros planes?	What are your plans?
LORENZO.—Pensamos ir a bailar el sábado.	We intend to go dancing this Saturday.
ELISA.—Pero por la pierna no vas a poder venir.	But you won't be able to come because of your leg.
PILAR.—¿Cómo que no? Mira, ya no estoy cojeando.	What do you mean I can't? Look. I'm not limping any more.

LENGUA (Ver 48, 49.)

MODISMOS Y VOCABULARIO ADICIONAL

no dormir nada   not to sleep a wink or at all
pedir (III) **hora**   to ask for an appointment
estar comunicando   to be busy (telephone)
pensar (I) **en**   to think about
pensar en las musarañas   to daydream
tener razón   to be right
costar (I) **caro**   to cost dearly, to really pay (for)
Que pasen.   Have them come in.
faltar a clase   to miss class
hacer una pregunta   to ask a question
ya no   no longer, not...any more

la **altura** height
el **bebé** baby
   descansar to rest
   gritar to shout
el **grito** shouting, shout

la **industria** industry
el **río** river
   seguir* (III) to continue, to follow
la **ventaja** advantage

The preterit of **estar**:

estuve, estuviste, estuvo, estuvimos, estuvisteis, estuvieron

EJERCICIOS ORALES

1. Seguir el ejemplo, usando **qué, cuál,** o **cuáles**, según el sentido de la frase dada. (48.)

    Ejemplo: EL PROFESOR.—un teléfono
           EL ALUMNO.— ¿**Qué es un teléfono?**

la industria principal	una suegra
esto	las ventajas
lo que compraron	la altura
la capital de Méjico	eso
las señas de Elisa	una pistola
el río que pasa por Madrid	las noticias
los mejores pintores	un teléfono

2. Dar el gerundio de los siguientes verbos. (49a.)

entrar	comunicar	oir	pensar
doler	costar	telefonear	leer
cojear	decir	mirar	hacer
hablar	mejorar	faltar	caer
pedir	ir	pintar	asistir

3. (48b.) *Ejemplo:* EL PROFESOR.—Ese chico estudia mucho.
              EL ALUMNO.—**Pues no está estudiando ahora.**

Esas chicas fuman mucho.	Ustedes leen mucho.
Ellos ven la televisión mucho.	Tú descansas mucho.
El bebé duerme mucho.	Usted piensa en ella mucho.
Esa chica habla mucho.	Él hace mucho ejercicio.
Pepe, yo trabajo mucho.	Ese chico estudia mucho.

* See Spelling Changes in the **Addendum**.

DIÁLOGO 14

4. Terminar las oraciones con gerundios. (49b.)

Ejemplo: EL PROFESOR.—El niño entró en casa _____.
   EL ALUMNO.—**El niño entró en casa llorando (cantando, gritando, etc.).**

La pierna le sigue _____.
Ella no estaba mirando lo que estaba _____.
Es lo que siempre te estoy _____.
Lentamente está _____.
¿Sigues _____?
Cuando llamé, su teléfono estaba _____.
Los gritos me están _____.
El niño entró en casa _____.

PREGUNTAS SOBRE EL DIÁLOGO

1. ¿Qué le está doliendo a Pilar? 2. ¿Durmió Pilar mucho anoche? 3. ¿A quién estuvo telefoneando su madre? 4. ¿Para qué estuvo telefoneando al médico? 5. ¿Qué pregunta el padre? 6. ¿Qué es lo que el padre siempre le está diciendo a Pilar? 7. ¿Quién tiene razón? 8. Según la madre, ¿quién tuvo la culpa? 9. ¿Qué dice la doncella? 10. ¿Quiénes son los amigos de Pilar? 11. ¿Está mejorando Pilar? ¿Cómo? 12. ¿Quién está faltando a clase? 13. ¿Cuál es la excusa de Pilar? 14. ¿Cuáles son los planes de los chicos? 15. ¿Puede ir Pilar a bailar? 16. ¿Qué es lo que ya no hace Pilar?

El autobús de Toledo

DIÁLOGO 15

La maleta

Personajes: Pepe, Ricardo, Lorenzo, un taxista

(*Pepe y Lorenzo entran en el dormitorio de Ricardo. Pepe es primo de Ricardo y va con él a Toledo.*)

PEPE.—¡Pero no has hecho aún la maleta!

(*Pepe and Lorenzo enter Ricardo's dorm room. Pepe is Ricardo's cousin and is going to Toledo with him.*)

But you haven't packed your suitcase yet!

62

DIÁLOGO 15

RICARDO.—Hay tiempo de sobra. Aún faltan más de dos horas.

There is plenty of time. There are still more than two hours.

LORENZO.—¿Sí? Son las diez menos veinte.

Oh yeah? It's twenty of ten.

RICARDO.—¡Tan tarde! No me había dado cuenta de la hora. He dormido a pierna suelta.

So late! I hadn't realized what time it was. I've slept like a log.

PEPE.—¡Ya! Y te has levantado ahora mismo. Venga, date prisa. Tenemos que salir para la estación antes de media hora.

I'll bet! And you've just now gotten up. Come on, shake a leg. We must leave for the station in less than a half hour.

RICARDO.—No me he afeitado.

I haven't shaved.

PEPE.—Mientras te afeitas, te hacemos la maleta.

While you shave, we'll pack your suitcase.

RICARDO.—Gracias. Siento no haberla hecho anoche. (*Sale.*)

Thanks. I'm sorry I didn't pack it last night. (*He goes out.*)

LORENZO.—¿Cómo se dobla una americana?

How does one fold a suitcoat?

PEPE.—Así, con las mangas hacia atrás. Pero primero se meten los pantalones.

Like this, with the sleeves behind. But first you put the trousers in.

LORENZO.—Encima, las camisas, y en los rincones, los calcetines.

On top, the shirts, and in the corners, the socks.

PEPE.—Tiene más de treinta corbatas.

He has more than thirty ties.

RICARDO.—(*Entrando.*) Bueno, ya estoy listo. ¿Hubo sitio para todo en la maleta?

(*Entering.*) Well, I'm ready. Was there room for everything in the suitcase?

PEPE.—Sí. Vámonos.

Yes. Let's go.

LORENZO.—Adiós, yo me quedo. Buen viaje.

Good-by. I'll stay here. Pleasant trip.

RICARDO.—No se dice "adiós" sino "hasta luego".

One doesn't say "good-by," but "until later."

LOS TRES.—Hasta luego.
(*En la calle.*)

Until later.
(*In the street.*)

PEPE.—¡Taxi, taxi!

TAXISTA.—¿Dónde vamos?

PEPE.—A los autobuses para Toledo. ¡De prisa! (*El coche arranca.*)

RICARDO.—¡Mi maleta! ¡Nos hemos dejado mi maleta!

Taxi, taxi!

Where to?

To the Toledo bus station. And fast! (*The car starts off.*)

My suitcase! We've left my suitcase!

LENGUA (Ver 50, 51.)

MODISMOS Y VOCABULARIO ADICIONAL

hacer la maleta   to pack (one's suitcase)
de sobra   plenty of, more than enough
falta(n) ____ **hora(s)**   there is (are) still ____ hour(s)
darse cuenta de   to realize
dormir a pierna suelta   to sleep like a log
ahora mismo   just now, right now
¡Venga!   Come on!
darse prisa   to hurry
antes de (media hora)   in less than (a half hour)
¡Vámonos!   Let's go!
sino   but (= but rather)

arreglar to fix	**preparar** to prepare
la **cena** supper	**pronto** early, soon
encontrar (I) to meet, to find	**triste** sad
la **palabra** word	**ya** already

Present indicative of **haber** (to have):

he, has, ha, hemos, habéis, han

EJERCICIOS ORALES

1. (50.)   *Ejemplo:* EL PROFESOR.—¿Cuándo va usted a comer?
          EL ALUMNO.—**Ya he comido.**

¿Cuándo va usted a estudiar?
¿Cuándo van ustedes a arreglarlo?

¿Cuándo va su madre a preparar la cena?
¿Cuándo van sus padres a visitarlos?

DIÁLOGO 15

¿Cuándo va usted a salir?	¿Cuándo van ellos a hacerlo?
¿Cuándo vas a decírselo?	¿Cuándo va ella a dártelo?
¿Cuándo vais a comprarlo?	¿Cuándo va usted a comer?

2. Expresar en el pasado las siguientes oraciones. (50.)

Ejemplo: EL PROFESOR.—Estoy triste porque no han venido.

EL ALUMNO.—**Estaba triste porque no habían venido.**

Sé que ha llegado.
Dicen que no has telefoneado.
Tú no comprendes por qué he faltado a clase.
Nos dice que ha bailado toda la noche.
Estamos cansados porque hemos trabajado mucho.
Me dicen que habéis sido buenos.
No saben que tu pierna ha mejorado.
No he podido dormir porque me han molestado mucho.
Estoy triste porque no han venido.

3. Preguntar a varios alumnos "¿Qué ha hecho usted esta mañana?" (50.)

Ejemplo: EL PROFESOR.—¿Qué ha hecho usted esta mañana?

EL ALUMNO.—**He escrito una carta.**

Variar el ejercicio preguntando "¿Qué ha hecho usted hoy?" seguido de "¿Qué hizo usted ayer?"

PREGUNTAS SOBRE EL DIÁLOGO

1. ¿Quién es Pepe? 2. ¿Quiénes van a Toledo? 3. ¿Qué es lo que no ha hecho Ricardo? 4. ¿Por qué no ha hecho la maleta? 5. ¿Qué hora es? 6. ¿Es pronto o es tarde para ir a la estación? 7. ¿Por qué no se había dado cuenta Ricardo de la hora? 8. ¿Cuándo se ha levantado Ricardo? 9. ¿Cuándo tienen que salir para la estación? 10. ¿Qué van a hacer Pepe y Lorenzo mientras se afeita Ricardo? 11. ¿Cómo se hace una maleta? 12. ¿Cuántas corbatas tiene Ricardo? 13. ¿Hubo sitio para todo en la maleta? 14. ¿Quién se queda? 15. ¿Se dice "adiós"? 16. ¿Encuentran un taxi? 17. ¿Cuáles son las últimas palabras de Ricardo?

DIÁLOGO 16

El tejano

Personajes: Lorenzo, Pilar, Ricardo, Elisa, el tejano (*Texan*)

LORENZO.—¿Queréis que os presente a un amigo mío de Tejas?

Would you like me to introduce you to a friend of mine from Texas?

PILAR.—Sí. Espero que sea rico y guapo.

Yes. I hope he is rich and good-looking.

LORENZO.—Me ha dicho que vaya a la biblioteca esta tarde a buscarle. Sugiero que vengáis conmigo.

He told me to go to the library this afternoon to get him. I suggest you all come with me.

RICARDO.—¿Te ha pedido que le des clase de español?

Did he ask you to tutor him in Spanish?

LORENZO.—No, pero temo que me lo pida.

No, but I fear that he will ask me.

ELISA.—¿Por qué lo temes?

Why do you fear that?

LORENZO.—Porque no sé explicar gramática. No es tan fácil como parece.

Because I don't know how to teach (*explain*) grammar. It's not as easy as it seems.

PILAR.—Me alegro que lo reconozcas.

I'm glad you admit that.

ELISA.—Posiblemente él sabe más que tú.

He may know more than you.

(*Más tarde en la biblioteca.*)

(*Later on at the library.*)

ELISA.—Cuéntanos algo de tu país.

Tell us something of your country.

TEJANO.—Te agradezco que me pidas que hable de ese tema.

I thank you for asking me to speak on that matter.

66

La Biblioteca Nacional está en el Paseo de la Castellana.

ELISA.—(*Aparte.*) ¡Ahí va! ¿No te decía? ¡Emplea el subjuntivo mejor que yo!

(*Aside.*) Eeee gads! Wasn't I telling you? He uses the subjunctive better than I!

TEJANO.—Para daros una idea (*se infla*), se puede subir a un tren en Tejas, viajar dos días seguidos en el tren y aún no se ha salido de Tejas.

In order to give you an idea (*he puffs up*), one can get on a train in Texas, ride for two days straight and still one hasn't left Texas.

PILAR.—Aquí también hay trenes lentos. (*El tejano se desinfla.*)

There are also slow trains here. (*The Texan is "deflated."*)

RICARDO.—Siento que hayas dicho una tontería. No creo que este chico nos vuelva a dirigir la palabra.

I'm sorry you made a foolish remark. I don't believe this fellow will speak to us again.

PILAR.—(*Al tejano.*) Perdona. No trataba de tomarte el pelo.

(*To the Texan.*) Pardon me. I wasn't trying to pull your leg.

TEJANO.—Prefiero que lo olvides. De todas formas, lo merezco* por ser jactancioso.

I prefer that you forget it. Anyway, I deserve it for being a braggart.

* **Merecer, reconocer, agradecer** like **conocer.**

LENGUA (Ver 52.)

MODISMOS Y VOCABULARIO ADICIONAL

dar clase de   to teach, to tutor (someone) in
volver a/infinitivo   verb/again
dirigir la palabra   to speak to
tomar el pelo   to pull one's leg
de todas formas   anyway

leer to read	**recoger** to pick up
mal badly	**seguidos** straight, consecutive

Present subjunctive of **hablar, comer, vivir, tener,** and **pedir** (III):

hablø	comø	vivø	tengø	pidø
habl*e*	com*a*	viv*a*	teng*a*	pid*a*
habl*es*	com*as*	viv*as*	teng*as*	pid*as*
habl*e*	com*a*	viv*a*	teng*a*	pid*a*
habl*emos*	com*amos*	viv*amos*	teng*amos*	pid*amos*
habl*éis*	com*áis*	viv*áis*	teng*áis*	pid*áis*
habl*en*	com*an*	viv*an*	teng*an*	pid*an*

The present subjunctive (except for class I and II verbs, and **dar, estar, haber, ir, saber,** and **ser**) is formed by striking off the **o** of the **yo** form of the present indicative, and adding the appropriate endings. Note that **E** and **I** verbs have the same endings.

Present subjunctive of **ser** and **ir**:

ser: **sea, seas, sea, seamos, seáis, sean**
ir: **vaya, vayas, vaya, vayamos, vayáis, vayan**

EJERCICIOS ORALES

1. (52.)   *Ejemplo:* EL PROFESOR.—Nos vamos.
     EL ALUMNO.—**Siento que ustedes se vayan.**

Vivimos lejos.	No lo hacemos.
Salimos poco.	No cantamos bien.
Estudiamos poco.	No venimos.
Trabajamos mucho.	No lo tenemos.
Escribimos mal.	Nos vamos.

DIÁLOGO 16

2. (52.) *Ejemplo:* EL PROFESOR.—Él no quiere recogerlo.

                EL ALUMNO.— **¿Quiere usted que yo lo recoja?**

                       ¿Quiere usted que nosotros lo recojamos?

Él no quiere comprarlas.	Él no quiere ir allí.
Ella no quiere llamarlos.	Ella no quiere leerlo.
Ella no quiere hacerlo.	Ellos no quieren enviarlo.
Pepe no quiere escribirles.	Él no quiere recogerlo.

3. (52.) *Ejemplo:* EL PROFESOR.—¿Van a venir hoy?

                EL ALUMNO.—**Dudo que vengan hoy.**

¿Van a llamar mañana?	¿Van a terminarlo pronto?
¿Van a ir esta tarde?	¿Van a pedir más?
¿Van a comer aquí?	¿Van a subir esta tarde?
¿Van a salir esta noche?	¿Van a venir hoy?

4. (52.) *Ejemplo:* EL PROFESOR.—¿Por qué no lo hace usted hoy?

                EL ALUMNO.—**Ella prefiere que lo haga mañana.**

¿Por qué no lo escribe usted hoy?	¿Por qué no me lo dice usted hoy?
¿Por qué no sale usted hoy?	¿Por qué no viene usted hoy?
¿Por qué no los invita usted hoy?	¿Por qué no lo abre usted hoy?
¿Por qué no se va usted hoy?	¿Por qué no lo hace usted hoy?

PREGUNTAS SOBRE EL DIÁLOGO

1. ¿De dónde es el amigo de Lorenzo? 2. ¿Qué espera Pilar? 3. ¿Dónde van a buscarle? 4. ¿Qué pregunta Ricardo a Lorenzo? 5. ¿Qué teme Lorenzo? 6. ¿Sabe Lorenzo explicar gramática? 7. ¿De qué se alegra Pilar? 8. ¿Sabe el tejano más gramática española que Lorenzo? 9. ¿Habla bien el español el tejano? 10. ¿Qué pide Elisa al tejano? 11. ¿Qué emplea bien el tejano? 12. ¿Qué dice el tejano de Tejas? 13. ¿Dónde son lentos los trenes? 14. ¿Qué siente Ricardo? 15. ¿Trataba Pilar de tomarle el pelo? 16. ¿Fue jactancioso el tejano?

DIÁLOGO 17

Mala suerte

Personajes: Tere, Jaime, Pilar, un empleado del garaje*

TERE.—¿Por qué tanta prisa? Aún falta hora y media para los toros.

Why the big rush? There's still an hour and a half before the bullfight.

JAIME.—¿No te dije que necesito todo ese tiempo para ir a la Plaza de Toros en este cacharro? Subir.

Didn't I tell you that I need all that time to go to the Bull Ring in this jalopy? Get in.

PILAR.—¿Cuándo te dieron el carnet (*pronounced* carné) de conducir?

When did they give you your driver's license?

JAIME.—No recuerdo, pero he pasado muchos meses de un tirón sin coger el volante.

I don't remember, but I've gone many months in a row without driving (*getting hold of the steering wheel*).

TERE.—¡Cuidado! No hables mientras conduces.

Be careful! Don't talk while driving.

JAIME.—Avisarme si veis un surtidor de gasolina.

Let me know if you see a gas pump.

PILAR.—Da la vuelta a la derecha. En ese garaje hay uno.

Turn to the right. In that garage there is one.

EMPLEADO.—¿En qué puedo servirles?

What can I do for you?

* *garaje*—garage where cars are parked, housed, or washed and greased; *taller de reparaciones*— a repair garage.

70

La corrida

JAIME.—Ponga diez litros de gasolina, por favor, y un litro de aceite en el motor.

(*El empleado lo hace.*)

EMPLEADO.—¿Algo más?

JAIME.—No gracias. Cóbrese. (*Le da dos billetes de cien pesetas.*)

Put in ten liters of gas, please, and one liter of oil in the motor.

(*The attendant does it.*)

Anything else?

No, thanks. Take it out of this. (*He gives him two* 100 **peseta** *bills.*)

71

EMPLEADO.—Son ciento veinte pesetas. Tome la vuelta.

It's 120 *pesetas*. Here's (*take*) your change.

(*Jaime le da una propina.*)

(*Jaime gives him a tip.*)

EMPLEADO.—Gracias.

Thanks.

TERE.—Bueno, y ahora derechitos a la Plaza de Toros.

Well, now let's head straight for the Bull Ring.

PILAR.—Te di las entradas, ¿verdad?

I gave you the tickets, didn't I?

TERE.—Sí. Míralas.

Yes. Look (*at them*).

TODOS.—¿Qué ha sido eso?

What was that?

JAIME.—¡Un pinchazo! (*Para el coche, saca el gato y cambia la rueda.*) La cubierta está completamente estropeada. Menos mal que tenía una rueda de repuesto.

A flat tire! (*He stops the car, gets out the jack and changes the wheel.*) The tire is completely ruined. It's a good thing I had a spare wheel.

TERE.—¿Qué pasa ahora? ¿No puedes encender el motor?

What's the matter now? Can't you start the motor?

JAIME.—Algo no funciona. No sé si es el encendido, las bujías, o el carburador.

Something doesn't work. I don't know whether it is the ignition, the spark plugs, or the carburetor.

PILAR.—Llama a un taller de reparaciones. Pide que manden una grúa.

Call a garage. Ask them to send a towtruck.

TERE.—Toma, Jaime. Aquí tienes tu entrada. Nosotras vamos a tomar el Metro.

Take this, Jaime. Here is your ticket. We're going to take the subway.

PILAR.—Los toros son la única cosa puntual en España y no queremos llegar tarde.

Bullfighting is the only thing in Spain that begins on time and we don't want to arrive late.

JAIME.—Hoy parece que me he levantado por los pies de la cama.

Today it seems that I got up on the wrong side of the bed.

LENGUA (Ver 53.)

DIÁLOGO 17

MODISMOS Y VOCABULARIO ADICIONAL

¿Por qué tanta prisa? Why the big rush (so much haste)?
de un tirón in a row, in a stretch
¡Cuidado! Be careful!
dar la vuelta to turn
¿En qué puedo servirle? What can I do for you?
por favor please
¿Algo más? Anything (something) else?
_____ de repuesto spare _____
aquí tiene usted _____ here is _____
levantarse por los pies de la cama to get up on the wrong side of the bed
tener prisa to be in a hurry

Preterit of **dar** and **decir**:

dar: **di, diste, dio, dimos, disteis, dieron**
decir: **dije, dijiste, dijo, dijimos, dijisteis, dijeron**

EJERCICIOS ORALES

1. (53.) *Ejemplo:* EL PROFESOR.—Usted le pregunta.
                EL ALUMNO.—**Pregúntele usted.**

Tú la llamás por teléfono.	Ustedes le preguntan al profesor.
Ustedes salen por aquí.	Vosotros tratáis de terminarlo.
Vosotros coméis todo.	Tú lo practicas* bien.
Usted me paga más tarde.	Usted le pregunta.

2. (53.) *Ejemplo:* EL PROFESOR.—Lo hacemos.
                EL ALUMNO.—**No lo hagan ustedes ahora.**

Los buscamos.*	Lo pagamos.*
Salimos.	Nos vamos.
Lo bebemos.	Lo pido.
Lo miramos.	Salgo.
Lo hago.	Me lo pongo.
Lo busco.*	Lo hacemos.

* Refer to Spelling Changes in the **Addendum** for **A** verbs whose stem ends in **c** or **g**.

3. (53.) *Ejemplo:* EL PROFESOR.—¿Lo compro ahora o mañana?
        EL ALUMNO.—**Cómprelo mañana.**

¿Lo escribo ahora o mañana?	¿Me afeito ahora o mañana?
¿Lo leemos ahora o mañana?	¿Lo leo ahora o mañana?
¿Se lo envío ahora o mañana?	¿Lo compro ahora o mañana?
¿Lo estudiamos ahora o mañana?	

PREGUNTAS SOBRE EL DIÁLOGO

1. ¿A dónde van Tere, Pilar, y Jaime? 2. ¿Por qué tiene prisa Jaime? 3. ¿Tiene Jaime un buen coche? 4. ¿Recuerda Jaime cuándo le dieron el carnet de conducir? 5. ¿Conduce Jaime el coche con frecuencia? 6. ¿Qué dice Tere que no haga Jaime mientras conduce? 7. ¿Qué quiere Jaime que las chicas le avisen? 8. ¿Dónde hay un surtidor de gasolina? 9. ¿Cuántos litros de gasolina pide Jaime? 10. ¿Qué más necesita? 11. ¿Cuánto pidió el empleado por la gasolina y el aceite? 12. ¿Cuánto dinero le dio Jaime al empleado? 13. ¿A quién había dado Pilar las entradas? 14. Después del pinchazo, ¿cómo estaba la cubierta? 15. ¿Cómo van las chicas a la Plaza de Toros? 16. ¿Cuál es la única cosa puntual en España? 17. ¿Ha tenido Jaime buena o mala suerte?

DIÁLOGO 18

En la parada del tranvía

Personajes: Elisa, Pilar, una mujer, dos hombres

PILAR.—Como hay pocos tranvías en esta línea, todos vienen llenos.

ELISA.—Es necesario que tomemos el primero. Es muy tarde.

PILAR.—¡Anda! Puse el monedero en mi bolso nuevo y he cogido el viejo. ¡No tengo dinero!

Well, I'll be! I put my coin purse in my new bag and I've picked up my old one.

ELISA.—Yo te pago el tranvía, que a propósito ya es hora que venga.
(*Pasa un tranvía lleno de gente sin pararse.*)

I'll pay your car fare, and speaking of the streetcar, it is time for it to come.

MUJER.—Es inútil que esperemos más. Han pasado tres llenos.

It is useless for us to wait any longer.

HOMBRE 1º.—Parece mentira que en una ciudad como Madrid haya aún tranvías tan viejos.

It seems incredible that in a city like Madrid there are still such old streetcars.

75

HOMBRE 2º.—Van desapareciendo poco a poco. Casi todos son ya trolebuses.

They are gradually disappearing.

PILAR.—Ahí viene otro. Es posible que podamos subirnos.

ELISA.—¡Qué disparate! Fíjate en cómo viene la gente colgada por fuera.

Nonsense! Notice how the people come, hanging on outside.

MUJER.—¡Parece imposible que no se caigan!

It's a wonder they don't fall off!

PILAR.—Es mejor que tratemos de subir.*

* **Subir** may or may not be reflexive.

Un tranvía de los antiguos

DIÁLOGO 18

ELISA.—No es seguro que podamos,
pero vamos a tratar de hacerlo.

(*Pilar sube al tranvía. Al ir a subir Elisa,
la mujer y los dos hombres se interponen
y suben antes que ella. El tranvía se pone
en marcha antes que Elisa pueda subir.*)

(*Pilar gets on the streetcar. When Elisa
is about to get on, the woman and two
men step in front and get on. The streetcar
starts up before Elisa can get on.*)

PILAR.—(*Desde el tranvía.*) ¡Elisa, Elisa,
no tengo dinero!

LENGUA (Ver 54.)

MODISMOS Y VOCABULARIO ADICIONAL

a propósito   speaking of (matter already mentioned)
poco a poco   little by little, gradually
fijarse en   to notice
ponerse en marcha   to start, to start up
al parecer   apparently

coger   to pick up
feo   ugly
la **línea**   line
lleno   full
pararse   to stop, come to a stop

el **ruido**   noise
la **tardanza**   delay, tardiness
tirar   to throw, throw away
vender   to sell

Present and preterit of **caer** (to fall; v.r., to fall down, to fall off):

caigo, caes, cae, caemos, caéis, caen
caí, caíste, cayó, caímos, caísteis, cayeron

EJERCICIOS ORALES

1. (54.)   *Ejemplo:* EL PROFESOR.—Es absurdo hacerlo.
                         EL ALUMNO.—**Es absurdo que usted lo haga.**

Es mejor venderlo.
Es preferible tomar el Metro.
No es necesario ir.
Es lástima tirarlo.

No es posible venir más pronto.
Es preciso levantarse antes de las seis.
Conviene ser puntual.
Es absurdo hacerlo.

2. Expresar en subjuntivo la idea dada en las oraciones, usando *extraña, molesta, gusta,* o *conviene.* (54.)

Ejemplo: EL PROFESOR.—Elisa sale.

EL ALUMNO.—**Me gusta que Elisa salga.**

Sus hermanos no vienen.	(*me extraña*)
Hacen tanto ruido.	(*me molesta*)
Siempre llega a tiempo.	(*me gusta*)
Nosotros trabajamos mucho.	(*me gusta, me extraña*)
Lo envían mañana.	(*me conviene*)
Los ponen aquí.	(*me molesta*)
Tienen sólo uno.	(*me extraña*)
Elisa sale.	

3. (54.)   *Ejemplo:* EL PROFESOR.—Al parecer no te gustan.

EL ALUMNO.—**No es que no me gusten.**

Al parecer usted no tiene tiempo.
Al parecer no os gusta.
Al parecer ustedes no tienen tiempo.
Al parecer es fea.
Al parecer no funciona bien.
Al parecer son feos.
Al parecer no funcionan bien.
Al parecer le molesta a usted.
Al parecer les extraña a ustedes mi tardanza.
Al parecer les molestan a ustedes.
Al parecer no te gustan.

PREGUNTAS SOBRE EL DIÁLOGO

1. ¿Cuántos tranvías hay en la línea? 2. ¿Cómo vienen todos los tranvías? 3. ¿Por qué es necesario que Elisa y Pilar tomen el primero? 4. ¿Dónde puso Pilar el monedero? 5. ¿Qué bolso ha cogido? 6. ¿Quién le va a pagar el tranvía a Pilar? 7. ¿Cómo viene el primer tranvía? 8. ¿Se paró el primer tranvía? 9. ¿Por qué dice la mujer que es inútil que esperen más? 10. ¿Qué es lo que va desapareciendo poco a poco? 11. ¿Cómo viene alguna gente en el tranvía? 12. ¿Quiénes pudieron subir al tranvía? 13. ¿Cuándo se puso en marcha el tranvía? 14. ¿Por qué no ha subido Elisa? 15. ¿Por qué estaba preocupada Pilar?

DIÁLOGO 19

El sereno

Personajes: Pilar, Tere, Mari, Papá, Mamá, Jaime, Sereno

(*En casa de los señores Martínez Aparicio.*)

PAPÁ.—Espero que la cena esté pre-
parada pronto.

MAMÁ.—La cena está, pero Tere ha
invitado a Jaime a cenar esta noche y
tenemos que esperarle.

Supper is ready . . .

PAPÁ.—Parece raro que tarde tanto.
Son ya las diez.

It seems strange he delays so.

TERE.—Es posible que Jaime piense que
le invité para otro día. O se le ha
olvidado.

Or it has
slipped his mind.

MAMÁ.—Dudo que se le haya olvidado.

PILAR.—No hay quien pueda olvidarse
de ir a casa de la novia.

MARI.—Espero que te dé una buena
excusa por su tardanza.

I hope he gives you a good excuse for
his delay.

TERE.—Mamá, ¿quieres que diga a la
doncella que empiece a servir la cena?

Mama, do you want me to tell the maid
to begin to serve supper?

MAMÁ.—Si a papá no le importa, es mejor que esperemos.

(*En la calle, delante del portal cerrado de la casa donde viven Tere y Pilar con sus padres.*)

JAIME.—No creo que el sereno esté muy lejos. (*Hace palmas y llama.*) ¡Serenooooo!

(*He claps his hands and calls.*)

SERENO.—(*Apareciendo por la esquina de la calle.*) ¡Vaaa!

I'm coming!

El sereno

DIÁLOGO 19

JAIME.—Voy al tercer piso, a casa de los señores Martínez Aparicio.

SERENO.—(*Abriendo el portal.*) Subo con usted.

I'll go up with you.

JAIME.—No se moleste. No es preciso que suba conmigo. Soy casi de la familia.

Don't bother.

I'm like one of the family.

SERENO.—Diga usted lo que quiera. Después de cerrar el portal, no puede subir nadie que no sea inquilino de la casa.

Say what you like. After the entrance door is closed, no one can go up unless he is a tenant of the building.

(*Llegan al piso y llaman al timbre. Abre la puerta Pilar.*)

(*They arrive at the apartment and ring the bell.*)

PILAR.—¡Jaime con el sereno! ¿Qué pasa?

What's the matter?

SERENO.—¿Conoce usted a este joven?

. . . young man?

TERE.—(*Saliendo.*) Por supuesto. Pasa Jaime. Te estamos esperando para cenar.

PILAR.—Me alegro que al fin hayas llegado.

MARI.—Pero, ¿qué pasó? ¿Te caíste por las escaleras?

Did you fall down the stairs?

JAIME.—No. Es que estaba el portal cerrado y el sereno tuvo que subir conmigo.

TERE.—Parece mentira que no sepas que cierran el portal a las diez.

It's unbelievable that you don't know that they close the entrance door at ten.

PAPÁ.—O una de dos; o los españoles cenamos demasiado tarde o cierran los portales demasiado pronto.

It's either one or the other; either we Spaniards eat supper too late or they close the entrance doors too early.

LENGUA (Ver 52, 54, 55.)

MODISMOS Y VOCABULARIO ADICIONAL

hacer palmas   to clap
llamar al timbre   to ring the doorbell
olvidarse (a uno)   to slip one's mind
olvidarse de/infinitivo   to forget/infinitive
al fin   finally

aparecer   to appear
cenar   to dine, to have supper
el **portal**   entrance door
el **sereno**   night watchman

servir (III)   to serve
tercero   third
usar   to use

Present subjunctive of **estar, dar, haber, saber, poder** (I), and **pensar** (I):

estar: **esté, estés, esté, estemos, estéis, estén**
dar: **dé, des, dé, demos, deis, den**
haber: **haya, hayas, haya, hayamos, hayáis, hayan**
saber: **sepa, sepas, sepa, sepamos, sepáis, sepan**
poder: **pueda, puedas, pueda, podamos, podáis, puedan**
pensar: **piense, pienses, piense, pensemos, penséis, piensen**

Note: the same vowel changes occur in the present indicative and the present subjunctive of class I verbs.

EJERCICIOS ORALES

1. Expresar las siguientes oraciones negativamente. (55.)

   Ejemplo: EL PROFESOR.—Tengo otro que es mejor.
             EL ALUMNO.—**No tengo otro que sea mejor.**

   Tengo otro que funciona.
   Tengo otros que funcionan.
   Tengo otro que escribe bien.
   Tengo otros que escriben bien.

   Tengo otro que se puede usar.
   Tengo otros que se pueden usar.
   Tengo otros que son mejores.
   Tengo otro que es mejor.

2. Contestar negativamente. (55.)

   Ejemplo: EL PROFESOR.—¿Hay algo que yo pueda hacer?
             EL ALUMNO.—**No hay nada que usted pueda hacer.**

82

DIÁLOGO 19

¿Hay alguien que lo haga?	¿Hay alguno que haya terminado?
¿Hay algo que sirva?	¿Hay alguien que sepa leerlo?
¿Hay alguno que tenga más?	¿Hay alguno que le guste a usted?
¿Hay alguien que esté contento aquí?	¿Hay algo que yo pueda hacer?

3. Expresar la oración, usando el pronombre dado como sujeto del segundo verbo. (52, 54, 55.)

> *Ejemplo:* EL PROFESOR.—Es posible hacerlo. **yo**
>   EL ALUMNO.—**Es posible que yo lo haga.**

Juan quiere hacerlo. **yo**
Mi padre prefiere quedarse. **nosotros**
Me gusta cantar. **ella**
Es ridículo creerlo. **ellos**
Esperamos llegar mañana. **usted**
Siento no conocerle. **ustedes**
Es necesario dármelo hoy. **él**
Me alegro de estar aquí. **tú**
Tememos decirle la verdad. **vosotros**
Es posible hacerlo. **yo**

PREGUNTAS SOBRE EL DIÁLOGO

1. ¿Qué es lo que espera el padre? 2. ¿Por qué no cenan? 3. ¿Qué es posible que piense Jaime? 4. ¿Por qué no se le ha olvidado? 5. ¿Cómo estaba el portal de la casa donde vive Tere? 6. ¿Dónde puede estar el sereno? 7. ¿Cómo llama Jaime al sereno? 8. ¿Qué contesta el sereno? 9. ¿Por qué tiene que subir el sereno? 10. ¿Quién abre la puerta del piso? 11. ¿Se cayó alguien por las escaleras? 12. ¿Qué es lo que parece mentira que no sepa Jaime? 13. ¿Cree usted que los españoles cenan demasiado tarde? 14. ¿O es que los españoles cierran los portales demasiado pronto?

DIÁLOGO 20

En el Puerto de Navacerrada*

Personajes: Lorenzo, Ricardo, Elisa, Pilar, el tejano

LORENZO.—Hemos tardado solamente hora y media desde Madrid.

It took us only an hour and a half from Madrid.

RICARDO.—El autobús venía de bote en bote, y siguen llegando más autobuses con esquiadores.

The bus was jammed . . .

ELISA.—Espero que este año dure la nieve hasta febrero.

LORENZO.—El año pasado no hubo nieve más que en los meses de diciembre y enero.

Last year there was snow only in the months . . .

PILAR.—Tenemos que ir al club para alquilar los esquís antes que haya más gente.

to rent the skis . . .

RICARDO.—Y reservar una mesa en el restorán.

TEJANO.—Cuando no se conoce bien España, no se imagina que los deportes de nieve se practiquen† con tanto entusiasmo.

snow sports . . .

* A mountain pass north of Madrid.
† See Spelling Changes in the **Addendum** for **A** verbs whose stem ends in **c**.

84

El Puerto de Navacerrada

LORENZO.—Por extraño que parezca, tampoco son los toros el espectáculo más popular.

However strange it may seem, neither is bullfighting the most popular spectacle.

RICARDO.—Por supuesto, los españoles vamos al fútbol. Los toros se quedan para los turistas.

Of course, we Spaniards go to soccer games. Bullfighting is left for the tourists.

ELISA.—A menos que sea una corrida buenísima.

PILAR.—Bueno, bueno, que hemos venido al Puerto de Navacerrada para esquiar, no para que habléis de toros. (*Se van a alquilar los esquís.*)

All right, all right, we came to Navacerrada Pass to ski . . .

TEJANO.—¿Quieres decirme, por favor, cómo se llaman todas estas prendas del equipo para esquiar?

items of ski gear?

ELISA.—Esquís, ligaduras para los esquís, botas, calcetines de lana . . .

bindings, boots, wool socks . . .

RICARDO.—Pantalón de sierra, jersey y encima del jersey, el anorak.

Ski pants, sweater, and on top of the sweater, the parka.

PILAR.—Gorro, gafas oscuras, manoplas, y bastones.

Cap, sun glasses, mitts, and poles.

TEJANO.—Voy a escribirlo en caso de que se me olvide.

RICARDO.—Vamos a coger el telesilla para subir a las pistas.

cablechair . . . (*ski*) trails.

ELISA.—Hay que ir de dos en dos.

It's necessary to go two at a time.

LORENZO.—Tener cuidado, hay que cogerlo en marcha. (*Se suben al telesilla.*)

Be careful, you have to catch it in motion.

PILAR.—¡Mirar aquéllos! No van a cogerlo.

TEJANO.—¿Es posible que prefieran subir andando?

DIÁLOGO 20

(*Llegan a la cumbre.*)

(*They arrive at the top.*)

PILAR.—Es una vista preciosa de toda la sierra.

It's a wonderful sight of the entire mountain range.

TEJANO.—Este ejercicio al aire libre va a servir para que duerma a pierna suelta esta noche.

ELISA.—¡Pues, de cabeza hacia abajo!

Well, it's down we go!

LENGUA (Ver 56.)

MODISMOS Y VOCABULARIO

tardar (tiempo)   to take (time)
de bote en bote   completely filled, jammed packed
no más que   only
de dos en dos   two at a time
tener cuidado   to be careful
hay que/infinitivo   it is necessary/infinitive
en marcha   in motion
al aire libre   outdoors
de cabeza hacia abajo   head downward

la **corrida** bullfight	el **nacimiento** birth
deportivo (*adj*) sport	la **nieve** snow
durar to last	**olvidar** to forget
el **esquiador** skier	la **píldora** pill
la **fecha** date	**practicar** to practice
nacer* to be born	**reservar** to reserve

Los meses: **enero, febrero, marzo, abril, mayo, junio, julio, agosto, septiembre, octubre, noviembre, diciembre**

Present subjunctive of class II verbs, using **dormir** and **preferir** as examples:

duerma	**durmamos**	**prefiera**	**prefiramos**
duermas	**durmáis**	**prefieras**	**prefiráis**
duerma	**duerman**	**prefiera**	**prefieran**

Note the change from **o** to **u** and **e** to **i** in the **nosotros** and **vosotros** forms.

* Like **conocer**

87

EJERCICIOS ORALES

1. Cambiar el sujeto del verbo de la oración dependiente, según se indica. (56.)

Ejemplo: EL PROFESOR.—Hágalo antes que *él* vuelva. **los otros**
EL ALUMNO.—**Hágalo antes que los otros vuelvan.**

Hágalo antes que *él* vuelva.	**nosotros, yo, mis hermanos, ella, ellos, los otros, él**
Me da la píldora para que *yo* duerma bien.	**usted, vosotros, ellas, nosotros, tú, yo**
Pienso ir con tal que *usted* me acompañe.	**ustedes, ella, tú, vosotros, mis padres, mi amigo, usted**
Le compramos esto a menos que *usted* prefiera otra cosa.	**ustedes, tú, vosotros, ellos, su madre, usted**

2. Cada alumno tiene que dar su fecha de nacimiento.*

Ejemplo: EL PROFESOR.—¿En qué fecha nació usted?
EL ALUMNO.—**Nací el diez de febrero de mil novecientos cuarenta y cinco.**

* If you need to review numbers, refer to the **Addendum**, section 3.

3. (56.) *Ejemplo:* EL PROFESOR.—¿Puedo ir con usted?
EL ALUMNO.—**Sí, pero a condición de que usted sea puntual.**

¿Podemos ir con usted?	¿Podemos ir mi hermano y yo con usted?
¿Puede ir ella con usted?	¿Pueden ir ellas con usted?
¿Pueden ir ellos con usted?	¿Puede ir mi hermano con usted?
¿Puede ir él con usted?	¿Puedo ir con usted?

PREGUNTAS SOBRE EL DIÁLOGO

1. ¿Dónde están los chicos? 2. ¿Cuánto han tardado desde Madrid? 3. ¿En qué han venido? 4. ¿Cómo venía el autobús? 5. ¿Qué es lo que van a hacer? 6. ¿Hasta cuándo espera Elisa que dure la nieve? 7. ¿En qué meses hubo nieve el año pasado? 8. ¿Para qué tienen que ir al club? 9. ¿Qué es lo que no se imagina uno si no conoce bien España? 10. ¿Son los toros el espectáculo más popular en España? 11. ¿Quiénes van a los toros? 12. ¿A qué espectáculo deportivo van los españoles? 13. ¿Cómo se llaman las prendas del equipo para esquiar? 14. ¿Qué va a hacer el tejano con toda esa información? 15. ¿Qué tienen que coger para subir a las pistas? 16. ¿Por qué hay que tener cuidado? 17. ¿Cómo es la vista desde la cumbre? 18. ¿Para qué va a servir el ejercicio al aire libre?

DIÁLOGO 21

El Acueducto de Segovia

Personajes: Pilar, Lorenzo, Elisa, el tejano, Ricardo

PILAR.—¿Es seguro que iremos el domingo a Segovia?

LORENZO.—Sí. El tejano dijo que nos llevaría en su coche.

he would take us . . .

PILAR.—Es simpatiquísimo ese chico.

ELISA.—Así tendré ocasión de contarle la leyenda del acueducto romano.

Then (*thus*) I'll have the opportunity to tell him the legend of the Roman aqueduct.

LORENZO.—Ahora mismo podrás contársela. Mírale, aquí viene.

You'll be able to tell it to him right now.

TEJANO.—(*Se acerca con un libro en la mano.*) Estoy leyendo este libro sobre Segovia.

RICARDO.—Pues estarás más informado que nosotros.

Well, you are probably more informed than we.

TEJANO.—Me enfado conmigo mismo por lo despacio que leo. Es interesantísimo.

I get mad at myself because of how slowly I read. It is very interesting.

RICARDO.—¿Me permites verlo?

May I see it?

DIÁLOGO 21

TEJANO.—Sobre el acueducto estoy leyendo ahora, pero aún no sé quién lo ordenó construir.

ELISA.—Yo te lo contaré. Une dos colinas a bastante distancia.

TEJANO.—Sí, mide ochocientos trece metros de largo.

ELISA.—Y las piedras están sobrepuestas sin cemento.

TEJANO.—Y justamente en el arco central falta una piedra.

LORENZO.—Elisa te contará por qué falta esa piedra.

ELISA.—(*A sí misma.*) Si me deja hablar.

RICARDO.—No habrá otro país que tenga más materia prima para leyendas que España.

PILAR.—Las invasiones de los fenicios, griegos, romanos dieron lugar a muchas de ellas.

RICARDO.—Y sobre todo las de los cartagineses, los bárbaros, y los árabes.

ELISA.—No me dejarán contarle la leyenda.

LORENZO.—Veo que tendrás que dejar que los segovianos se la cuenten.

ELISA.—¡Qué va! Se la voy a hacer oir a la fuerza.

but I still don't know who had it built.

It joins two hills quite a distance apart.

Yes, it measures 813 meters in length.

And the stones are laid one on top of the other . . .

And exactly in the middle arch a stone is missing.

(*To herself.*)

There probably isn't another country that has more raw material for . . .

Phoenicians, Greeks, Romans gave occasion to . . .

And especially those of the Carthaginians, the Barbarians, and the Arabs.

I see that you will have to let the Segovians tell it to him.

Of course not! I'm going to make him hear it by force.

Acueducto de Segovia

LENGUA (Ver 57–60.)

MODISMOS Y VOCABULARIO ADICIONAL

el domingo (el lunes) Sunday, on Sunday (Monday, on Monday)
tener ocasión de to have the occasion or opportunity to
enfadarse con to get mad at
de largo in length, long
dar lugar a to give occasion to (for)
a la fuerza by force

brillante brilliant, bright	**fuerte** strong
el **cemento** cement	la **invasión** invasion
el **color** color	**medir** (III) to measure
la **fiesta** party	**oscuro** dark

The following endings, when added to the infinitive (**ir** *used as a model*), express futurity:

Future (posterior to the present—"shall," "will")		**Retro-Future** (posterior to a past moment—"would")	
iré	iremos	iría	iríamos
irás	iréis	irías	iríais
irá	irán	iría	irían

To form the future and retro-future of the following verbs, modify the infinitive as indicated by the forms in parentheses:

haber (**habr**)	poner (**pondr**)	decir (**dir**)
poder (**podr**)	salir (**saldr**)	hacer (**har**)
querer (**querr**)	tener (**tendr**)	
saber (**sabr**)	venir (**vendr**)	

EJERCICIOS ORALES

1. Contestar afirmativamente.

Ejemplo: EL PROFESOR.—¿Pasarán ustedes mucho tiempo allí?
     EL ALUMNO.—**Sí, pasaremos mucho tiempo allí.**

¿Comprará usted el coche?	¿Saldrán ellos esta tarde?
¿Estará usted en casa?	¿Me lo dirá usted más tarde?
¿Tendré que esperar mucho?	¿Comerán ellos antes de las dos?

DIÁLOGO 21

¿Vendrán ustedes inmediatamente? ¿Irás conmigo?
¿Podré yo ir a la fiesta? ¿Lo haréis si os ayudo?
¿Podremos ir nosotros? ¿Pasarán ustedes mucho tiempo allí?

2. *Ejemplo:* EL PROFESOR.—¿Lo hizo él?

        EL ALUMNO.—**No sé. Dijo que lo haría.**

¿Vino él? ¿Lo compraron ellos?
¿Se lo dijo Elisa? ¿Se lo contó Lorenzo?
¿Salieron anoche? ¿Le llevaron al médico?
¿Lo midieron? ¿Aprendió a conducir un coche?
¿Fueron allí? ¿Lo hizo él?

3. (59.) *Ejemplo:* EL PROFESOR.—Es un chico simpático.

        EL ALUMNO.—**Sí, es simpatiquísimo.**

Es un tren lento. Es un libro interesante.
Es una lección difícil. Es un acueducto largo.
Es un color brillante. Es un hombre fuerte. (fortísimo)
Es una noche oscura. Es una casa grande.
Son novelas malas. Es un chico simpático.
Son niños sucios. (sucísimos)

PREGUNTAS SOBRE EL DIÁLOGO

1. ¿A dónde irán los chicos? 2. ¿Cuándo irán? 3. ¿Quién dijo que los llevaría?
4. ¿Cómo es el tejano? 5. ¿Para qué tendrá ocasión Elisa? 6. ¿Quién viene en este
momento? 7. ¿Qué tiene en la mano? 8. ¿Sobre qué está leyendo el tejano?
9. ¿Por qué se enfada el tejano consigo mismo? 10. ¿Cómo es el libro? 11. ¿Quién
quiere verlo? 12. ¿Sabe el tejano quién ordenó construir el acueducto? 13. ¿Qué
une el acueducto? 14. ¿Cuánto mide de largo el acueducto? 15. ¿Cómo está hecho
el acueducto? 16. ¿Qué falta en el arco central? 17. ¿Por qué hay muchas leyendas
en España? 18. ¿Cómo se llama la gente de Segovia?

DIÁLOGO 22

El Cid

Personajes: Elisa, Pilar, Lorenzo, Ricardo, y el tejano

LORENZO.—A todos nos llega un momento en la vida en el que tenemos que decidir.

RICARDO.—Ese momento ha llegado. ¿Qué hacemos esta tarde?

LORENZO.—Vamos al cine.

Let's go to the movies.

ELISA.—Pilar y el tejano, que acaban de volver del cine, no van a querer ir otra vez.

RICARDO.—¿Qué película habéis visto?

PILAR.—*El Cid*, que nos ha gustado mucho.

LORENZO.—Es la película de que estábamos hablando hace un momento.

It's the picture we were talking about a moment ago.

RICARDO.—Hay escenas de batallas en las que se siente uno como si se estuviera de verdad tomando parte.

There are battle scenes where one feels as if he really were taking part.

TEJANO.—Me parece que no se ha seguido mucho la leyenda del Cid, que es la figura histórica a la que más admiro.

Una escena de batalla

LORENZO.—Desde el siglo XII en que se escribió el *Cantar de Mío Cid*, Rodrigo Díaz de Vivar no ha dejado de excitar la imaginación.

PILAR.—Y no podía por menos de atraer a Hollywood.

Since the twelfth century when the *Cantar de Mio Cid* was written, Rodrigo Diaz de Vivar has not stopped exciting the imagination.

And he couldn't help attracting Hollywood.

95

RICARDO.—Pero en los romances del siglo XV, en el teatro del Siglo de Oro y del romanticismo, el Cid es el símbolo del pueblo español.

But in the ballads . . .
Golden Age and of Romanticism, the Cid is the symbol of the Spanish people.

ELISA.—Y de aquí en adelante, cuando pensemos en el Cid, que de todas formas sería alto y rubio, nos vendrá a la mente Charlton Heston.

And from now on, when we think about the Cid, who surely must have been tall and blond, Charlton Heston will come to mind.

TEJANO.—Pues yo, desde que he visto esa película, comprendo mejor la actitud de los españoles de hoy día.

PILAR.—No sé de qué hablas.

TEJANO.—Los españoles, que ya has visto de lo que eran capaces de hacer entonces, están descansando ahora.

The Spaniards, whose capability you have already seen. . .

ELISA.—¡Tiras con bala, chico!

A poignant dig, boy!

LENGUA (Ver 61–62.)

MODISMOS Y VOCABULARIO ADICIONAL

otra vez   again
hace un momento   a moment ago
dejar de/infinitivo   to stop/present participle
no poder por menos de/infinitivo   to not be able to help/present participle
de aquí en adelante   from now on
de todas formas   anyway, surely
hoy día   at the present time, nowadays
tirar con bala   to make a sharp "dig"

el **actor** actor		la **parte** part	
la **colina** hill		el **señor** gentleman, man	
la **figura** person, figure		el **siglo** century	
histórico historical			

Check the ordinal numbers in the **Addendum.**

96

DIÁLOGO 22

EJERCICIOS ORALES

1. Contestar, modificando el sustantivo con una oración, usando verbos ya aprendidos. (61.)

> *Ejemplo:* EL PROFESOR.—¿Es ése el hombre?
> EL ALUMNO.—**Sí, es el hombre que vi.** (entró, lo robó, etc.)

¿Es ése el libro?	¿Es ése el chico?
¿Son ésos los libros?	¿Son ésos los dos capitanes?
¿Es ésa la carta?	¿Es ese señor el autor?
¿Son ésas las pinturas?	¿Es ésa la película?
¿Es ésa la pulsera?	¿Es ése el hombre?

2. Expresar la oración dada, usando pronombres relativos. (62.)

> *Ejemplo:* EL PROFESOR.—Se casó con esa chica.
> EL ALUMNO.—**Es la chica con la que se casó.**

Iba a hacerlo por ese profesor.	Me gusta hablar con ese chico.
Van a esa tienda a comprar.	Te hablé de esa pintura.
Admira a esos pintores modernos.	Lo compramos en esa tienda de muebles.
Vamos a vivir en esa ciudad.	Admiro a ese actor de cine.
Se ve el río desde esa colina.	Se casó con esa chica.

PREGUNTAS SOBRE EL DIÁLOGO

1. ¿Por qué no querrán ir al cine Pilar y el tejano? 2. ¿Qué película han visto? 3. ¿De qué película estaban hablando hace un momento? 4. ¿Cómo son las escenas de batallas? 5. ¿Se ha seguido en la película la leyenda del Cid? 6. ¿Quién es la figura histórica a la que más admira el tejano? 7. ¿Cómo se llamaba el Cid? 8. ¿Cuándo se escribió el *Cantar de Mío Cid*? 9. ¿Por qué la leyenda del Cid no podía por menos de atraer a Hollywood? 10. ¿Es el Cid el símbolo del pueblo español? 11. ¿Qué comprende mejor el tejano desde que ha visto la película? 12. ¿Qué están haciendo los españoles ahora? 13. ¿Ha visto usted la película *El Cid*? 14. ¿Le ha gustado? 15. ¿Quién fue el actor principal de la película? 16. ¿Cómo sería el Cid?

DIÁLOGO 23

El estreno

Personajes: Pepe, Lorenzo, Ricardo, el tejano
(*A la salida del teatro.*)   (*Just after leaving the theater.*)

PEPE.—El estreno de la comedia de nuestro amigo ha sido un fracaso.

The première of our friend's play was a failure.

LORENZO.—De todas formas me alegro que nos dieran entradas gratis y de haber venido a verla.

Anyway I'm glad we were given free tickets . . .

RICARDO.—Y además, como el autor es amigo nuestro, era necesario que le aplaudiéramos.

PEPE.—Pobre chico. Dudo que piense escribir más obras de teatro.

RICARDO.—No puedo decir que la obra sea mala del todo. Tiene unas cosas malas y otras buenas.

I can't say that the work is completely bad.

LORENZO.—Pero no hay quien entienda el desenlace.

But there isn't anyone who can understand the conclusion.

TEJANO.—Yo, al menos, no me enteré de nada.

I, at least, didn't understand anything.

PEPE.—Los críticos son quienes volverán a decir mañana en la prensa que el teatro español está pasando una crisis.

will again say . . .

is going through a crisis.

98

RICARDO.—Y es que nadie ha escrito nada decente después de 1936. Con García Lorca y Alejandro Casona se acabó el teatro.

anything worthwhile . . . The theater ended with . . .

LORENZO.—¡Hombre! ¡No tanto! Buero Vallejo ha escrito cosas muy buenas.

Man! I wouldn't go that far!

TEJANO.—Ahora se está representando en Madrid *La dama del alba* de Casona.

The Lady of the Dawn (i.e., Death).

LORENZO.—Ya era hora que la viéramos los españoles. Se estrenó en Buenos Aires en 1944 y, por razones políticas, no se podía representar en España.

It was time that we Spaniards saw it. It had its première in . . .

El estreno de La dama del alba *en un teatro de Madrid*

PEPE.—Y a pesar de que la escribió lejos de España, es una obra muy española en su doble plano de fantasía y realidad.

TEJANO.—Bueno, hace demasiado fresco para estar parados hablando. ¿Qué hora es?

Well, it's too cool to be standing around talking.

PEPE.—Las dos de la madrugada.

2:00 a.m.

TEJANO.—¡Qué horas de salir de un teatro! No puedo creer que los españoles duerman tan poco.

What a time to be getting out of a theater!

RICARDO.—Siento que te demos la impresión de juerguistas, pero lo corriente a la salida del teatro es ir a tomar chocolate con churros.*

I'm sorry that we give you the impression of being carousers, but it's customary, after the theater . . .

TEJANO.—Insisto en que en España hagamos como los españoles. (*A sí mismo.*) Espero que no nos entretengamos mucho. Empiezo a tener sueño.

(*To himself.*) I hope we don't dally too long. I'm beginning to feel sleepy.

* A thin fritter in the form of a loop.

LENGUA (Ver 63–65.)

MODISMOS Y VOCABULARIO ADICIONAL

a la salida   just after leaving, upon leaving
al menos   at least
enterarse de   to understand, to find out
pasar una crisis   to go through a crisis
a pesar de   in spite of
hacer fresco   to be cool (weather)
lo corriente   what is customary
tener sueño   to be sleepy, to feel sleepy

además   besides
aplaudir   to applaud
azul   blue
barato   cheap

el **gusto**   flavor
el **helado**   ice cream
jugar (I)   to play
la **obra**   work

DIÁLOGO 23

el **crítico** critic	el **plano** plane, level
doble double	**político** political
entender (I) to understand	la **prensa** press
el **éxito** success	la **realidad** reality
la **fantasía** fantasy	**representar** to put on

The retro-subjunctive of all verbs:

hablar	**vivir**	**leer**	**ir** or **ser**
(*hablaroɴ*)	(*vivieroɴ*)	(*leyeroɴ*)	(*fueroɴ*)
hablara	viviera	leyera	fuera
hablaras	vivieras	leyeras	fueras
hablara	viviera	leyera	fuera
habláramos	viviéramos	leyéramos	fuéramos
hablarais	vivierais	leyerais	fuerais
hablaran	vivieran	leyeran	fueran

The retro-subjunctive forms of all verbs are very simply derived. Add **a, as, a, amos, ais, an** to the 3d, plural, preterit form, after striking off the **on**.* Due to the fact that the stress falls on the same vowel, an accent mark is required on the **nosotros** form.

* There is also another form, derived by striking off **ron**, instead of **on**, and adding **se, ses, se, semos, seis, sen**. This form seems to be gradually falling into disuse.

EJERCICIOS ORALES

1. Repetir las frases, omitiendo el sustantivo la segunda vez. (63a.)

Ejemplo: EL PROFESOR.—los trenes lentos y los trenes rápidos
EL ALUMNO.—**los trenes lentos y los rápidos**

unas fotos grandes y unas fotos pequeñas
una camisa barata y una camisa cara
el libro de historia y el libro de arte
las obras históricas y las obras de fantasía
estos chicos franceses y esos chicos alemanes
los amigos nuestros y los amigos tuyos
ese coche azul y el otro coche verde
un helado de chocolate y un helado de tres gustos
los alumnos que estudian y los alumnos que juegan
los trenes lentos y los trenes rápidos

2. (63b, c.)   *Ejemplo:* EL PROFESOR.—¿Lo hicieron ellos?

　　　　　　EL ALUMNO.—**Sí, fueron ellos quienes lo hicieron.**

　　　　　　Sí, fueron ellos los que lo hicieron.

¿Elisa te lo dijo?　　　　　　　　¿Le dijo ella la verdad?

¿Se lo envió su amigo?　　　　　　¿Le contó a usted su profesor esa historia?

¿La vio Juan?　　　　　　　　　　¿Pudo hacerlo su madre?

¿Le aplaudieron los amigos?　　　　¿Lo hicieron ellos?

3. Expresar en el pasado las siguientes oraciones. (65.)

Ejemplo: EL PROFESOR.—No hay quien te entienda.

　　　　EL ALUMNO.—**No había quien te entendiera.**

Es posible que lo compren.

Es probable que vuelva a verles.

Dudo que lo hagan.

Quieren que les llamemos a las cuatro.

Prefieren que todos vengan pronto.

No hay nada que me guste más.

Voy a poner la lámpara aquí para que veas mejor.

No hay quien te entienda.

PREGUNTAS SOBRE EL DIÁLOGO

1. ¿De dónde salen los chicos? 2. ¿Ha sido un éxito el estreno de la comedia? 3. ¿De qué se alegra Lorenzo? 4. ¿Por qué era necesario que aplaudieran? 5. ¿Es la obra mala del todo? 6. ¿Quién entiende el desenlace? 7. ¿De qué se enteró el tejano? 8. ¿Qué volverán a decir los críticos? 9. ¿Qué ha pasado al teatro español desde 1936? 10. ¿Qué se está representando en Madrid ahora? 11. ¿Quién escribió *La dama del alba*? 12. ¿Dónde se estrenó? 13. ¿Hace calor o frío? 14. ¿Es por la tarde o por la noche cuando salen del teatro? 15. ¿Dónde van los españoles a la salida del teatro? 16. ¿En qué insiste el tejano?

DIÁLOGO 24

La tirana

Personajes: Madre, Padre, Tere, Pilar, Mari, y Jaime
(*En el comedor de los señores Martínez Aparicio.*)

MADRE.—Cuando traigan el televisor lo
pondremos en la sala.

PADRE.—No. En el comedor de manera
que podamos ver los telediarios
mientras cenamos.

In the dining room so that we
can see the newscasts while we eat
supper.

MADRE.—Si tuviéramos una alfombra
en el comedor. . . .

TERE.—¿Qué dices si trajéramos la
alfombra de la sala que está bastante
gastada?

What do you say if we brought the
living room rug which is rather worn?

PILAR.—¿Y compráramos otra nueva
para la sala?

And bought another (new) . . .

MARI.—Vamos a medirla a ver si viene
bien.

Let's measure it to see if it will do.

JAIME.—¿Dónde está la cinta métrica?

measuring tape?

MADRE.—Aquí la tienes.

Here it is.

TERE.—Aunque fuera algo grande para
el comedor, se podría doblar.
(*Se van a medirla.*)

it could be folded.

Calle del General Pardiñas

JAIME.—Tres metros por cuatro y medio.

(*about* 10′ × 15′)

MADRE.—En cuanto queráis, podéis traerla. Llevo años queriendo poner una alfombra en el comedor.

You can bring it as soon as you want. For years I have been wanting to put a rug in the dining room.

104

DIÁLOGO 24

TERE.—Necesitamos un par de sillones cómodos para ver la televisión después de cenar.

PILAR.—De modo que podemos comprar nuevos para la sala y traer los de la sala aquí.

PADRE.—Ahora comprendo por qué llaman a la televisión la "Nueva Tirana".

JAIME.—Y es que necesita distancia, perspectiva, alfombra, y hasta sillones cómodos.

PADRE.—Pero mientras sea yo el padre de familia, el único tirano aquí soy yo.

But as long as I'm the head of the house, I am the only tyrant here.

MADRE.—Hasta que venga mañana, hay tiempo para decidir dónde lo ponemos.

PADRE.—Siempre que no aumentéis el gasto. Es un aparato bastante caro en sí mismo.

As long as you don't increase the expense. It is a rather expensive apparatus in itself.

MARI.—Si no se pensara siempre en lo que cuestan las cosas, se disfrutarían más.

If one didn't always think about what things cost, one would enjoy them more.

PADRE.—Si no fuera por lo que llamáis mi tacañería, estaríamos comiendo la sopa boba.

If it weren't for what you call my stinginess, we would be eating handouts.

LENGUA (Ver 66.)

MODISMOS Y VOCABULARIO ADICIONAL

venir bien   to fit, to suit
llevar (tiempo)   for (time)
de modo (*or* **manera**) **que**   so that (then)
la sopa boba   handout, free food given to the poor

bajar to go or come down	el **periódico** newspaper
la **distancia** distance	la **perspectiva** perspective
feliz happy	**querer** (I) to love, to want
mientras while, as long as	el **televisor** TV set
el **par** pair, couple, two	el **tirano** the tyrant

Present and preterit of **traer** (to bring):

traigo, traes, trae, traemos, traéis, traen
traje, trajiste, trajo, trajimos, trajisteis, trajeron

EJERCICIOS ORALES

1. Expresar las siguientes oraciones en el pasado. (66.)

Ejemplo: EL PROFESOR.—Rosa toca el piano de modo que él pueda oírla.
   EL ALUMNO.—**Rosa tocó el piano de modo que él pudiera oírla.**

Nos dicen que saldrán aunque haga fresco.
Lorenzo lo pone de manera que no se pueda caer.
Dice que me lo dirá cuando vuelva.
Hace todo porque sean felices.
Dice que comerán mientras haya dinero.
Pueden tener postre siempre que coman las verduras.
Por mucho que estudie, no podrá pasar el examen.
Rosa toca el piano de modo que él pueda oírla.

2. Cambiar las oraciones según el ejemplo. (66.)

Ejemplo: EL PROFESOR.—Rosa siempre espera hasta que él vuelve.
   EL ALUMNO.—**Rosa esperará hasta que él vuelva.**

Ellos siempre escriben cuando tienen tiempo.
Rosa siempre me escribe cuando puede.
Juan siempre nos llama en cuanto llega.
Ellas siempre salen en cuanto ven mi coche.
Los niños siempre se acuestan después que salimos.
Nosotros siempre nos quedamos hasta que cenan.
Yo siempre bajo cuando traen el periódico.
Rosa siempre espera hasta que él vuelve.

106

3. (66.) *Ejemplo:* EL PROFESOR.—Es guapa.

                    EL ALUMNO.—**Aunque es guapa, no me gusta.**

                    EL PROFESOR.—No es guapa.

                    EL ALUMNO.—**Aunque fuera guapa, no me gustaría.**

Tiene dinero.	No tiene dinero.
Son inteligentes.	No son inteligentes.
Puede hacerlo.	No puede hacerlo.
Sabe bailar bien.	No sabe bailar bien.
Está hecho con huevos.	No está hecho con huevos.
Te quieren.	No te quieren.
Juega al fútbol.	No juega al fútbol.
Cuesta poco.	No cuesta poco.
Es guapa.	No es guapa.

PREGUNTAS SOBRE EL DIÁLOGO

1. ¿Dónde quiere la madre poner el televisor cuando lo traigan? 2. ¿Por qué quiere el padre ponerlo en el comedor? 3. ¿Qué es lo que le gustaría a la madre tener en el comedor? 4. ¿Cómo está la alfombra de la sala? 5. ¿Dónde la van a poner? 6. ¿Qué alfombra van a poner en la sala? 7. ¿Con qué miden la alfombra? 8. ¿Cuánto mide la alfombra? 9. ¿Cuándo pueden cambiar la alfombra? 10. ¿Qué quiere la madre poner en el comedor? 11. ¿Qué necesitan para ver la televisión después de cenar? 12. ¿Cómo llaman a la televisión? 13. ¿Por qué la llaman la "Nueva Tirana"? 14. ¿Quién es el tirano en esa familia? 15. ¿Qué es lo que hay tiempo para decidir? 16. ¿Cómo se disfrutarían más las cosas?

DIÁLOGO 25

El Rastro, un domingo por la mañana

Personajes: Pilar, Lorenzo, Ricardo, Elisa, un desconocido

PILAR.—Aquí se vende y se compra de todo.

Here everything is bought and sold.

LORENZO.—¡Cómo está esto de gente! Hay miles de personas.

How crowded this place is! There are thousands of people.

RICARDO.—Ponte la cartera en sitio seguro, pues aquí se la roban al más listo.

they steal it from the most alert person.

LORENZO.—Ten cuidado tú. Nos la pueden robar a todos.

(*Alguien, al pasar, empuja a Lorenzo sobre Ricardo.*)

DESCONOCIDO.—¡Perdóneme!

PILAR.—No discutamos. Tenemos poco tiempo. Yo quiero ver las galerías de antigüedades.

Let's not argue. the antique shops.

ELISA.—A mí me interesan los libros de viejo.

I'm interested in secondhand books.

PILAR.—Pues cada uno va a lo suyo y podemos reunirnos aquí dentro de hora y media.

Well, each one can go to do what he wants, and we can meet here within an hour and a half.

El Rastro, un domingo por la mañana

RICARDO.—Muy bien. Vente conmigo, Elisa. Vamos a ver los libros. Adiós. (*Se van.*)

LORENZO.—Pili, te acompaño a las galerías.

(*En los puestos de libros de viejo, hojeando libros.*)

(*At the secondhand book stalls, leafing through books.*)

ELISA.—Hazme el favor de dejarme tu pluma. Esto es interesante. Quiero anotarlo.

Please let me use your pen. I want to make a note of it.

RICARDO.—¡Mi pluma! Si la tenía en el bolsillo. ¡Me la han robado!

Why, I had it in my pocket! It has been stolen from me!

ELISA.—¿Pero cómo no nos hemos dado cuenta? Busca bien.

But how come we didn't realize it? Look carefully.

RICARDO.—No, no la tengo. Cincuenta mil veces me he dicho que no debía de llevarla en el bolsillo de la americana. Es una Parker que me regaló mi padre y tiene mis iniciales grabadas.

my initials engraved.

(*Al cabo de hora y media se reúnen, Elisa y Ricardo cabizbajos.*)

PILAR.—¿Qué os pasa?

What's wrong with you two?

ELISA.—Le han robado la pluma.

LORENZO.—Mira. Ve al sitio donde acabo de comprar esta Parker. Ha sido una ganga.

Look. Go to the place where I've just bought this Parker pen. It was a bargain.

RICARDO.—Déjamela ver. ¡Lorenzo! ¡Si es mi pluma! Dime la verdad. ¿Me la has quitado tú?

Why, it's my pen!

PILAR.—Te está tomando el pelo.

RICARDO.—Esto pasa ya de la raya.

This has gone too far.

LORENZO.—(*A las chicas.*) Parece que no le ha hecho gracia la broma.

It seems that he didn't find the joke very funny.

ELISA.—¡No te enfades, Ricardo!

RICARDO.—Me las vas a pagar. Vaya susto que me has hecho pasar.

You'll pay me for this. What a scare you gave me.

110

DIÁLOGO 25

LENGUA (Ver 67.)

MODISMOS Y VOCABULARIO ADICIONAL

vender de todo   to sell all sorts of things
de viejo   secondhand, used
haz (haga) el favor de/infinitivo   please/verb
esto pasa de la raya   this has gone too far
hacer gracia   to be funny
me las vas a pagar   you'll pay me for this (that)
poner un telegrama   to send a telegram

cabizbajo dejected	**perdonar** to pardon
el **cabo** end	**quitar** to take away, to take off
la **cuenta** bill, account	**regalar** to give (as a gift)
el **desconocido** unknown person	**seguro** sure, safe
empujar to push	**sobre** on, upon, about
la **estrella** star	

The irregular affirmative commands (**tú** form) of **decir, hacer, ir, poner, salir, ser, tener,** and **venir**:

di (tell)	**pon** (put)	**ten** (have)
haz (do)	**sal** (leave)	**ven** (come)
ve (go)	**sé** (be)	

EJERCICIOS ORALES

1. (67a.)   *Ejemplo:* EL PROFESOR.—Quitaron a Lorenzo su pluma.
           EL ALUMNO.—**Se la quitaron.**

Regaló a su novia el reloj.	No hable usted a Ricardo.
Dirán a su padre la verdad.	No pongan ustedes el telegrama ahora.
Empujó a la alumna.	¿Han enviado las cuentas este mes?
El desconocido robó la cartera.	Yo daría a usted el libro si fuera mío.
Compramos unos libros de viejo.	Quitaron a Lorenzo su pluma.

111

2. (67b.)   *Ejemplo:* EL PROFESOR.—Siguiendo la estrella, llegarían a Belén.
EL ALUMNO.—**Siguiéndola, llegarían a Belén.**

Diga al policía sus señas.
Nos gusta leer las novelas inglesas.
Se aprende estudiando las lecciones.
Cuenten la historia a los niños.
Tráiganme los otros, por favor.
Nos alegramos de no haber comprado la casa.
Es bastante inteligente para hacer el trabajo.
Siguiendo la estrella, llegarían a Belén.

3. (67c.)   *Ejemplo:* EL PROFESOR.—Están llamando a Juan.
EL ALUMNO.—**Le están llamando.**
Están llamándole.

Sabe cantar la canción.
No pude abrir las ventanas.
Volveremos a ver a nuestros amigos.
¿Quieres poner esta ropa en mi dormitorio?
Iban a escribir las cartas.
Le dejaron poner la maleta allí.
¿Tienen que devolver las entradas?
Hemos venido a buscar a mi hermano.
Están llamando a Juan.

PREGUNTAS SOBRE EL DIÁLOGO

1. ¿Qué se vende y se compra en el Rastro? 2. ¿Cuánta gente hay? 3. ¿Por qué hay que ponerse la cartera en sitio seguro? 4. ¿Quién empujó a Lorenzo? 5. ¿Qué hace Lorenzo cuando le empujan sobre Ricardo? 6. ¿Qué quiere ver Pilar? 7. ¿A dónde va cada uno? 8. ¿Cuándo se van a reunir? 9. ¿Dónde? 10. ¿Con quién va Elisa? 11. ¿Con quién va Pilar? 12. ¿Dónde tenía Ricardo la pluma? 13. ¿De qué no se han dado cuenta? 14. ¿Quién le regaló la pluma? 15. ¿Quién le quitó la pluma? 16. ¿Le ha hecho gracia a Ricardo la broma?

DIÁLOGO 26

Un antiguo compañero de colegio

Personajes: Carlos, Ricardo, Lorenzo, una camarera

(*Lorenzo y Ricardo están sentados en la barra de una cafetería de la Gran Vía. Carlos se acerca.*)

. . . at the counter of a snack bar on the Gran Vía.

CARLOS.—Hola Lorenzo. Hola Ricardo. No os había reconocido.

LORENZO.—Hola Carlos. ¡Tanto tiempo sin verte!

I haven't seen you in ages!

RICARDO.—Uno se hace viejo, pero es fácil reconocerse.

One can turn old, but it's easy to recognize one another.

CARLOS.—Yo me estoy volviendo calvo.

I'm becoming bald.

RICARDO.—¿Qué es de tu vida?

How are things with you?

LORENZO.—Si no tienes prisa, vamos a sentarnos en una mesa fuera y charlamos.

If you aren't in a hurry, let's sit at a table outside and we can chat.

CARLOS.—Con mucho gusto.

CAMARERA.—¿Qué van a tomar?

What are you going to have?

LORENZO.—Un limón natural.

A lemonade.

CARLOS.—Un café solo.

Black coffee.

RICARDO.—Para mí con leche.

Make mine (*coffee*) with milk.

113

LORENZO.—¿Qué estudias?	What are you studying?
CARLOS.—Ingeniero industrial.	(*I'm studying to be an*) industrial engineer.
RICARDO.—Buena carrera. Puedes llegar a ser importante. (*Llega la camarera.*)	That's a good profession.

Un café al aire libre

Philip Gendreau Photo

DIÁLOGO 26

CAMARERA.—¿De quién es este zumo de naranja?

Whose is this orange juice?

LORENZO.—Lo que yo he pedido ha sido limón natural.

CAMARERA.—No sé qué me pasa hoy. No doy una. (*Al poner las tazas, tira café sobre la mesa.*) ¡Ay! ¡Perdón! Acabo de tirar jugo de tomate sobre el abrigo de una señorita y me he puesto tan nerviosa que no sé lo que hago.

I don't do anything right. (*On placing the cups, she spills . . .*)

RICARDO.—Se enfadaría, ¿no?

She probably got angry, didn't she?

CAMARERA.—Se puso hecha una fiera y dijo que me iba a enviar la cuenta del tinte. Ahora le traigo su limón.

CARLOS.—¿Qué tal es la carrera de Filosofía y Letras?

How's the Liberal Arts course?

RICARDO.—No es difícil, pero no se puede llegar a ser profesor en propiedad sin hacer oposiciones.

. . . but one cannot become a teacher with tenure without taking competitive exams.

LORENZO.—Y generalmente para cada vacante se presentan cincuenta o sesenta candidatos.

for each vacancy (of a permanent position).

CARLOS.—Eso pasa porque hay pocas universidades privadas.
(*Llega la camarera.*)

CAMARERA.—Aquí está su horchata.
(*La deja y se marcha.*)

Here's your *horchata* (*a milk drink made from chufa seeds*).

LORENZO.—¡Pero esa mujer se ha vuelto tonta!

Why, that woman has gone daffy!

LENGUA (Ver 68.)

MODISMOS Y VOCABULARIO ADICIONAL

¡Tanto tiempo sin verte!   I haven't seen you in ages!
¿Qué es de tu vida?   How are things with you?
No doy una.   I don't do anything right.
ponerse hecho una fiera   to become like a wild beast, to become very angry

antiguo old	**pasar** to happen
cada each, every	el **presidente** president
la **camarera** waitress	**privado** private
el **campeón** champion	**reconocer** to recognize
el **candidato** candidate	el **rey** king
el **enemigo** enemy	**rojo** red
el **jugo** juice	la **señorita** lady, Miss
el **miembro** member	el **sindicato** union
el **ministro** minister	el **tenis** tennis
nervioso nervous	el **torero** bullfighter

EJERCICIOS ORALES

1. (68a.)   *Ejemplo:* EL PROFESOR.—Ella se puso *bien.*   **malo**
      EL ALUMNO.—**Ella se puso mala.**

Ellos se pusieron *malos.*   **bien, pálido, rojo, triste, alegre, rabioso, contento, de mal humor, enfermo**

Ella se puso *bien.*   **pálido, rojo, triste, alegre, rabioso, contento, de mal humor, enfermo, malo**

2. (68a.)   *Ejemplo:* EL PROFESOR.—*Ella* se está volviendo loca.   **él**
      EL ALUMNO.—**Él se está volviendo loco.**

Su padre se volvió sordo.   **su madre, el profesor, yo, el pintor, el escritor, sus padres, mi hermano**

Ella se está volviendo loca.   **ellos, ellas, su hermano, la hermana, la reina, el rey, el escritor, la escritora, ella**

3. (68b.)   *Ejemplo:* EL PROFESOR.—¿Son amigos Elisa y Ricardo?
      EL ALUMNO.—**Sí. Se hicieron amigos el año pasado.**

¿Son ustedes amigos?
¿Son novios Elisa y Ricardo?
¿Es usted miembro del club?
¿Son ellos miembros del club?
¿Es tu padre miembro del sindicato?

¿Sois miembros del sindicato?
¿Él es rico?
¿Son ricos sus padres?
¿Son amigos Elisa y Ricardo?

116

DIÁLOGO 26

4. (68b.) *Ejemplo:* EL PROFESOR.—¿Fue un escritor de fama?

                 EL ALUMNO.—**No. Nunca llegó a ser un escritor de fama.**

¿Fue ministro?	¿Fue un pintor de fama internacional?
¿Fueron amigos?	¿Fue usted campeón de tenis?
¿Fue un torero famoso?	¿Fueron enemigos?
¿Fue presidente de la compañía?	¿Fue un escritor de fama?

PREGUNTAS SOBRE EL DIÁLOGO

1. ¿De quién es amigo Carlos? 2. ¿Es difícil reconocerse aunque uno se haga viejo? 3. ¿Qué se está volviendo Carlos? 4. ¿Dónde se sientan los tres amigos? 5. ¿Qué van a tomar? 6. ¿Qué puede llegar a ser Carlos? 7. ¿Quién ha pedido zumo de naranja? 8. ¿Qué acaba de hacer la camarera? 9. ¿Se enfadó la señorita? 10. ¿Qué tal es la carrera de Filosofía y Letras? 11. ¿Hay universidades privadas en España? 12. ¿Qué le trae la camarera a Lorenzo? 13. ¿Qué había pedido Lorenzo? 14. ¿Por qué dice Lorenzo que se ha vuelto tonta la camarera?

DIÁLOGO 27

El comilón

Personajes: Juanito, Mamá, Elisa, el médico don José Ocaña

JUANITO.—¡Ay, mamá! ¡Qué mal me siento! ¡Ay, mamá, estoy más malo de lo que crees!

MAMÁ.—El médico vendrá en seguida. En menos de media hora dijo que estaría aquí.

JUANITO.—¡Ay! Eso es más de lo que puedo esperar con estos dolores.

MAMÁ.—Calma, hijo. Hay que tener más paciencia de la que tú tienes.

Be calm, son. You have to be more patient than you are.

ELISA.—(*Entrando*.) Mamá, el doctor Ocaña está aquí.

MAMÁ.—Que pase. Ya ves, ha tardado menos de lo que pensábamos.

Have him come in. You see, he took less time than we thought.

(*El médico entra.*)

MAMÁ.—Buenas tardes, don José.

D. JOSÉ.—Buenas tardes. Vamos a ver, Juanito. ¿Qué te duele?

JUANITO.—El estómago, la garganta, y la cabeza. Los oídos me zumban y tengo náusea.

ring and I feel nauseated.

118

Un supermercado

D. José.—Con menos cosas de las que a ti te duelen, se puede estar muy grave. A ver. Saca la lengua. (*Le toma el pulso y le pone el termómetro.*) No tienes fiebre. ¿Qué has comido hoy?

Juanito.—Churros en el desayuno.

D. José.—¿Cuántos?

Juanito.—Comí más de una docena.

One can be gravely ill with less things than those that ail you. Let's see. Stick out your tongue.

. . . and he puts the thermometer in his mouth.)

Churros for breakfast.

119

ELISA.—¡Qué barbaridad! Y además, al mediodía te has comido más pasteles de los que te correspondían.

Good grief! And besides, at noontime you ate more cakes than your share.

MAMÁ.—Este niño, don José, come más de prisa de lo que debe. Lo come todo sin masticar.

faster than he should.

D. JOSÉ.—Pues, Juanito, estás mejor de lo que mereces. Vas a tomar un purgante. (*Escribe la receta*.) ¿A cuántos estamos?

ELISA.—A veinte y dos de noviembre.

MAMÁ.—¿Qué día de semana es hoy?

ELISA.—Jueves. Vienen a merendar mis amigos. ¿Hiciste las empanadillas?

MAMÁ.—Sí, hice más de las que me dijiste. Están ahí en el aparador.

ELISA.—(*Va a mirar*.) ¡Mamá, las empanadillas han desaparecido! (*Los tres miran a Juanito que hace gestos de dolor de estómago*.)

...makes grimaces of having a stomach ache.)

D. JOSÉ.—Aumentaré la dosis del purgante.

LENGUA (Ver 69–70.)

MODISMOS Y VOCABULARIO ADICIONAL

en seguida   immediately
Calma.   Be calm.
tener paciencia   to be patient
de prisa   fast
¿A cuántos estamos?   What is the date?

bastante   enough, sufficient, quite
comilón   glutton
la **docena**   dozen
la **dosis**   dosage, dose

120

DIÁLOGO 27

la **empanadilla**   turnover (meat or fruit)
el **estómago**   stomach
la **fiebre**   fever
la **garganta**   throat
  masticar   to chew
  merendar (I)   to have a snack or tea around 6 p.m., between dinner (2 p.m.) and
       supper (9:30 p.m.)
el **oído**   (inner) ear
el **pulso**   pulse
el **purgante**   laxative, purgative
la **receta**   prescription

EJERCICIOS ORALES

2. (69a.)   *Ejemplo:* EL PROFESOR.—Él no come de prisa.
               EL ALUMNO.—**Come más de prisa de lo que usted cree.**

La lección no es fácil.   Lorenzo no pinta bien.
El hablar español no es difícil. No tiene mucha fuerza.
Ella no estudia mucho.   Ella no sabe mucho.
Ellos no comen mucho.   Él no come de prisa.

1. Contestar, dando cualquier número apropiado. (69a.)

Ejemplo: EL PROFESOR.—¿Han hecho unas fotos?
          EL ALUMNO.—**Han hecho más de cien.**

¿Han leído algunos libros?   ¿Han escrito algunas cartas?
¿Han venido muchos alumnos?   ¿Han traído algunas sillas?
¿Han comido pasteles?   ¿Han faltado a muchas clases?
¿Han hecho bastantes empanadillas?   ¿Han hecho unas fotos?

3. (69a.)   *Ejemplo:* EL PROFESOR.—¿Tiene usted bastante dinero?
               EL ALUMNO.—**Más del que necesito.**

¿Tiene usted bastantes camisas?   ¿Tiene usted bastante gasolina?
¿Tiene usted bastante tiempo?   ¿Tienen ustedes bastante agua?
¿Tienen ustedes bastantes lápices?   ¿Tiene usted bastantes pasteles?
¿Tienen ustedes bastantes aspirinas? ¿Tiene usted bastante dinero?

121

4. (69b.)   *Ejemplo:* EL PROFESOR.—¿Cuál es mejor, éste o ése?
             EL ALUMNO.—**Éste es mejor que ése.**

¿Quiénes hicieron más, ustedes o los otros?
¿Quién sabe más, ella o él?
¿Qué sillón es más cómodo, éste o aquel?
¿Qué le gustan más, las empanadillas o los pasteles?
¿Quién come más, Ricardo o Lorenzo?
¿Cuál es más bonito, el suyo o el de Juan?
¿Cuál es mejor, éste o ése?

PREGUNTAS SOBRE EL DIÁLOGO

1. ¿Qué le pasa a Juanito? 2. ¿Cuándo vendrá el médico? 3. ¿Puede Juanito esperar? 4. ¿Tiene Juanito paciencia? 5. ¿Ha tardado mucho el médico? 6. ¿Qué le duele a Juanito? 7. ¿Qué hace el médico? 8. ¿Tiene Juanito fiebre? 9. ¿Cuántos churros ha comido? 10. ¿Cómo dice la mamá que come Juanito? 11. ¿Está Juanito muy enfermo? 12. ¿Qué escribe el médico? 13. ¿Sabe el médico la fecha? 14. ¿Quiénes vienen a merendar? 15. ¿Cuántas empanadillas hizo la mamá? 16. ¿Dónde están las empanadillas?

DIÁLOGO 28

En la Telefónica (Telephone Building)

Personajes: Pepe, la telefonista, Señor A, Señor B, el tejano, Manolo
(*In Madrid, if one does not have a private telephone at his disposal, he goes to the Telephone Building, on the* Gran Vía, *to make long distance calls. Only local calls are made from public phone booths.*)

PEPE.—Señorita, quiero una conferencia con Ávila.

Miss, I want to make a long distance call to Avila.

TELEFONISTA.—Tiene usted que esperar una media hora.

to wait about a half hour.

SEÑOR A.—Señorita, una conferencia con el número setenta y ocho treinta y cinco de París.

. . . to Paris, number 7-8-3-5.

TELEFONISTA.—París al habla. Pase usted al locutorio número cinco.

Paris on the phone. Go to booth number 5.

(*El tejano sale del locutorio número 1.*)

TEJANO.—¡Hola, Pepe! ¿Qué haces aquí?

PEPE.—Estoy esperando que me den una conferencia con Ávila. Estoy aquí desde hace casi una hora.

TEJANO.—Acabo de llamar a Dallas, Tejas, y me han puesto al habla en seguida.

connected me immediately.

123

Ávila

SEÑOR B.—Póngame, por favor, con el número noventa y cuatro diez y nueve de Londres. ¿Tengo que esperar mucho?

Connect me, please . . . London.

124

DIÁLOGO 28

TELEFONISTA.—No señor, en el acto se la damos. Pase al locutorio número tres.

... we'll connect you immediately. (**la** *means* **conferencia**)

PEPE.—Señorita, hace una hora que llegué y todavía estoy esperando mi conferencia. Ávila está sólo a cien kilómetros.

Avila is only 65 miles away.

TELEFONISTA.—Lo siento mucho. Su conferencia tiene demora. Hace bastante rato que la línea está ocupada.

I'm very sorry. Your call is delayed.

... the line (*to Avila*) has been busy.

TEJANO.—¡Hombre! Tengo una idea! (*Hablan por lo bajo.*)

(*They talk in a low voice.*)

PEPE.—(*A la telefonista.*) Señorita, anule mi conferencia con Ávila y póngame con el número setenta y cuatro trece de Lisboa.

cancel my call ...

Lisbon.

TELEFONISTA.—Lisboa al habla. Pase al locutorio número cinco.

PEPE.—(*Al teléfono.*) ¿Manolo? Soy Pepe.

MANOLO.—¡Hola! ¡Tanto tiempo sin saber de ti!

PEPE.—Quiero pedirte un favor. Desde hace más de una hora estoy tratando de conseguir una conferencia con Ávila.

MANOLO.—Ya comprendo. Quieres que llame yo a Ávila desde Lisboa.

PEPE.—Sí, por favor.

MANOLO.—Chico, eso es para morirse de risa.

Boy, is that a laugh!

LENGUA (Ver 71.)

MODISMOS Y VOCABULARIO ADICIONAL

querer una conferencia con   to want to make a long distance call to
una media hora   about a half hour
al habla   on the phone, speaking
poner al habla   to connect
en seguida   immediately
poner con   to connect with
en el acto   right away, immediately
tener demora   to be delayed
hablar por lo bajo   to speak in a low voice
es para morirse de risa   to be extremely laughable

    conseguir (like **seguir**)   to obtain, to get, to attain
    desayunarse   to breakfast, to have breakfast
la **telefonista**   the operator (telephone switchboard girl)

EJERCICIOS ORALES

1. Contestar, dando cualquier tiempo apropiado. (71a.)

   Ejemplo: EL PROFESOR.—¿Cuánto tiempo hace que usted lo tiene?
        EL ALUMNO.—**Hace dos años que lo tengo.**

¿Cuánto tiempo hace que usted la conoce?
¿Cuánto tiempo hace que usted está estudiando?
¿Cuánto tiempo hace que usted está leyendo?
¿Cuánto tiempo hace que usted está sentado ahí?
¿Cuánto tiempo hace que usted vive aquí?
¿Cuánto tiempo hace que usted está esperando?
¿Cuánto tiempo hace que estamos hablando?
¿Cuánto tiempo hace que usted lo sabe?
¿Cuánto tiempo hace que usted lo tiene?

2. Contestar, dando cualquier tiempo apropiado. (71a.)

   Ejemplo: EL PROFESOR.—¿Cuánto tiempo hacía que usted lo tenía?
        EL ALUMNO.—**Hacía dos años que lo tenía.**

¿Cuánto tiempo hacía que usted lo conocía?
¿Cuánto tiempo hacía que usted estaba estudiando?
¿Cuánto tiempo hacía que usted estaba leyendo?

¿Cuánto tiempo hacía que usted estaba sentado allí?
¿Cuánto tiempo hacía que usted vivía allí?
¿Cuánto tiempo hacía que usted estaba esperando?
¿Cuánto tiempo hacía que estábamos hablando?
¿Cuánto tiempo hacía que usted lo sabía?
¿Cuánto tiempo hacía que usted lo tenía?

3. Contestar, dando cualquier tiempo apropiado. (71a.)

Ejemplo: EL PROFESOR.—¿Hace mucho tiempo que lo tienen ustedes?
  EL ALUMNO.—**Lo tenemos desde hace dos años.**

¿Hace mucho tiempo que las conocen ustedes?
¿Hace mucho tiempo que lo usan ustedes?
¿Hace mucho tiempo que están casados?
¿Hace mucho tiempo que no han tenido ustedes carta?
¿Hace mucho tiempo que no han comido ustedes?
¿Hacía mucho tiempo que iban allí?
¿Hacía mucho tiempo que vivían ustedes allí?
¿Hace mucho tiempo que lo tienen ustedes?

4. Contestar, dando cualquier tiempo apropiado. (71b.)

Ejemplo: EL PROFESOR.—¿Cuándo se casaron ellos?
  EL ALUMNO.—**Hace trece años que se casaron.**
  Se casaron hace trece años.

¿Cuándo se fueron sus padres?   ¿Cuándo hizo usted los ejercicios para hoy?
¿Cuándo se levantó usted?   ¿Cuándo llegó usted a la clase?
¿Cuándo se desayunó usted?   ¿Cuándo estaba él aquí?
¿Cuándo comenzó esta clase?   ¿Cuándo se casaron ellos?

PREGUNTAS SOBRE EL DIÁLOGO

1. ¿Dónde está Pepe? 2. ¿Qué es lo que quiere? 3. ¿Con quién habla? 4. ¿Cuánto tiempo tiene que esperar? 5. ¿Qué quiere el señor A? 6. ¿Tiene que esperar mucho tiempo? 7. ¿Quién sale del locutorio número uno? 8. ¿Ha esperado mucho tiempo para tener una conferencia con Dallas? 9. ¿Qué quiere el señor B? 10. ¿Tiene que esperar mucho tiempo? 11. ¿Cuánto tiempo hace que está esperando Pepe? 12. ¿A qué distancia está Ávila? 13. ¿Por qué tardan tanto en darle la conferencia con Ávila? 14. ¿Cuál es la idea que tiene el tejano? 15. ¿Tardan mucho en darle la conferencia con Lisboa? 16. ¿Qué es para morirse de risa?

DIÁLOGO 29

Correos (Post Office)

Personajes: Ricardo, el tejano, Lorenzo, empleado A, empleado B, empleado C, empleado D

LORENZO.—Si quieres llevar ese paquete a correos, tienes que darte prisa. — to hurry up.

RICARDO.—¿No tomas a mal que no te acompañemos? — You won't mind (*take it badly*) if we don't . . .

TEJANO.—No. Voy a tomar el Metro. Adiós.
(*En Correos.*)

TEJANO.—¿Me hace el favor? ¿Para enviar un paquete al extranjero? — Pardon me. What must I do in order to send a package to a foreign country?

EMPL. A.—Tome uno de estos papeles. Tiene que rellenarlo, y después, vaya a pesar el paquete a aquella ventanilla. — You must fill it out . . . go to weigh the package at that window.

EMPL. B.—¿Para dónde es este paquete?

TEJANO.—Para los Estados Unidos.

EMPL. B.—Pesa exactamente un kilo. — (*kilo* = 2.2 *pounds*)

TEJANO.—Quiero certificarlo. — I want to register it.

128

DIÁLOGO 29

EMPL. B.—Tiene que llevarlo a aquella ventanilla donde pone "sellos", para el franqueo, y después, lo certifica en aquella otra ventanilla.

it says "stamps," for the postage, ...

(*En la ventanilla de los sellos.*)

EMPL. C.—Son treinta pesetas.

TEJANO.—Deme también diez aerogramas, por favor.

air letters, please.

EMPL. C.—Tiene que salir a la calle y entrar por la puerta de los buzones. Allí venden los aerogramas.

Los buzones en Correos

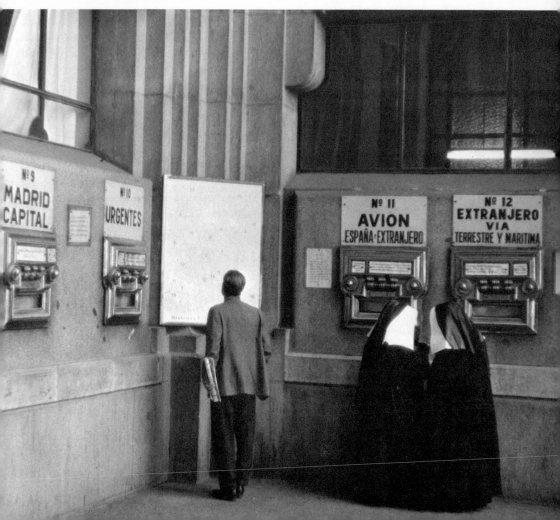

TEJANO.—¡Ah! Ahora a la ventanilla
para certificar. ¿Dónde está?

EMPL. C.—Al final de aquel corredor.

(*En la ventanilla de los certificados.*)

TEJANO.—Quiero certificar este paquete.

EMPL. D.—Hay que poner sus señas al
reverso. (*Él lo hace.*)

It is necessary to put your address on the
back.

TEJANO.—¿Tengo que llevar el paquete
a alguna otra ventanilla?

EMPL. D.—No, esto es todo. (*El tejano
se ríe.*) ¿De qué se ríe usted?

What are you laughing at?

TEJANO.—Anduve tanto llevando este
paquete de ventanilla en ventanilla
que se me ocurrió que sería más fácil
llevarle a mano que enviarle por
correo.

... that it occurred to me that it
would be easier to carry it by hand
than to send it by mail.

LENGUA (72.)

MODISMOS Y VOCABULARIO ADICIONAL

tomar a mal   to mind, to take badly
¿Me hace el favor?   Pardon me (precedes the asking a favor, e.g., requesting
directions, information, etc.)
de ____ en ____   from ____ to ____
a mano   by hand, at hand
reírse de   to laugh at
hacer una foto   to take a picture
hacer un viaje   to take a trip
echar(se)   to take a nap, to lie down
echar(se) la siesta   to take an afternoon nap (right after the noonday meal)
bañarse   to take a bath
aprovechar   to take advantage of

el **buzón**   mailbox
el **corredor**   hall, hallway
los **Estados Unidos**   United States

el **parque**   park
por   through
el **saldo**   sale

130

DIÁLOGO 29

Present and preterit of **reir** (III, to laugh)

río	reímos	reí	reímos
ríes	reís	reíste	reísteis
ríe	ríen	rio	rieron

Past participle—**reído**

Present participle—**riendo**

Preterit of **andar** (to walk)

anduve	anduvimos
anduviste	anduvisteis
anduvo	anduvieron

EJERCICIOS ORALES

1. (72.)   Formar una oración con las palabras dadas, usando el verbo *llevar* o *tomar*, según el sentido.

Ejemplo: EL PROFESOR.—El médico _____ el pulso a Juan.
  EL ALUMNO.—**El médico le tomó el pulso a Juan.**

El bedel _____ los libros a la biblioteca.
El policía _____ a Ricardo a la comisaría.
Ellos le _____ por un pintor famoso.
Por tener dolor de cabeza _____ aspirina.
_____ la falda al tinte.
Nosotros _____ un taxi porque era tarde.
Siempre lo han _____ en serio.
Hace cuatro horas que _____ la medicina.
Mi amigo me va a _____ a su casa.
El médico _____ el pulso a Juan.

2. Formar una oración con las palabras dadas.

Ejemplo: EL PROFESOR.—bañarse anoche
  EL ALUMNO.—**Me bañé anoche antes de cenar.**

hacer muchas fotos	hacer un viaje a España
echarse la siesta	llevar el paquete a Correos
dar un paseo por el parque	aprovechar los saldos
tomar clases particulares	bañarse anoche

131

3. Terminar la frase, usando "reirse de mí" en el tiempo indicado por el sentido de las palabras dadas.

Ejemplo: EL PROFESOR.—Anduvo por la calle.
   EL ALUMNO.—**Anduvo por la calle riéndose de mí.**

hace poco	ayer	siempre	no me gusta
es posible	es cierto	no quiero	no comprendo por qué
todavía	dudo	dígales	anduvo por la calle
sé	me dijeron	yo temía	

PREGUNTAS SOBRE EL DIÁLOGO

1. ¿A dónde va el tejano? 2. ¿Toma a mal que no le acompañen? 3. ¿Va andando o en Metro? 4. ¿A dónde va a enviar el paquete? 5. ¿Qué hay que hacer para enviar un paquete al extranjero? 6. ¿A dónde tiene que llevar el paquete para certificarlo? 7. ¿Cuánto cuesta enviar el paquete? 8. ¿Qué pide el tejano en la ventanilla de los sellos, después de pagar los sellos del paquete? 9. ¿Dónde venden los aerogramas? 10. ¿Dónde está la ventanilla de los certificados? 11. ¿Dónde hay que poner las señas? 12. ¿Tiene el tejano que llevar el paquete a alguna otra ventanilla? 13. ¿A cuántas ventanillas tuvo que llevar el paquete? 14. ¿De qué se ríe el tejano?

La Avenida de la Ciudad Universitaria

DIÁLOGO 30

El enemigo público número uno

Personajes: Pilar, Elisa, Lorenzo, Ricardo, Jaime, Tere
(*Al terminar las clases.*)

PILAR.—Vamos a volver a casa andando.   Let's walk home.

ELISA.—Hace un tiempo estupendo para invierno.

133

LORENZO.—Esperar a Ricardo.

PILAR.—¿Has estudiado la lección de historia para mañana?

LORENZO.—Hasta ahora no he podido por falta de tiempo.

RICARDO.—(*Llega.*) Gracias por haberme esperado.

ELISA.—Hemos decidido ir andando.

RICARDO.—Muy bien. Hace un tiempo de primavera.

(*Van andando por la Avenida de la Ciudad Universitaria. Un coche les pasa y se para.*)

PILAR.—¡Es el coche de Jaime, y mi hermana Tere va conduciendo! ... Tere is driving!

TODOS.—Hola, ¿qué hay? Hello, what do you say?

JAIME.—Subiros y os llevamos a donde queráis. Tere tiene que practicar para su examen del carnet de conducir. Get in ...

ELISA.—Pensábamos andar hasta casa, pero hace un poco aire. but it's a bit windy.

JAIME.—Subir. Hay sitio para todos.

(*Se suben.*)

RICARDO.—¿Qué tal se te da el volante, Tere? How are you getting along at the wheel, Tere?

TERE.—No se me da mal, para la poca experiencia que tengo.

JAIME.—Le di la primera lección hace solamente dos días.

134

DIÁLOGO 30

TERE.—Jaime me dijo: "Ponte al volante. Ahí tienes embrague, freno, acelerador, y cambio de velocidades."

"Get behind the wheel. There's the clutch, brake, gas pedal, and stick (*shift*)."

LORENZO.—Y darías marcha atrás.

And you probably put it in reverse.

TERE.—No. Pisé el acelerador y salí disparada por la calle sin pararme en ninguno de los pasos para peatones.

I stepped on the gas and zoomed down the street without stopping at any of the pedestrian crossings.

RICARDO.—¿Te pusieron una multa?

Were you fined?

TERE.—No. La gente me tomaba por loca, pero yo perdí el miedo.
(*Tere por poco atropella a un peatón.*)

(*Tere almost runs over a pedestrian.*)

ELISA.—Ahora que me acuerdo, tenemos que ir por las entradas para el concierto y estamos cerca del teatro. ¿Puedes parar?

JAIME.—Aparca allí, junto al bordillo de la acera y les esperamos.

Park over there, next to the curbing and we'll wait for them.

LORENZO.—No, gracias. No nos esperéis. Seguimos andando, que es buen ejercicio para la salud.

PILAR.—Yo no voy. Toma el dinero para mi entrada.

RICARDO.—Gracias por traernos.

TODOS.—Adiós.
(*Se bajan.*)

(*They get out.*)

TERE.—(*A Jaime.*) ¿Es que crees que se han asustado de mi manera de conducir?

Do you think that they were frightened by my driving?

LENGUA (73.)

MODISMOS Y VOCABULARIO ADICIONAL

¿Qué hay? What's up? What do you say?
¿Qué tal se te da ____?   How are you getting along with ____?
dar (ir) marcha atrás   to put (go) in reverse
poner una multa   to fine
asustarse de   to be frightened by
¿Qué (tal) tiempo hace? How's the weather?
Hace buen (mal) tiempo. It's nice (bad) weather.
Hace un día hermoso. It's a beautiful day.
Hacía mucho frío cuando entré. It was cold when I entered.
Hizo mucho calor ayer. It was very warm yesterday.
Va a hacer fresco esta noche. It is going to be cool this evening (tonight).
Hace sol. It is sunny. The sun is out.
¿Hace mucho aire (viento)? Is it very windy?

la **acera** sidewalk	el **invierno** winter
acordarse (I) de to remember	la **multa** fine
atrás backward	el **otoño** fall
la **avenida** avenue	la **primavera** spring
bajarse to get out of	**próximo** next
el **banco** bank	el **pueblo** town
el **caballero** gentleman, man	la **salud** health
la **Ciudad Universitaria** campus	el **sitio** place, room
el **concierto** concert	la **velocidad** speed
disparar to shoot	el **verano** summer
la **farmacia** drugstore	

EJERCICIOS ORALES

1. (73a1.) *Ejemplo:* EL PROFESOR.—¿Ese abrigo es para el otoño o para el invierno?
   EL ALUMNO.—**Es para el invierno.**

¿Ese sillón es para la sala o para el comedor?
¿Esta lección es para hoy o para la próxima vez?
¿Las cartas son para usted o para mí?
¿Partieron para Argentina o para Uruguay?
¿Las entradas son para el teatro o para el concierto?

DIÁLOGO 30

¿Los sellos son para las cartas o para el paquete?
¿La conferencia es para París o para Lisboa?
¿Este vaso es para vino o para cerveza?
¿Es un reloj para señora o para caballero?
¿Ese abrigo es para el otoño o para el invierno?

2. Dar una contestación apropiada, usando **para**. (73a2.)

Ejemplo: EL PROFESOR.—¿Qué tal es la escuela?
        EL ALUMNO.—**Muy buena para un pueblo tan pequeño.**

¿Qué tal marcha el coche?   ¿Qué tal se le da a usted el español?
¿Cómo conduce Tere?   ¿Qué tal escribe Juanito?
¿Qué tal se le da a usted el volante?   ¿Qué tal es el profesor de Historia?
¿Qué tal tiempo hace?   ¿Qué tal es la escuela?
¿Cómo es Tere?

3. Dar una contestación apropiada, usando **por**. (73b1.)

Ejemplo: EL PROFESOR.—¿Por qué no van?
        EL ALUMNO.—**No van por falta de dinero.**

¿Por qué lucharon?   ¿Por qué es importante?
¿Por qué fueron a la farmacia?   ¿Por qué es famoso el Museo del Prado?
¿Por quién lo ha hecho?   ¿Por qué le dieron una paliza?
¿Por qué van ustedes al banco?   ¿Por qué le estiman?
¿Por qué fue su hermana a Correos?   ¿Por qué no van?

4. Contestar.

Ejemplo: EL PROFESOR.—¿Qué tal tiempo hace?
        EL ALUMNO.—**Hace muy buen tiempo.**

¿Qué tiempo hizo ayer?   ¿Hizo sol ayer?
¿Qué tiempo va a hacer mañana?   ¿Va a hacer sol mañana?
¿Hacía frío cuando se levantó usted?   ¿Hace aire?
¿Hizo mucho calor el verano pasado?   ¿Hizo aire ayer?
¿Hace calor en esta sala?   ¿Hará aire mañana?
¿Va a hacer un día hermoso hoy?   ¿Hizo mucho frío anoche?
¿Hace sol?   ¿Qué tal tiempo hace?

PREGUNTAS SOBRE EL DIÁLOGO

1. ¿Por qué van a volver a casa andando? 2. ¿Por qué no ha podido estudiar Lorenzo la lección de Historia? 3. ¿Por qué da las gracias Ricardo? 4. ¿De quién es el coche? 5. ¿Quién va conduciendo? 6. ¿Para qué tiene que practicar Tere? 7. ¿Hay sitio para todos en el coche? 8. ¿Qué tal se le da el volante a Tere? 9. ¿Cuándo le dio Jaime la primera lección? 10. ¿Qué le dijo Jaime? 11. ¿Qué pasó cuando Tere pisó el acelerador? 12. ¿Conduce Tere mejor ahora? 13. ¿De qué se acuerda Elisa? 14. ¿Dónde va a aparcar? 15. ¿Por qué no quiere Lorenzo que les esperen? 16. ¿Quiénes se bajan del coche? 17. ¿Por qué se han bajado?

DIÁLOGO 31

El botijo versus el frigorífico

Personajes: Lorenzo, Ricardo, Pilar, Elisa, Alicia, camarero

(*Pilar y Elisa están sentadas en un café al aire libre en la Castellana. Ricardo y Lorenzo se acercan.*)

(*Pilar and Elisa are seated in a sidewalk cafe on the Castellana Boulevard.*)

LORENZO.—¡Qué casualidad!

What a coincidence!

RICARDO.—Tomando el sol, ¿eh?

Sunning yourselves, eh?

PILAR.—Esperando a Alicia. Ya sabéis que ha vuelto de los Estados Unidos.

LORENZO.—Sí, la vi ayer.

RICARDO.—Se cuentan tantas cosas de los Estados Unidos que me gustaría oir sus impresiones.
(*Alicia se acerca.*)

You hear so many things . . .

TODOS.—¡Hola! ¿Qué tal?

ALICIA.—¡Vaya, la reunión ha sido aumentada!
(*Alicia y los dos muchachos se sientan. Ricardo hace palmas. Viene el camarero.*)

Well, the gathering has grown (*been increased*)!

RICARDO.—¿Qué vais a tomar?

TODOS.—Cerveza.

RICARDO.—Cuatro cañas.

Four small beers.

CAMARERO.—Muy bien. Se le servirá en seguida.

Vendiendo botijos en una calle de Madrid

DIÁLOGO 31

ELISA.—¿A que no hay cafés al aire libre en los Estados Unidos?

I'll bet there aren't sidewalk cafes in the United States.

ALICIA.—No, y se los echa de menos.

No, and you miss them.

PILAR.—Allí no se come muy bien, ¿verdad?

ALICIA.—En los restoranes baratos, no, pero en los caros, sí.

ELISA.—¿Y en las casas particulares?

ALICIA.—Las comidas son guisadas por las madres y generalmente son buenas.

PILAR.—¿No hay muchachas como aquí?

ALICIA.—No. El trabajo duro es hecho por las máquinas.

LORENZO.—Las máquinas no me convencen.

I'm not sold on appliances.

RICARDO.—A mí tampoco. El agua fresca es más agradable si la muchacha la sirve de un botijo que si es sacada por mí del frigorífico.

Nor am I.

ALICIA.—¡Los españoles no tenéis arreglo!

You Spaniards are hopeless!

ELISA.—Nuestras casas han sido construidas con la idea que siempre seremos servidos por muchachas.

PILAR.—Las habitaciones de servicio han sido colocadas tan lejos del comedor que es más fácil pedir el agua que levantarse por ella.

(Service quarters = **cocina** and **despensa**, i.e., kitchen and pantry.)

LORENZO.—Y además, una muchacha y un botijo cuestan menos que un frigorífico.

RICARDO.—Has dado en el clavo.

You hit the nail on the head.

141

LENGUA (46, 74, 75.)

MODISMOS Y VOCABULARIO ADICIONAL

al aire libre outdoor
tomar el sol to sun oneself, to sit in the sun
¿A que . . . ? I'll bet . . .
echar de menos to miss
dar en el clavo to hit the nail on the head

el **botijo** water jug
el **camarero** waiter
descubrir to discover
duro hard
enseñar to teach
fresco cool

el **frigorífico** freezer, refrigerator
la **lengua** language
menos less
la **muchacha** maid
sacar to take out
tan so

Present and preterit of **construir** (to construct):

construyo	construimos	construí	construimos
construyes	construís	construiste	construisteis
construye	construyen	construyó	construyeron

Present participle—**construyendo**
Like **construir**: **huir** (to flee), **sustituir** (to substitute), **destruir** (to destroy).

EJERCICIOS ORALES

1. (46, 74.) *Ejemplo:* EL PROFESOR.—Los romanos construyeron el acueducto.
   EL ALUMNO.—**El acueducto fue construido por los romanos.**

Los árabes tomaron el fuerte.
La muchacha cerró la ventana.
Juan escribió estos ejercicios.
Ricardo pidió las cañas.
Elisa hará las invitaciones.
La madre lavó la ropa.
Ella abrió las cartas.

Ellos rompieron los vasos.
Mi amiga guisó la comida.
El profesor ha llamado al alumno.
Los españoles descubrieron América.
Yo saqué el agua fresca.
Los romanos construyeron el acueducto.

DIÁLOGO 31

2. (46, 74.) *Ejemplo:* EL PROFESOR.—Va a ser arreglado por mi hermano.

   EL ALUMNO.—**Mi hermano va a arreglarlo.**

Las maletas fueron hechas por Pepe.
Ella fue reconocida por el médico.
El reloj fue roto por su hermana.
La casa fue destruida por esos hombres.
Los otros serán hechos por sus padres.
Todo eso fue dicho por tu papá.

El camino fue cubierto por la nieve.
La pregunta fue hecha por un chico.
Fueron preparadas por mí.
Será terminada por otros.
Va a ser arreglado por mi hermano.

3. (75.) *Ejemplo:* EL PROFESOR.—Vamos a hacer las invitaciones hoy.

   EL ALUMNO.—**Se van a hacer las invitaciones hoy.**

Vamos a hacer los otros mañana.
Perdieron el papel.
Encontraron las pinturas.
Ellos cultivan muchas verduras.
Todos comieron muchos pasteles.
Las mujeres guisan las comidas en la cocina.
Uno debe prepararlos por la mañana.
Abren la tienda a las nueve y media.
Cierran la tienda a las siete y cuarto.
No enseñamos las lenguas modernas en esta escuela.
Vamos a hacer las invitaciones hoy.

PREGUNTAS SOBRE EL DIÁLOGO

1. ¿Dónde están sentadas Pilar y Elisa? 2. ¿Quiénes se acercan? 3. ¿A quién esperan? 4. ¿Quién ha vuelto de Estados Unidos? 5. ¿Por qué le gustaría a Ricardo oir las impresiones de Alicia? 6. ¿Por qué ha sido aumentada la reunión? 7. ¿Para qué hace palmas Ricardo? 8. ¿Qué es lo que van a tomar? 9. ¿Qué se echa de menos en los Estados Unidos? 10. ¿Se come bien en Estados Unidos? 11. ¿Las muchachas hacen el trabajo duro en Estados Unidos? 12. ¿Por qué no convencen las máquinas a Ricardo? 13. ¿Por qué no tienen arreglo los españoles? 14. ¿Con qué idea han sido construidas las casas españolas? 15. ¿Dónde han sido colocadas las habitaciones de servicio? 16. ¿Qué es lo que cuesta menos que un frigorífico?

Aquí se venden los décimos de la lotería.

DIÁLOGO 32

La lotería de Navidad

Personajes: Elisa, Ricardo, Pilar, Lorenzo, el tejano

ELISA.—Las vacaciones de Navidad
empiezan pronto.

DIÁLOGO 32

RICARDO.—¡Quién pudiera irse mañana! Pero aún tenemos dos días más de clases.

PILAR.—Así estás aquí para el veinte y dos de diciembre que es el sorteo de la lotería.

LORENZO.—A lo mejor te toca.

Perhaps you'll win.

RICARDO.—Imposible. No juego.

ELISA.—¿Qué dices?

PILAR.—¿No juegas a la lotería de Navidad?

ELISA.—Pues quizá seas el único español que no juegue.

LORENZO.—La lotería es uno de los mayores ingresos para el Estado.

The lottery is one of the biggest revenues for the (Spanish) government.

RICARDO.—Sí, es un impuesto voluntario. Precisamente por eso no me gusta.

PILAR.—¡Qué poco patriótico!

How unpatriotic!

LORENZO.—El Estado se queda con el treinta por ciento aproximadamente. Lo que queda se reparte en premios.

The government keeps approximately 30%. The rest is distributed as prizes.

RICARDO.—Si la gente quiere hacerle ese regalo al Estado, que se lo haga.

let them do it.

ELISA.—Acaso tengas razón, pero quisiera hacerte ver que la emoción de la lotería es antes del sorteo.

PILAR.—Cuando treinta millones de españoles están pensando "¡Ojalá me toque el premio gordo!"
(*El tejano se acerca.*)

TODOS.—¡Hola!

LORENZO.—(*Al tejano.*) ¿Cuáles son tus planes para las Navidades?

TEJANO.—Pues si me tocan los quince millones del gordo* . . .

of the first prize . . .

TODOS.—(*Interrumpiéndole.*) ¡Tú también!

* *El (premio) gordo* is worth about $250,000. ($1.00 = about 60 *pesetas.*)

LENGUA (76.)

MODISMOS Y VOCABULARIO ADICIONAL

a lo mejor   perhaps
jugar a   to play (a game)
quedarse con   to keep
por ciento   per cent
el premio gordo   first prize

la **carta**   playing card, letter
la **emoción**   emotion
   gordo   stout, fat
el **impuesto**   tax
el **ingreso**   revenue
   interrumpir   to interrupt
la **lotería**   lottery
el **millón**   million
la **Navidad**   Christmas
las **Navidades**   Christmas holidays
la **pelota**   ball
   precisamente   precisely
el **regalo**   gift
el **sorteo**   drawing
   tocar (a uno)   to win
las **vacaciones**   vacation
   voluntario   voluntary

146

DIÁLOGO 32
EJERCICIOS ORALES

1. Los tiempos de *jugar*.

   Ejemplo: EL PROFESOR.—jugué a la lotería

   EL ALUMNO.—**jugué a la lotería, jugaste a la lotería, jugó a la lotería, jugamos a la lotería, jugasteis a la lotería, jugaron a la lotería**

he jugado a la lotería	había jugado al tenis
juego a la pelota	jugué a la lotería
jugaré al fútbol	

2. (76c.) *Ejemplo:* EL PROFESOR.—Está lloviendo.

   EL ALUMNO.—**¡Ojalá que no estuviera lloviendo!**

Hace frío.	Están aquí.
Ellos vienen esta tarde.	Somos pobres.
Tengo que hacerlo.	Bebe mucho.
Hay examen hoy.	Nos interrumpen.
Juegan demasiado.	Está lloviendo.

3. (76c.) *Ejemplo:* EL PROFESOR.—¿Va a llover?

   EL ALUMNO.—**Ojalá que no llueva.**

¿Van a venir?	¿Lo va a romper?
¿Habrá examen mañana?	¿Van a vivir cerca?
¿Va a hacer calor?	¿Tienes que hacerlo?
¿Los van a tirar?	¿Va a llover?

4. Expresar como posibilidad las siguientes frases. (76e.)

   Ejemplo: EL PROFESOR.—Pueden venir.

   EL ALUMNO.—**Acaso (tal vez) puedan venir.**

Será mejor.	Lo harán.
Quieren comprarlos.	Comeremos en un restorán.
Recibiré carta hoy.	Jugarán al tenis esta tarde.
Nos pagarán lo que nos deben.	Pueden venir.

PREGUNTAS SOBRE EL DIÁLOGO

1. ¿Cuándo empiezan las vacaciones de Navidad? 2. ¿Por qué no puede irse Ricardo mañana? 3. ¿Qué pasa el veintidós de diciembre? 4. ¿Por qué no puede tocarle la lotería a Ricardo? 5. ¿Juegan todos los españoles a la lotería de Navidad? 6. ¿Qué es la lotería? 7. ¿Por qué no le gusta a Ricardo? 8. ¿Con cuánto dinero se queda el Estado? 9. ¿Cuál es la emoción de la lotería? 10. ¿Ha jugado el tejano a la lotería? 11. ¿Llegamos a saber cuáles son sus planes para las Navidades? 12. ¿Por qué le interrumpen? 13. ¿Qué haría usted si le tocaran los quince millones del premio gordo de la lotería de Navidad?

DIÁLOGO 33

La Nochebuena (Christmas Eve)

Personajes: Juan, Elisa, Papá, Mamá, la muchacha

(*En casa de Elisa, sobre las diez de la noche, la familia está sentada a la mesa, terminando la cena de Nochebuena.*)   *around ten*

JUAN.—Lo que más me gusta de las Navidades es la cena de Nochebuena.

ELISA.—Claro. Sopa de almendra, besugo, pavo, y de postre turrón y mazapán.   Naturally. Almond soup, sea bream, turkey, and for dessert, almond nougat and marchpane.

PAPÁ.—No todos somos tan comilones como tú. Disfrutamos de la Nochebuena por otras razones.

MAMÁ.—A mí me gusta la cena de Nochebuena tanto como a ti, hijo, pero por razones distintas. Me gusta veros a todos como ahora, sentados a la mesa con tanta alegría y salud como el año pasado.

PAPÁ.—Y con la esperanza de que el año que viene sea aún mejor.

149

JUAN.—¿Qué quieres decir, que el pavo va a ser más grande?

MUCHACHA.—(*Entrando.*) Señora, el sereno viene pidiendo el aguinaldo. Me ha dado esta tarjeta.

PAPÁ.—Dale diez pesetas.

ELISA.—(*Leyendo la tarjeta.*) "El sereno de esta calle le desea Felices Pascuas y un Próspero Año Nuevo".

MUCHACHA.—Esta mañana han venido el basurero, el cartero, el fontanero, y los barrenderos.

garbageman, the mailman, the plumber, and the street cleaners.

MAMÁ.—No han venido tantos como el año pasado.

ELISA.—La más divertida de todas las tarjetas de felicitación es la de los engrasadores del ascensor, que desde hace dos días no funciona.

The funniest of all the greeting cards is that of the elevator greasers...

MAMÁ.—Terminar de comer lo más pronto posible porque vamos a cantar villancicos delante del Nacimiento.

JUAN.—¿No vamos a la Misa del Gallo?

Midnight Mass?

PAPÁ.—Sí, pero antes vamos a cantar.

ELISA.—Vamos a empezar con el que más me gusta.

TODOS.—(Cantando.)
En Belén tocan a fuego,
del portal salen las llamas
porque dicen que ha nacido
el Redentor de las almas.

Brincan y bailan los peces en el río,
Brincan y bailan de ver al Dios nacido.
Brincan y bailan los peces en el agua.
Brincan y bailan de ver nacida el alba.

150

Cards of several workers, presented at Christmas time when asking for the Aguinaldo (a gift, usually money)

El trapero de esta casa

FELICITA a Vd. las PASCUAS

— PERFECTUS.—López Silva, 3.—

LOS BARRENDEROS DE ESTA CALLE

felicitan a Vd. las Pascuas
y le desean un feliz y
próspero Año Nuevo

ASCENSORES D. S. R.

Los Engrasadores del Ascensor

Felicitan a Vd. las Pascuas y le desean un feliz y próspero Año Nuevo.

En Belén tocan a fuego (*Villancico popular de Castilla*)

Allegro tranquilo

En Be - lén to - can a fue - go del por - tal sa - len las lla - mas por-que

di - cen que___ ha na - ci - do el Re - den - tor de las al - mas.

Un poco más movido

Brin-can y bai-lan los pe-ces en el rí - o brin-can y bai-lan de ver al Dios na - ci - do

Brin-can y bai-lan los pe-ces en el a-gua brin-can y bai-lan de ver na-ci-do el al-ba.___

LENGUA (Ver 77–79.)

MODISMOS Y VOCABULARIO ADICIONAL

querer decir   to mean
venir (pidiendo)   to be here (asking for)
Felices Pascuas   Merry Christmas, Season's Greetings
tocar a fuego   to ring the fire alarm

el **aguinaldo**   gift (usually money given to servants, mailman, etc.)
la **alegría**   happiness
el **barrendero**   streetcleaner
el **basurero**   garbage man
brincar   to jump
el **cartero**   mailman
distinto   different
la **esperanza**   hope

el **fontanero**   plumber
el **fuego**   fire
la **llama**   flame
el **nacimiento**   birth, Bethlehem scene
el **pez**   fish
próspero   prosperous
el **Redentor**   Redeemer
la **tarjeta**   card
el **villancico**   Christmas carol

EJERCICIOS ORALES

1. (77.)   *Ejemplo:* EL PROFESOR.—Han venido muchos.
   EL ALUMNO.—**No tantos como el año pasado.**

Hay muchas cartas.
Les ha gustado mucho.
Ha trabajado mucho este año.
Has disfrutado mucho.

Hay mucha nieve.
Ha llovido mucho.
Hemos comprado muchos regalos.
Han venido muchos.

2. (78.)   *Ejemplo:* EL PROFESOR.—El pavo del año pasado fue grande.
   EL ALUMNO.—**Éste es más grande.**

El año pasado fue próspero.
La cena del año pasado fue buena.
Las tarjetas del año pasado fueron divertidas.
Las obras de teatro del año pasado fueron malas.
La corrida del año pasado fue emocionante.
El torero del año pasado fue valiente.
El accidente del año pasado fue trágico.
El pavo del año pasado fue grande.

DIÁLOGO 33

3. (78.)   Hacer una oración corta con las palabras dadas.

Ejemplo: EL PROFESOR.—más despacio
   EL ALUMNO.—**Ella habla más despacio que yo.**

más caros	más interesante	más rápido	más rubia
más de prisa	más blancas	mejores	más despacio
peor	más guapa		

4. (79a.)   *Ejemplo:* EL PROFESOR.—Ella anda más de prisa que yo.
   EL ALUMNO.—**Ella anda tan de prisa como yo.**

La máquina de él es mejor que la mía.
Él está más ocupado que ella.
Ricardo es más alto que Lorenzo.
Mi casa es más grande que la suya.
Sus libros son más interesantes que los míos.
Su hijo es más inteligente que el nuestro.
Elisa es más guapa que Pilar.
Ella anda más de prisa que yo.

5. (79b.)   *Ejemplo:* EL PROFESOR.—Hágalo bien.
   EL ALUMNO.—**Lo haré lo mejor que pueda.**

Termínelo pronto.	Hable claro.
Póngalos cerca.	Léalo rápido.
Sujételo firmemente.	Hágalo bien.
Colóquelo alto.	

PREGUNTAS SOBRE EL DIÁLOGO

1. ¿Qué es lo que más le gusta a Juanito de las Navidades? 2. ¿Qué comen en la cena de Nochebuena? 3. ¿Es Juanito un comilón? 4. ¿Son todos en la familia comilones? 5. ¿Por qué le gusta a la mamá la cena de Nochebuena? 6. ¿Qué esperanza tiene el papá? 7. ¿En qué está pensando siempre Juanito? 8. ¿Qué aguinaldo va a recibir el sereno? 9. ¿Han venido muchos pidiendo aguinaldo? 10. ¿Por qué es la tarjeta de los engrasadores del ascensor la más divertida? 11. ¿Por qué tienen que terminar de comer lo más pronto posible? 12. ¿Cuándo van a ir a la Misa del Gallo? 13. ¿Qué villancico van a cantar primero?

DIÁLOGO 34

De compras

Personajes: Mamá, Elisa, dependiente

MAMÁ.—La semana pasada te compré el regalo de Reyes,* pero aún no he comprado los de tu padre y tu hermano. Los regalos para los hombres son más difíciles de elegir.

ELISA.—Como el lunes próximo es el día de Reyes, pocos días te quedan para ir de tiendas.

Since next Monday is the twelfth night, only a few days are left to go shopping.

MAMÁ.—Me temo que no me dé tiempo a ir esta tarde. Los viernes tengo hora en la peluquería.

ELISA.—¿Por qué no vamos ahora a las tiendas de la Calle de Serrano? Tienen cosas monísimas.

MAMÁ.—Pues vamos de prisa. Son las nueve y media. Tenemos tiempo hasta la hora de la comida.

. . . .

(*Al salir de una tienda.*)

ELISA.—Me alegro que le hayamos comprado una máquina fotográfica a Juanito. Hace tiempo que quería una.

* Spaniards do not give gifts on Christmas day but on the 6th of January, the *twelfth night*, when the three kings (*reyes*) arrived at Bethlehem with their gifts.

154

Una tienda durante las fiestas de Navidad

MAMÁ.—Vamos a entrar en esa tienda para el regalo de papá. La señora de Ramos me ha dicho que tienen cosas muy buenas.
(*Entran.*)

DEP.—¿Qué desean las señoras?

MAMÁ.—Camisas de caballero de la talla treinta y ocho* y jerseys de caballero de tamaño mediano. Los queremos de la mejor calidad.

Men's shirts, size 15, and men's sweaters, medium size.

ELISA.—¡Mira, mamá! Al final de mes rebajan los precios en la sección de señoras y tienen los bolsos de señora baratísimos.

MAMÁ.—(*Al dependiente.*) Vamos a ver los bolsos primero.

ELISA.—Este marrón de piel de cocodrilo es precioso.

MAMÁ.—¿Qué precio tiene?

What is the price of it?

DEP.—Setecientas pesetas.

MAMÁ.—Es caro, pero es precioso.

ELISA.—Este otro es más barato y es muy mono también.

MAMÁ.—Ése es más de jovencita. Mira, son verdaderas gangas. Te compro ése a ti y para mí el de cocodrilo.

That is more for a young person.

ELISA.—¿Y el regalo para papá?

MAMÁ.—Tendré que comprarle una corbata. Ya no me queda dinero.

I don't have any money left.

* Sizes are in centimeters.

LENGUA (Ver 80.)

MODISMOS Y VOCABULARIO ADICIONAL

(ir) de compras (or de tiendas)   (to go) shopping
difícil de/infinitivo   difficult/infinitive
dar(le a uno) tiempo a/infinitivo   to have time/infinitive
quedar(le a uno)   to have left
¿Qué precio tiene?   What is the price of it?

la **calidad**   quality
el **cocodrilo**   crocodile
la **máquina fotográfica**   camera
  marrón   brown
  mono   cute
la **nariz**   nose

la **peluquería**   barber shop, beauty parlor
la **piel**   skin
el **precio**   price
  rebajar   to reduce, lower
la **sonrisa**   smile
  temerse = temer   to fear

ADJECTIVES OF CHARACTER AND PERSON

limpio   clean
sucio   dirty
cuidadoso   careful
descuidado   careless
cortés   courteous
descortés   discourteous
prudente   prudent
imprudente   imprudent
inteligente   intelligent
tonto   foolish

bien educado   well-mannered
mal educado   bad-mannered
culto   educated
inculto   uneducated
simpático   nice
antipático   disagreeable
hábil   skillful
torpe   clumsy
bien vestido   well-dressed
mal vestido   badly-dressed

ADJECTIVES OF PHYSICAL FEATURES

alto   tall
bajo   short
delgado   thin
esbelto   slender
flaco   skinny
gordo   fat, stout
bonito   pretty
guapo   good-looking, handsome

lindo   pretty
feo   ugly
moreno   dark complexioned
rubio   blond
rubio jaro   red head
fino   fine, refined

157

EJERCICIOS ORALES

1. Dar una descripción corta de cualquier persona.

(*The student should prepare this oral exercise before class, preferably in written form, and memorize it in order to be able to give it without reading.*)

Por ejemplo:

Mi hermana es joven, delgada y rubia jara.
Tiene los ojos verdes, nariz fina y una sonrisa muy bonita.
Está bien educada, es inteligente y habla correctamente.
Siempre está bien vestida y no se pinta mucho.

PREGUNTAS SOBRE EL DIÁLOGO

1. ¿Cuándo compró la mamá el regalo de Reyes para Elisa? 2. ¿Ha comprado los regalos para su marido y su hijo? 3. ¿Cuándo es el día de Reyes? 4. ¿Cuántos días quedan para ir de tiendas? 5. ¿Por qué la mamá temía que no le diera tiempo a ir de compras esa tarde? 6. ¿Dónde fueron de compras? 7. ¿Qué tienen en las tiendas de la Calle de Serrano? 8. ¿Cuándo tenían que volver a casa? 9. ¿Qué regalo le han comprado a Juanito? 10. ¿Para qué entraron en la tienda? 11. ¿Le compraron al papá una camisa y un jersey de la mejor calidad? 12. ¿Dónde rebajan los precios al final de mes? 13. ¿Cuál era el bolso que más les gustó? 14. ¿Eran los bolsos caros, baratos, o eran gangas? 15. ¿Cuántos bolsos compraron? 16. ¿Para quién será el de cocodrilo? 17. ¿Por qué tendrán que comprarle al papá una corbata?

DIÁLOGO 35

La Noche Vieja

Personajes: el Sr. y la Sra. Martínez Aparicio, Pilar, Tere, Jaime, Elisa, Ricardo, Pepe, Lorenzo, el tejano, y el locutor de radio

(*En casa de Pilar, la Noche Vieja. Entran Lorenzo, el tejano, Ricardo, y Pepe.*)

PILAR.—Mamá, te voy a presentar a Pepe Aldecoa. Es primo de Ricardo.

PEPE.—Tengo mucho gusto en conocerla, señora.

MAMÁ.—El gusto es mío.

(*Se dan la mano.*)

TEJANO, RICARDO, Y LORENZO.—¿Cómo está usted, señora?

MAMÁ.—(*Les da la mano a los tres.*)—¿Qué tal? Me alegro mucho que hayan venido.

TEJANO.—(*Al papá.*) Buenas noches, señor Martínez.

PAPÁ.—Hola. Pasen, pasen. Los chicos están bailando en la sala, divirtiéndose un ratito.

RICARDO.—Señor Martínez, permítame que le presente a mi primo, Pepe Aldecoa.

PAPÁ.—Encantado de conocerle, Pepe. (*Le da unas palmaditas en la espalda.*) Espero que se divierta esta noche.

PEPE.—Muchas gracias. Son ustedes muy amables en haberme invitado.

RICARDO.—(*A Pilar.*) He traído los discos que me pediste.

159

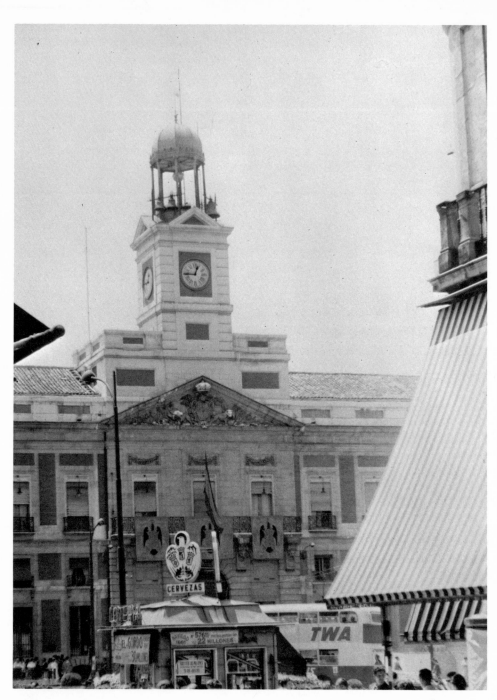

El reloj de Gobernación, Puerta del Sol

DIÁLOGO 35

PILAR.—¡Ah! Gracias. Tengo ganas de oírlos.

(*Entran en la sala. Varias parejas están bailando.*)

PILAR.—Creo que conocéis a todo el mundo.

LORENZO.—(*Se acerca a Elisa.*) ¿Bailamos, Elisa?

ELISA.—Si te digo la verdad, tengo miedo de bailar estos bailes modernos. Tanto saltito no me gusta.

LORENZO.—No hay más que tener cuidado para no caerse encima de otra pareja. ¡Vamos!

(*Bailan.*)

TERE.—(*Bailando con Jaime.*) ¡Uf! ¡Qué calor tengo!

JAIME.—Tienes razón. Debemos abrir una ventana. Voy a parar el tocadiscos también. Son cerca de las doce. (*Jaime abre una ventana, para el tocadiscos, y pone la radio.*) Atención todo el mundo. Hemos puesto la radio para oir las doce campanadas del reloj de Gobernación.*

PILAR.—(*Repartiendo cestitas, cada una con doce uvas, a todos sus amigos.*) Aquí están las uvas de la suerte.

TEJANO.—¿Qué he de hacer con ellas?

TERE.—Tienes que comer una uva a cada campanada, pero con cuidadito para que no te atragantes.

EL LOCUTOR DE RADIO.—Señoras y señores, en este momento son las doce. (*Suenan las doce campanadas. Todos tratan de comer una uva a cada campanada, y después de la última campanada, decir al mismo tiempo:* ¡**Feliz Año Nuevo**!)

LENGUA (Ver 81.)

---

* Official time in all Spain is provided by the clock of **Gobernación**, a government building facing the **Puerta del Sol**, the center of Madrid.

MODISMOS Y VOCABULARIO ADICIONAL

la Noche Vieja   New Year's Eve
dar la mano   to shake hands
dar palmaditas   to pat
todo el mundo   everybody
haber de   to be to, to be supposed to

tener {
(mucho) calor	to be (very) warm or hot
la culpa	to be at fault
(mucho) cuidado	to be (very) careful
(mucha) envidia	to be (very) envious
(mucho) frío	to be (very) cold
(muchas) ganas	to be (very) anxious, to feel like
(mucho) gusto	to be (very) glad
(mucha) hambre	to be (very) hungry
(mucho) miedo	to be (very) scared or afraid
(mucha) prisa	to be in a (big) hurry
(mucha) razón	to be (so) right
(mucha) sed	to be (very) thirsty
(mucho) sueño	to be (very) sleepy
(mucha) suerte	to be (very) lucky

atención   attention
atragantarse   to choke
el **baile**   dance
la **campanada**   stroke of a bell
la **cesta**   basket
el **disco**   record
divertirse (II)   to have a good time
encantado   delighted, charmed,
   glad to meet you

la **espalda**   back
el **locutor**   announcer
la **pareja**   partner, couple
poner   to turn on (radio)
el **salto**   jump, hop
el **tocadiscos**   record player, phonograph
la **uva**   grape

EJERCICIOS ORALES

1. Grupos de alumnos deben practicar las siguientes escenas:

   a) Presentando a dos personas mayores—

   Sr. X.—Sra. de García, permítame que le presente al Sr. López. Sr. López, la señora de don Rafael García.
   Sr. López.—Tengo mucho gusto en conocerla, señora.
   Sra. de García.—El gusto es mío.

162

DIÁLOGO 35

b) Presentando a dos jóvenes—

SRTA. X.—Luisita, voy a presentarte a mi primo, Rafael López. Rafael, mi compañera de clase, Luisita Sánchez.

RAFAEL.—Encantado. (*or* Mucho gusto.)

LUISITA.—Encantada. (*or* Mucho gusto.)

c) Presentando un joven a una persona mayor—

PILAR.—Mamá, te voy a presentar a Pepe Aldecoa.

PEPE.—Tengo mucho gusto en conocerla, señora.

MAMÁ.—El gusto es mío.

. . . .

RICARDO.—Sr. Martínez, permítame que le presente a mi primo, Pepe Aldecoa.

SR. MARTÍNEZ.—Encantado. (*or* Mucho gusto.)

PEPE.—El gusto es mío.

2. Contestar apropiadamente, usando modismos con el verbo **tener**.

Por ejemplo: EL PROFESOR.—¿Por qué quiere usted ir ahora mismo a verles?

EL ALUMNO.—**Porque tengo muchas ganas de verles.**

¿Por qué se ha quitado usted el abrigo?

¿Por qué le pidió a usted perdón?

¿Por qué se han puesto ellos el jersey?

¿Por qué quieren ustedes comer tan pronto?

¿Por qué no da ella palmaditas al perro?

¿Por qué quieren ellos volver hoy en vez de mañana?

¿Por qué le cree usted a él y no a ella?

¿Por qué ha bebido usted tanta agua?

¿Por qué se acuesta usted tan pronto?

¿Por qué quiere usted ir ahora mismo a verles?

PREGUNTAS SOBRE EL DIÁLOGO

1. ¿A quién presenta Pilar a su mamá? 2. ¿Quién es Pepe? 3. ¿Qué estaban haciendo los chicos en la sala? 4. ¿Qué ha traído Ricardo? 5. ¿Tenía ganas Pilar de oir los discos? 6. ¿De qué tenía miedo Elisa? 7. ¿Qué hay que hacer para no caerse al bailar? 8. ¿Por qué ha parado Jaime el tocadiscos? 9. ¿Para qué han puesto la radio? 10. ¿Cuántas son las uvas de la suerte? 11. ¿Cómo se comen las doce uvas? 12. ¿Qué dijo el locutor de radio? 13. ¿Cuántas campanadas sonaron? 14. ¿Qué hicieron nuestros amigos mientras sonaban las doce campanadas? 15. ¿Qué dijeron todos al mismo tiempo, después de la última campanada?

LENGUA

NOTA PRELIMINAR

A word should be said about a few grammatical terms that we employ in this section. For years now, a number of linguists have been keenly aware of the inappropriateness of much grammar nomenclature, but only recently have better or at least more descriptive terms been suggested or used. The terminology applied to "tenses," in particular, seems to need a revamping. We like the modified terminology suggested by William Bull in his *Time, Tense and the Verb*, but since it is obvious that prior public acceptance is necessary in order that this or any text enjoy complete success, we have taken a moderate position. The minimum changes that we felt should be made are:

NEW TERMINOLOGY	TRADITIONAL TERMINOLOGY
actor	subject (of verb)
retro-future	conditional tense
retro-subjunctive	imperfect subjunctive
with-verb pronoun	pronoun object

The term, with-verb pronoun, has been reluctantly borrowed from *Modern Spanish: A Project of the Modern Language Association*. It is an awkward label, but certainly more accurate than the one it replaces. The same holds true for retro-future, borrowed from Dr. Bull. It means a future oriented to some past moment. Likewise, retro-subjunctive is applied to an action related with a past moment.

167

1. NOUNS AND DEFINITE ARTICLES

el padre the father	**la madre** the mother
el policía the policeman	**la vaca** the cow
el toro the bull	**la universidad** the university
el año the year	**la costumbre** the custom
el respeto the respect	**la especie** the species
	la religión the religion
	la mesa the table

Nouns naming male beings and those that end in **o** are of masculine gender. *Exceptions*: **la mano** (the hand), **la radio** (the radio).

Nouns naming female beings and those that end in **ad, umbre, ie, ión** and most nouns ending in **a** are of feminine gender. *Exceptions*: **el avión** (the airplane), **el guión** (the hyphen), **el camión** (the truck), and **el pie** (the foot).

The gender of other nouns must be checked in a dictionary or in the vocabulary at the end of this text.

2. FORMATION OF THE PLURAL OF NOUNS AND DEFINITE ARTICLES

la escuela the school	**las escuelas** the schools
el libro the book	**los libros** the books
el coche the car	**los coches** the cars

Add **s** to words ending in **a**, **o**, or **e** to form the plural.

el papel the paper	**los papeles** the papers
la ciudad the city	**las ciudades** the cities
el maniquí the manikin	**los maniquíes** the manikins
el zulú the Zulu	**los zulúes** the Zulus

Add **es** to all other words to form the plural, except **el lunes** (Monday), **el martes** (Tuesday), **el miércoles** (Wednesday), **el jueves** (Thursday), and **el viernes** (Friday). The plural of these terms is noted by the definite article—**los lunes, los martes**, etc.

3. THE MASCULINE PLURAL

los niños   the boys, the boys and girls, the children
los padres   the fathers, the parents

The masculine plural of personal nouns (and pronouns) can represent an all male group or a mixed-gender group.

4. A, AN, ONE, SOME

un examen   a test, one test, an exam, one exam
unos exámenes   some tests

5. THE QUESTION

¿Dónde vive tu amiga?   Where does your friend live?
¿Cuándo llegan tus padres?   When are your parents arriving?
¿En qué compañía trabaja su hermano?   At what company does her brother
                                         work?

The actor follows the verb in questions that begin with an interrogative. In such questions, the voice rises on the accented vowel of the interrogative term and then falls to normal pitch.

¿Tiene Elisa hermanos?⎫
¿Elisa tiene hermanos?⎭   Does Elisa have any brothers or sisters?

In a *yes-no* type of question, the actor usually follows the verb, although it may precede. In this type of question, the voice generally rises on the first stressed vowel and then descends gradually, with a slight rise at the end.

6. NEGATION

¿Qué mujer no habla mucho?   What woman doesn't talk a lot?
Pepe no va a la Universidad.   Pepe doesn't go to the University.

A **no** before the verb makes the sentence negative.

7. MANNER OF EXPRESSING POSSESSOR
AND TYPE OR KIND

la familia de Elisa	Elisa's family
una compañía de seguros	an insurance company
una casa de pisos	an apartment house

The pattern *noun 1 | de | noun 2* means that *noun 2* limits or modifies *noun 1*. This construction expresses the possessor, or type or kind.

8. *AL (a + el)*

Va al Instituto.	He goes to the *Instituto*.
Habla al profesor.	He speaks to the teacher.

Whenever **el** follows **a**, the two words fuse to form **al**.

9. THE INFINITIVE

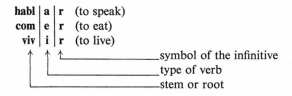

The stem states the action (*run, sleep, seem, be, etc.*). The type tells what set of endings is required to express person, number, mode, aspect (*perfected, imperfected*), and order (*anterior, simultaneous, posterior*).

170

10. SUBJECT PRONOUNS AND THE PRESENT OF REGULAR VERBS

yo	hablo	I
	como	
	vivo	
tú	hablas	you
	comes	
	vives	
él	habla	he
ella	come	she
usted	vive	you
nosotros	hablamos	
	comemos	we
nosotras	vivimos	
vosotros	habláis	
	coméis	you
vosotras	vivís	
ellos	hablan	they
ellas	comen	they
ustedes	viven	you

speak(s), eat(s), live(s)

do(es) speak, eat, live

am (is, are) speaking, eating, living

See **Addendum I** for the difference between **tú-vosotros** and **usted-ustedes**.

11. *DEL (de + el)*

| la parada del trolebús | the trolley bus stop |
| la cartera del profesor | the teacher's briefcase |

De plus a following **el** fuse to give **del. De**, however, does not fuse with the **El** of a proper name—**la capital de El Salvador** (*the capital of El Salvador*).

12. OMISSION OF *UN* AND *UNA* AFTER *SER*

a) Soy profesor de idiomas.   I am a language teacher.
    Es médico (carpintero).   He is a doctor (carpenter).
    —¿Es usted español?   Are you Spanish (*a Spaniard*)?
    —No, soy americano.   No, I'm American (*an American*).
    Esto es piedra.   This is rock.

When merely identifying a person or thing with a group or class, the indefinite article is not used in Spanish. Note that the English equivalent sometimes uses the article.

b) —¿Quién es ése que habla tanto?   —Who is that fellow who talks so much?
    —Es un americano.   —He's an American.
    Es amigo de Juan.   He is Juan's friend.
    Es un amigo de Juan.   He is a friend of Juan.
    Es un pintor famoso.   He is a famous painter.
    Eres tonto.   You are foolish.
    Eres un tonto.   You are a fool.

Most all other times, Spanish and English follow the same pattern. Words that may be either nouns or adjectives (**tonto, español**, *etc.*), function as nouns when preceded by the indefinite article.

13. GENDER AND NUMBER OF ADJECTIVES

a) un chico guapo   a good-looking boy
    chicos guapos   good-looking boys
    una chica guapa   a good-looking girl
    chicas guapas   good-looking girls

Spanish dictionaries list only the masculine, singular form of an adjective. If this form ends in **o**, the feminine ends in **a**. To get the plural, add **s**. This type of adjective always agrees in gender and number with the noun or pronoun it modifies.

b) un niño español   a Spanish child *or* boy
    niños españoles   Spanish children *or* boys
    una niña española   a Spanish girl
    niñas españolas   Spanish girls
    un niño catalán   a Catalonian boy
    niños catalanes   Catalonian boys

LENGUA

una niña catalana	a Catalonian girl
niñas catalanas	Catalonian girls
un niño llorón	a crybaby *m.*
una niña llorona	a crybaby *f.*
un niño encantador	a charming boy
una niña encantadora	a charming girl

An adjective denoting nationality or geographic division, whose masculine, singular form ends in a consonant, adds an **a** to make the feminine. Adjectives ending in **ón, án,** and **dor** also show gender in the same manner.

c) un libro interesante	an interesting book
novelas interesantes	interesting novels
una cosa fácil	an easy matter (*thing*)
ejercicios fáciles	easy exercises

All other adjectives show agreement only in number.

14. PERSONAL *A*

¿Ves **al** chico de gris?	Do you see the fellow in the gray suit?
Quiere **a** Elisa.	He loves Elisa.
Pega **al** pobre animal.	He beats the poor animal.

If the direct object of a verb is a substantive representing a definite person or persons, or anything looked upon as if it had feelings, the substantive is preceded by **a**.

15. USES OF THE SUBJECT PRONOUNS WITH VERBS

1. —No tenemos el horario.
   —**Yo** lo tengo.
   —We don't have the schedule.
   —I have it.
2. **Nosotros** hablamos español y **ellos** hablan francés.
   We speak Spanish and they speak French.
3. —¿Lo dice **ella** o **él**?
   —**Ella** lo dice.
   —Does she or he say so?
   —She says so.
4. ¿Va **usted** esta tarde?
   Are you going this afternoon?
5. Va a empezar pronto.
   It is going to start soon.
6. Es la clase de primer año.
   It's the first year class.
7. ¡Qué pisos! De verdad son pequeños.
   What apartments! They really are small.

173

In most cases, natives tend not to use subject pronouns. They, however, do use them (1) to stress an actor, (2) to contrast one actor with another, and (3) in a 3d person "either or" combination and the subsequent choice. **Usted** and **ustedes** (4) seldom are omitted because their use is a sign of courtesy.

In view of the fact that Spanish subject pronouns refer only to persons, there is no Spanish equivalent for "it" (5, 6) or "they" (7), referring to things.

16. SPANISH GIVEN AND FAMILY NAMES

Lorenzo Ortiz Álvarez

baptismal name⏌

father's family name⏌

mother's maiden name⏌

The Spaniard normally has three names. The middle name is the father's family name. The man, illustrated above, would be addressed as **Sr. Ortiz**. If this man's sister, **Carmen Ortiz Álvarez**, should marry **Antonio Alonso Forteza**, she would drop her mother's maiden name (*Álvarez*) and would add her husband's father's family name (*Alonso*). She would be called **Sra. Carmen Ortiz de Alonso**.

17. *A LA(S)*—at (clock time)

Va a empezar **a la** una.	It is going to begin at one.
Es **a las** nueve.	It is at nine.

The feminine definite article is used with clock time. **La** precedes **una**, and **las** any other number representing a clock hour.

18. CLOCK TIME

a) ¿Qué hora es?	What time is it?
Es la una.	It is one o'clock.
Es la una y diez.	It is ten after one.
Es la una menos cuarto.	It is twelve forty-five (*a quarter of one*).
Son las dos.	It is two o'clock.
Son las tres y media.	It is three-thirty.
Son las cuatro y quince.	It is four-fifteen.
Son las seis y cuarto	It is a quarter after six.
Son las doce menos veinte.	It is twenty of twelve.
Son las siete en punto.	It is seven on the dot.

LENGUA

In expressing clock time, the form of **ser** is singular when **la una** (**y** or **menos** *minutes*) follows. Otherwise, the form is plural. Use the **y** construction when the minute hand is in the right half of the clock, and the **menos** construction when it is in the left half.

b) Son las ocho de la mañana.　　　　It is 8:00 a.m.
　　Son las cinco de la tarde.　　　　　It is 5:00 p.m.
　　Son las once de la noche.　　　　　It is 11:00 p.m.

Note: **noche** begins about the time the street lights are turned on.

19. PREPOSITION/INFINITIVE

Voy **a preguntar**.　　　　　　　　　　I'm going to ask.
Tenemos una hora libre **para ir** al bar.　　We have a free hour (in order) to go to
　　　　　　　　　　　　　　　　　　　the snack bar.
Va **a comer** antes **de salir**.　　　　　He's going to eat before leaving.

A verb used immediately after a preposition is in its infinitive form. Note that when "to" means "in order to," the Spanish equivalent is **para**.

20. ADJECTIVE PLACEMENT

a) **AFTER noun**

1) **Selection**

un día hermoso　　　　　　a beautiful day
el piso bajo　　　　　　　　the ground floor
una hora libre　　　　　　　a free hour
otro vaso limpio　　　　　　another clean glass
pocos ejercicios fáciles　　few easy exercises
mucho aire frío　　　　　　a lot of cold air

The native places descriptive adjectives AFTER the noun whenever he expresses SELECTION, that is, to distinguish the referent (*of the noun modified*) from another or others of the same category—one floor from another, one glass from another or other glasses, etc.

un chico rubio, alto y guapo　　　a blond, tall, and good-looking boy
un chico alto, rubio y guapo　　　a tall, blond, and good-looking boy
un chico guapo, alto y rubio　　　a good-looking, tall, and blond boy

When two or more adjectives, denoting selection, modify the same noun, they may be in any order with respect to each other, the last one being linked by **y**.

175

2) In close-knit units

los jefes militares rivales	the rival military chiefs
¿Conoces un empleado público honrado?	Do you know an honest public servant?

Occasionally, the adjective forms a close-knit unit with the noun it modifies. The two together (**jefes militares, empleado público**) form a nucleus, the adjective placed immediately AFTER the noun. Any other adjective (**rivales, honrado**), used for the purpose of selection, follows the unit just as it does a simple noun. Note that it is not linked by an **y,** just as we would not say in English "the rival and military chiefs" or "an honest and public servant."

b) BEFORE noun

el conocido actor Charlot	the well-known actor Charlie Chaplin
la célebre novela *Don Quijote*	the famous novel *Don Quixote*
un buen café; una buena tela	a good coffee; a good cloth
un mal olor; una mala idea	a bad odor; a bad (*poor*) idea
algún día; algunas veces	some day; some times
ningún sitio; de ninguna manera	no place; by no means

As a general rule, an adjective NOT USED TO SHOW SELECTION comes BEFORE the noun. **Conocido** is not used in the first example to distinguish one **Charlot** from another or other **Charlots** because there is only one. Likewise, **célebre** does not distinguish one **Don Quijote** from others because there is only one novel by that name. Consequently, the use of the adjectives is non-selective.

With a few exceptions, all determiners (*articles, possessive and demonstrative adjectives, and adjectives of quantity and number*) always come BEFORE the noun.

Note that **bueno, malo, alguno,** and **ninguno** drop the **o** before a masculine, singular noun.

21. ADJECTIVE PLACEMENT AND MEANING

¡**Pobre** hijo! Tienes frío.	You poor child! You're cold.
Es un niño **pobre** que viene pidiendo limosna.	It's a poor child who is begging.
Es un **gran** general.	He is a great general.
Es una casa **grande.**	It is a large house.
Tengo un reloj **nuevo.**	I have a new watch.
La **nueva** reina viste el traje de novia.	The new queen is wearing her wedding gown.

176

LENGUA

Some adjectives communicate different meanings, depending on whether they are used before or after the noun.

	BEFORE	AFTER
cierto	(*a*) certain	sure
grande	great, grand	large, big
nuevo	new (*recently acquired, installed, elected, etc.*)	new (*brand new, unused*)
pobre	poor (*to be pitied*)	poor (*impoverished*)
puro	pure (*nothing but, just, only*)	pure (*without impurities*)
único	only, sole	only (*unique*)

Grande becomes **gran** before a singular noun.

22. ¿NO?, ¿VERDAD?, ¿NO ES CIERTO?

Tienen un hijo, ¿no?	They have a son, don't they?
Vamos a tomar cerveza, ¿verdad?	We're having beer, right?
Vamos mañana, ¿no es cierto?	We're going tomorrow, aren't we? (*Isn't that right?*)

Any one of the three expressions can be used in each of the sentences given as examples. The native uses these expressions when asking that his statement be confirmed.

23. SABER versus CONOCER

¿Sabes mis señas?	Do you know my address?
No saben escribir.	They don't know how to write.
¿Conoces al novio de Pili?	Do you know Pili's fiancé?
No conozco la canción.	I don't know the song.

SABER means "to know" when reference is to the capacity to impart information or to the capacity to perform a skill or any acquired ability—"know how."

CONOCER means "to know" when reference is to the capacity to recognize through acquaintance or association—"to be familiar with."

177

24. MULTIPLE NEGATIVES

—¿Hay algo en mi ojo?	Is there something in my eye?
—**No** hay **nada**.	There isn't anything.
—¿Ves a alguien?	Do you see anybody (anyone)?
—**No** veo a **nadie**.	I don't see anybody (anyone).
—¿Conoces algún buen restorán?	Do you know any good restaurant?
—**No** conozco **ninguno**.	I don't know any.
—Tienes que creer o a él o a ella.	You have to believe either him or her.
—**No** creo **ni** a él **ni** a ella.	I don't believe either him or her.
Yo siempre envío algo.	I always send something.
Ella **nunca** envía **nada**.	She never sends anything.
Sale **sin** decir **nada**.	He leaves without saying anything.
No están aquí **tampoco**. ⎤ **Tampoco** están aquí. ⎦	⎧They aren't here either. ⎩Neither are they here.
Yo **no** bebo **nada nunca**. ⎤ **Nunca** bebo **nada**. ⎦	⎧I don't ever drink anything. ⎩I never drink anything.

The bold faced terms are negative and, consequently, indicate that the multiple negative is correct Spanish. Note that only one negative ever appears before the verb.

25. USES OF *ESTAR*

1. Estoy en la biblioteca.	I'm in (at) the library.
No está lejos (cerca).	It isn't far away (nearby).
Están con las niñas.	They are with the girls.
Está en la luna.	He's daydreaming. (He's on the moon.)
2. Está boca abajo (arriba).	It is face down (up).
Están cara a cara.	They are face to face.
3. El agua está fría (caliente).	The water is cold (hot).
La cena está preparada.	Supper is ready.
La puerta está abierta.	The door is open.
4. —¿Cómo estás?—Estoy bien.	—How are you?—I'm well.
No estoy cansado.	I'm not tired.
¿Estáis preocupados?	Are you worried?
5. Él está tonto hoy.	He's silly today.
¡Qué amable estás!	How kind you are! (*Sarcasm.*)

6. El día está hermoso.   The day is beautiful.
—¿Cómo estoy?   —How am I? (*How do I look?*)
—Estás guapísima.   —You're (*look*) beautiful.
Las gambas están riquísimas.   The shrimps are (*taste*) simply delicious.
Los zapatos son grandes pero le están pequeños.   The shoes are large (*size*) but they are small for him. (They are size 12 but he wears size 13.)

Joaquín está más esbelto.   Joaquin is (*has become*) more slender.

ESTAR is used when expressing:

1. LOCATION—an exact place, one relative to another, or a figurative place
2. POSITION
3. STATE OR CONDITION OF THINGS
4. STATE OF BODY OR MIND
5. BEHAVIOR—when acting out of rôle
6. "has turned out," "looks," "tastes," "relative fitting of one item to another," "has become"

Discounting idiomatic expressions (**hacer buen tiempo**—to BE good weather, etc.) and the above uses of **estar**, the English verb *to be* is expressed by the verb **ser**. See **Addendum II** if a contrast of **ser** and **estar** is desired.

26. PERSONAL PRONOUNS AFTER PREPOSITIONS

No es para ella. Es para mí.   It's not for her. It's for me.
Pienso en ti a menudo.   I think of you often.
Salen sin él.   They go out without him.
Contamos con usted.   We are counting on you.
Hace todo por ellos.   He does everything for them.

Subject pronouns, other than **yo** and **tú**, are used after prepositions. **Mí** (me) and **ti** (you) correspond to the **yo** and **tú** pronouns. **Conmigo** (with me) and **contigo** (with you) are irregular. A common exception: **un secreto entre tú y yo** (a secret between you and me). With the preposition **entre** (between, among), **tú** and **yo** are used instead of **ti** and **mí**.

27. EXCLAMATIONS

¡Qué conferencia tan interesante!	What an interesting lecture!
¡Qué película tan emocionante!	What a thrilling picture!
¡Qué niños tan sucios!	What dirty children!

Notice the position of the adjective in Spanish.

28. DEFINITE ARTICLE WITH TITLES

Conozco a los señores Roca.	I know Mr. and Mrs. Roca.
El coronel Silva no está.	Colonel Silva is not in.
Soy la señorita Ramos.	I am Miss Ramos.

But:

Buenos días, doctor Fabra.	Good morning, Doctor Fabra.

The definite article precedes all titles of persons *not* directly addressed. The titles **don**, **doña** (*no translation*), **san**, **santo**, and **santa** (saint) do not take the article.

29. PRE-POSITION POSSESSIVE ADJECTIVES

Tus libros están en la mesa.	Your books are on the table.
Nuestra casa es pequeña.	Our house is small.
Vuestro jardín está precioso.	Your garden looks beautiful.
¿Tiene usted su coche?	Do you have your car?
Ella tiene su coche.	She has her car.

mi (my)	**nuestro** (our)
tu (your)	**vuestro** (your)
	su (his, her, its, their, your)

30. POST-POSITION POSSESSIVE ADJECTIVES

1. Muy señor mío:	Dear Sir:
Hija mía, ¿por qué lloras?	(My) child, why do you cry?
2. Son amigos nuestros.	They are friends of ours.
Esa actitud tuya molesta.	That attitude of yours is annoying.
3. Ese dinero es suyo.	That money is theirs.
¿Son suyas las fotos?	Are the pictures yours?
4. Su coche es como el tuyo.	His car is like yours.
Tus ideas y las mías.	Your ideas and mine.
5. Todo lo vuestro es nuevo.	Everything you have is new.
Hablemos de lo nuestro.	Let's talk about our affair (problem, situation, etc.).

180

LENGUA

The adjectives **mío, tuyo, suyo, nuestro,** and **vuestro** are used:

1. In formal address to show courtesy, and in familiar address to express a certain degree of endearment.
2. To mean "of mine," "of yours," "of his," etc.
3. After a form of **ser,** with the meaning "mine," "yours," "theirs," etc. The difference between **son nuestros** (they are ours) and **son los nuestros** (they are ours) lies in the number of different owners involved. In the first case, we are the sole owners of the items. In the second case, we are the owners of only some of the items.
4. With the definite articles to form constructs that function as pronouns and mean "mine," "yours," "his," etc.
5. With **lo** to form constructs that function as substantives and refer to "one's belongings" or to "what concerns one."

31. ALTERNATE FOR *SU* AND *SUYO*

Éste es el vaso de ella, y ése es de él.	This is her glass, and that one is his.
Éstos son los suyos.	These are yours.
Ésos son los de ellos.	Those are theirs.

Usual Construction	Alternate Construction
	(los zapatos) **de él**
	(los zapatos) **de ella**
sus (zapatos)	(los zapatos) **de ellos**
	(los zapatos) **de ellas**
	(los zapatos) **de usted**
	(los zapatos) **de ustedes**

The alternate construction is also used to replace **suyo, suya, suyos, suyas.**

The several possible meanings of **su** and **suyo** (his, her, their, your) are cause for ambiguity at times. This ambiguity can be avoided by employing the alternate forms.

32. DEMONSTRATIVE ADJECTIVES AND PRONOUNS

a) Esta pluma es de Elisa.	This pen is Elisa's.
Son simpáticos esos chicos.	Those boys are nice.
Están en aquellos pupitres.	They are (seated) at those desks.
¡Éste está mal de la cabeza!	This fellow is off his rocker!
Ése es un buen sitio.	That (place) is a good spot.
¿Aquél de la barba?	That fellow with the beard?

181

	ADJECTIVE	PRONOUN
este	this	this (one, fellow, "guy," etc.)
esta	this	this (one, girl, "gal," etc.)
ese, aquel	that	that (one, fellow, "guy," etc.)
esa, aquella	that	that (one, girl, "gal," etc.)
estos	these	these (people, men, etc.)
estas	these	these (girls, women, etc.)
esos, aquellos	those	those (people, men, etc.)
esas, aquellas	those	those (girls, women, etc.)

In the printed or written form, the demonstrative carries an accent mark over the **e** (never final **e**), when it functions as a pronoun.

When what is spoken about *is considered* distant or remote, in time or space, from the speaker and person spoken to, the **aquel** forms are used, instead of the more common **ese** forms.

b) Esto es lo más importante.　　This matter is the most important.
¿Qué es esto?　　What is this?
Eso suena a inglés.　　That sounds like English.

Esto and **eso** are neuter pronouns and are used to refer to an utterance, thought, idea, matter, affair, situation, or to an unidentified thing or things.

33. *ALLÍ, AHÍ*—there

aquellos alumnos allí　　those students over there
Me van a enviar allí.　　They are going to send me there.
Esos ahí son buenos.　　Those there are good.
¿Qué tienes ahí?　　What do you have there?

Allí refers to a place *considered* remote from the person addressed. **Ahí** refers to the latter's environs—the space, the room, the building, the city, part of country, or the country in which he is located. The difference between **allí** and **ahí** parallels the difference between **aquel** and **ese**.

34. WITH-VERB PRONOUNS

	1st person		2d person		3d person					
DIRECT	me	nos	te	os	lo	le	la	los	les	las
INDIRECT	,,	,,	,,	,,		le			les	
REFLEXIVE	,,	,,	,,	,,			se			
RECIPROCAL		,,		,,			se			

A with-verb pronoun is one that, whenever used, must come immediately before (*unattached*) or after (*attached to*) a verb.

a) DIRECT OBJECT

Me conocen bien.	They know me well.
Van a llamarnos.	They are going to call us.
Os queremos a los dos.	We love you both.
¿La conoces?	Do you know her?
Voy a verle esta tarde.	I'm going to see him this afternoon.

Lo, le, los, and **les,** as direct objects, may refer to masculine persons or masculine things.

b) INDIRECT OBJECT

Me dan el dinero.	They give me the money.
Papá te va a hacer otro.	Dad is going to make another for you.
Ella le guisa, le cose, y le lava la ropa.	She cooks for him, sews for him, and washes his clothes (washes clothes for him).
Les digo la verdad.	I'm telling you the truth.

183

c) **REFLEXIVE**

Me lavo.	I wash (myself).
Ella se lava las manos.	She washes her(self the) hands.
Me voy a preparar una bebida.	I'm going to fix myself a drink.
La historia se repite.	History repeats itself.
Va a comprarse un coche.	He's going to buy himself a car.

When whatever the actor does, affects himself (herself, etc.) in any degree—totally or partially, directly or indirectly—the Spanish construction uses the with-verb pronoun that corresponds to the actor.

d) **RECIPROCAL**

¿Ustedes se conocen?	Do you know each other?
¿No os escribís?	Don't you write each other?
Nos vemos en el espejo.	We see each other (*or* ourselves) in the mirror.

The reflexive and reciprocal constructions are alike. In case of ambiguity, the speaker may add **el uno al otro (las unas a las otras,** *etc.*):

Nos miramos el uno al otro.	We look at each other (*not* at ourselves).

35. TWO SUCCESSIVE WITH-VERB PRONOUNS

a) Si se me presenta la oportunidad ... (1)   If I get the opportunity (If the opportunity presents itself to me) ...

Nadie puede comparársele. (1)	No one can compare himself to him.
Me lo imagino. (2)	I can imagine. (I can imagine it to myself.)
Te la plancho hoy. (3)	I'll iron it for you today.
¿Nos los pueden enviar? (3)	Can you send them to us?

It will be observed that the relative order of with-verb pronouns is REFLEXIVE—INDIRECT—DIRECT. Because no more than two with-verb pronouns are ever used in succession, there are three possible patterns:

REFLEXIVE—INDIRECT (1)
REFLEXIVE—DIRECT (2)
INDIRECT—DIRECT (3)

b) No se lo van a contar.	They aren't going to tell it to him (her, them, you).
Se las compran.	They buy them from (for) him (her, them, you).

184

In the event that both pronouns are 3d person in the INDIRECT—DIRECT pattern, the first pronoun is expressed as **se**, never as **le** or **les**.

Note that **lo**, as a neuter term, may represent an idea, thought, matter, utterance, situation, action, or an unidentified item.

36. THE REFLEXIVE WITH-VERB PRONOUN

Me pongo el abrigo.	I put on my coat.
¿Por qué no te sientas?	Why don't you sit down?
Elisa se levanta.	Elisa gets up.
Ella se pone enferma.	She becomes ill.
Se van mañana.	They are going away tomorrow.

In dictionaries, the abbreviations *r.*, *vr.*, or *v.r.* (*verbo reflexivo*) mean that **me, te, nos, os, se**, corresponding to the actor, must accompany the verb, whether the action is reflexive or not. Observe the following:

poner   to put, to place; *r.* to put on, to become

sentar   to seat, to fit, to suit; *r.* to sit down

levantar   to lift, to raise; *r.* to get up, to rise

ir   to go; *r.* to leave, to go away, to depart, to go

Verbs requiring reflexive pronouns may also be denoted by a **se** attached to the infinitive, i.e., **ponerse** = **poner**, *r.*

37. THE INDEFINITE ACTOR

¿**Se puede** pasar?	Can I (*one*) come in?
Se debe comer despacio.	One should eat slowly.
Desde aquí **se oye** bien.	From here you (*one*) can hear well.
Se dice que no torea más.⎫	They say (*it is said*) he's not going to fight bulls
Dicen que no torea más. ⎭	anymore.
Se le va a fusilar. ⎫	⎧They are going to shoot him.
Le van a fusilar. ⎭	⎩He is going to be shot.

An indefinite actor commonly is expressed by **se**/*verb* (*3d, singular*). When the action is a substitute for *to be*/*past participle*, and the actor is not expressed, the construction sometimes is *verb* (*3d, plural*).

185

38. SELECTION AND CONTRAST

Le hablo a usted. (1)

I speak to you. (Not to him, her, or the others.)

No podemos verle. Ni él vernos a nosotros. (2)

We can't see him. Nor can he see us.

A plus an appropriate pronoun (see par. 26) are used to express (1) a selection (*one or several from a group*), or (2) a contrast. The construction is *generally* accompanied by the corresponding indirect with-verb pronoun.

39. USE OF THE PRETERIT

Después que llegamos, llovió.	After we arrived, it rained (or began to rain).
Lo compró ayer.	He bought it yesterday.
¿Cuándo viste a Paco?	When did you see Paco?
No me levanté a tiempo.	I didn't get up on time.
Perdí la cabeza. Le insulté.	I lost my head. I insulted him.
Murió el año pasado.	He died last year.
Hablé con ella muchas veces.	I spoke to her many times.
Vivieron aquí tres años.	They lived here (for) three years.

The preterit expresses anteriority and perfection. It communicates the notion that an action, either in toto or any segment of it, was perfected (*occurred*) before what is considered the present moment. If an action was repeated, but not as a habit, the preterit is employed with the necessary numerical modifier.

40. *GUSTAR*—to like

Me gusta mucho.	I like it a lot.
¿Os gusta nuestra idea?	Do you like our idea?
No me gustaron nada.	I didn't like them at all.
Te van a gustar los míos.	You are going to like mine.
A Luis no le gusta el vino.	Luis doesn't like wine.

Gustar means approximately *to appeal* or *to be pleasing* and usually translates the English verb *to like*. In view of the meaning of **gustar**, the Spanish construction is different from the English. *I like her* can be thought of in Spanish as *she appeals to me*—**Ella me gusta**. Likewise, *she likes me* is *I appeal to her*—**Yo le gusto**. The formula is:

	Spanish	*Indirect Object* / **gustar** /	*Actor*
		↑	↑
	English	*Actor* / *like* / *Direct Object*	

Note that the actor, if a personal pronoun, comes before the verb. There is freedom to place a noun-actor before or after the verb, but it normally is placed after the verb.

41. *EN, A*—at

Abone usted en caja.	Pay at the cash register.
En la esquina se encontró con un hombre.	He met a man at the corner.
No como en casa hoy.	I'm not eating at home today.
Están en la playa.	They are at the beach.
No puedo en este momento.	I can't at this moment.
El perro anda a su lado.	The dog walks at his side.
¿Quién llama a la puerta?	Who knocks at the door?

En is used to indicate the place or moment *within* which something exists, is located, or takes place. Most all other times, **a** is the equivalent to "at."

42. ADVERBS FORMED WITH -*MENTE*

Es precisamente lo que busco.	It's precisely what I'm looking for.
Habla clara y enfáticamente.	He speaks clearly and emphatically.

correcta + **mente** = **correctamente**   correctly
elegante + **mente** = **elegantemente**   elegantly

Linking the feminine singular of an appropriate adjective to the feminine noun **mente** (mind), forms an adverb. In a series, **mente** is attached only to the last adjective.

43. THE USES OF THE IMPERFECT

a) La veía con frecuencia.   I used to see her frequently.
  Siempre que venía, nos daba pirulíes.   Whenever he came, he would give us lollipops.

The imperfect can express what **was habitual**.

b) Cuando la guerra, vivíamos en Granada.　During the war, we were living in Granada.

En noviembre estaba yo en Río de Janeiro.　In November, I was in Rio de Janeiro.

Le vimos muchas veces pero no le conocíamos.　We saw him many times but we didn't know him.

Cuando eran ricos, tenían dos coches.　When they were rich, they had two cars.

The imperfect can express what **was in effect during the time that is being recalled**.

c) Volvían al día siguiente.　They were returning on the following day.

Dijo que se marchaba pronto.　He said that he was leaving soon.

Yo sabía que si se enteraba, me mataba.　I knew that if she found out, I was a dead duck (i.e., she would kill me).

The imperfect can express **retro-futurity** with such verbs as **volver, marcharse, ir, irse** (leave), and in **si** (if) statements. Usually the actions were to take place relatively soon.

d) ¿Qué hora era cuando volvió?　What time was it when he returned?

Era de día cuando llegamos.　It was daylight (daytime) when we arrived.

The imperfect is used to express **the time of day in the past**.

44. A COMPARISON OF THE IMPERFECT AND THE PRETERIT OF THE VERBS *PODER*, *QUERER*, *CONOCER*, AND *SABER*

Sabía que **podía** hacerlo.　I knew that I could do it. (had the capacity)

De puntillas **pude** ver por encima de la tapia.　On tiptoes I could see over the wall. (succeeded in . . .)

Querían escaparse.　They wanted to escape. (had the desire)

Quisieron escaparse.　They wanted to escape. (tried to escape)

No **quisieron** hacerlo.　They didn't want to do it. (refused, offered resistance)

La **conocía** bien.　I knew her well. (was acquainted with her)

La **conocí** el año pasado.　I met her last year. (made her acquaintance)

Mi padre **sabía** el secreto.　My father knew the secret. (had knowledge of)

¿Qué hizo cuando **supo** el secreto?　What did he do when he knew the secret? (learned, found out)

45. VERBS OF PERCEPTION/INFINITIVE

Le sentí entrar.	I heard him come in.
La oí llamar al sereno.	I heard her call the *sereno*.
Vio salir a tu futura con la mamá.	He saw your future wife go out with her mother.
Yo escuchando cantar, me duermo en seguida.	When I listen to someone sing, I fall asleep right away.
Sintieron temblar el suelo.	They felt the floor tremble (shake).

An action seen, heard, or felt is generally expressed as an infinitive. Note that **sentir** (II) may be used in place of **oir** when what is heard is a noise of some sort.

46. THE PAST PARTICIPLE

a)

$$\textbf{habl} + \textbf{ado} = \textbf{hablado} \quad \text{spoken}$$
$$\left.\begin{array}{c}\textbf{com} \\ \textbf{viv}\end{array}\right\} + \textbf{ido} \begin{array}{l} = \textbf{comido} \quad \text{eaten} \\ = \textbf{vivido} \quad \text{lived}\end{array}$$

The past participle is formed by adding the appropriate ending to the stem of the verb.

A number of common irregular past participles are:

abierto	(abrir)	opened	**puesto**	(poner)	put, placed
cubierto	(cubrir)	covered	**roto**	(romper)	broken
dicho	(decir)	said	**visto**	(ver)	seen
escrito	(escribir)	written	**vuelto**	(volver)	returned
hecho	(hacer)	done, made			

b)

un hombre condenado	a condemned man
Estamos cansados.	We are tired.
Ella sigue preocupada.	She is still (continues to be) worried.
Las ventanas están rotas.	The windows are broken.

A past participle, functioning as an adjective, agrees in gender and number with the noun it modifies.

47. SOME USES OF *LO*

a) **Lo peor** queda por venir. *The worst (part of it)* is yet to come.

Lo más interesante fue la última escena. *The most interesting part* was the last scene.

lo/adjective = *the*/adjective/*part*

b) ¡**Lo verde que** está la hierba!   *How green* the grass is!

  ¡**Lo cansados que** estamos!   *How tired* we are!

  Hay que ver **lo guapas que** son.   You should see *how pretty* they are.

  ¡**Lo bien que** comen!   *How well* they eat!

  ¡**Lo de prisa que** andas!   *How fast* you walk!

  Por **lo bien que** has salido en los exámenes, te llevo al teatro.   Because of *how well* you've done in your exams, I'm taking you to the theater.

lo	adjective adverb	**que**		*how*	adjective adverb

c) ¡Ahí va, **lo que** llueve!   Boy, *how* it rains! (Is it ever raining!)

  ¡**Lo que** se pinta esa mujer!   *How* that woman paints herself! (Does that woman ever put on the make-up!)

     ¡**lo que** . . . !   *how* . . . ! (= how much)

48. *QUÉ, CUÁL, LO QUE*—some translations for "what"

a) ¿**Qué** es su padre?—Médico.   *What* is your father?—A doctor.

  ¿**Qué** es un almanaque?   *What* is a calendar?

  ¿**Qué** es esto?   *What* is this?

  ¿**Qué** es lo que te falta?   *What* are you lacking?

  ¿**Qué** es lo importante?   *What* is the most important thing?

Qué is used when asking (1) a classification (*a label*), (2) a definition, or (3) when the predicate is or revolves about a neuter term, *i.e.*, **esto, eso, aquello,** or **lo.**

b) ¿**Cuál** es la carga máxima?   *What*'s the maximum load?

  ¿**Cuáles** son sus señas?   *What*'s his address?

  ¿**Cuáles** son tus planes?   *What* are your plans?

  ¿**Cuál** es la diferencia?   *What*'s the difference?

  ¿**Cuál** es el producto principal?   *What*'s the main product?

  ¿**Cuál** es el mejor camino?   *What*'s the best road?

Cuál is used when asking (1) a number (*address, quantity, etc.*), or (2) a detailed explanation, or (3) that an item or person be indicated by name or pointed out.

c) **Lo que** dices es verdad.   *What* you say is the truth.

  Les contó **lo que** pasó.   He told them *what* happened.

Non-interrogative "what" is **lo que.**

LENGUA

49. THE PRESENT PARTICIPLE

a)

$$\begin{aligned} \textbf{habl} + \textbf{ando} &= \textbf{hablando} & \text{speaking} \\ \left.\begin{array}{l}\textbf{com}\\\textbf{viv}\end{array}\right\} + \textbf{iendo} &= \textbf{comiendo} & \text{eating} \\ &= \textbf{viviendo} & \text{living} \end{aligned}$$

The present participle is formed by adding the appropriate ending to the stem of the verb. Exceptions:

1. Class II and III verbs change the stem vowel from **o** to **u**, or **e** to **i**—

   durmiendo   (*dormir*)
   sintiendo   (*sentir*)
   pidiendo   (*pedir*)

2. If the infinitive stem ends in a vowel, add **yendo** instead of **iendo**, e.g., **leyendo** (*leer*), **cayendo** (*caer*), **creyendo** (*creer*).

3. **Yendo** is the present participle of **ir**.
   Diciendo is the present participle of **decir**.
   Pudiendo is the present participle of **poder**.
   Viniendo is the present participle of **venir**.

b) (*Entrando.*)

Cantan, acompañándose de guitarras.

Tomando este camino se llega más pronto.
¿Sigues cojeando?
Me está doliendo.
Eso es lo que te estoy diciendo siempre.
No estaba mirando lo que estaba haciendo.

(Entering.)

They sing, accompanying themselves on the guitar.

(*By*) taking this road, you'll get there sooner.
Are you still limping?
It is hurting me.
That's what I'm always telling you.
He wasn't watching what he was doing.

The use of the present participle in Spanish and English is, with an exception or two, essentially the same.

Estar plus the present participle (**gerundio**) form the progressive construction that is used to express an "activity" going on, or to emphasize the activity's contemporaneity. Spanish does not follow the English progressive construction used to express future actions (*I'm returning tomorrow, I'm going to bring them, I'm eating out next Saturday*). In such cases, the Spaniard generally employs the simple present, or the construction **ir a**/*infinitive*.

50. PRESENT PERFECT AND PLUPERFECT CONSTRUCTIONS

a) **Present Perfect**

Todo ha variado.	Everything has changed.
Yo no he tenido nunca celos.	I have never been jealous.
Se han marchado esta tarde.	They left (*have left*) this afternoon.
¿Sabes lo que he decidido?	Do you know what I decided (*have decided*)?
¿Ha habido carta?	Was there a letter?
He dormido muy bien esta noche.	I slept very well last night. (This person has just gotten up and refers to last night as "this" night, still very close to him in time.)
Lo he comprado (compré) ayer.	I bought it yesterday.

English and Spanish present perfect constructions are similar when expressing that what has taken place *still* is of personal significance to the speaker. They are alike, also, when expressing what has never been true and *still* is not.

When expressing actions considered having occurred a relatively short time ago, the Spaniard almost invariably uses the present perfect, while the English-speaking native fluctuates between the simple past and the present perfect.

When using terms that denote past time, such as "yesterday," "last night," "last hour," etc., the English-speaking native employs the simple past. In Spanish, if the time element is considered relatively recent, the native will frequently use the present perfect.

In short, Spanish makes greater use of the present perfect construction than English does.

b) **Pluperfect**

Vi que ella había llorado.	I saw that she had cried.
Explicaron por qué no la habían visto.	They explained why they hadn't seen her.

In general, the use of the pluperfect in Spanish and in English is identical. Note that the imperfect of **haber** is employed in the construction. After **cuando**, the preterit is more common than the pluperfect. For example:

cuando terminó	when he had finished, or
	when he finished

51. *HABER*—there to be

Hay sólo uno.	There is only one.
Hay muchos.	There are many.
Ha habido sólo uno.	There has been only one.
Ha habido muchos.	There have been many.

Había sólo uno.	There was only one.
Había muchos.	There were many.
Hubo una explosión.	There was an explosion.
Va a haber muchos.	There are going to be many.

The various 3d, singular forms of **haber** translate "there is," "there are," "there was," "there will be," etc. **Y** (*"there" in old Spanish*) is attached only to **ha—hay**.

The difference between **había** and **hubo** is one of aspect. For example:

Había mucha gente cuando entré.	There were a lot of people when I entered. (They were there at the time to which reference is made.)
¿Hubo sitio para todo?	Was there space for all? (Reference is to a space that ceased being a space when it was filled.)

52. SUBJUNCTIVE—PATTERN I

No creo que **sea** difícil.	I don't think that it will be difficult.
Me alegro que todos **estén** bien.	I'm glad that all are well.
¿Quieres que yo le **escriba**?	Do you want me to write him?
Celebro que **puedan** venir.	I'm glad they can come.
Le he dicho que no los **compre**.	I have told him not to buy them.
No tolero que se **hable** más de este asunto.	I'll not tolerate that more be said of this matter.
Mi intención es que **tenga** lugar la semana que viene.	My intention is that it take place next week.
Le agradezco que usted me **acompañe**.	I'm grateful to you that you accompany me.

When a clause depends on an expression (*determiner*) that indicates a disposition of "mind," "heart," or "will," the conjugated verb in the dependent clause is in the subjunctive mode. This point of syntax may be diagramed as follows:

DETERMINER		DEPENDENT CLAUSE
Me alegro	que	todos **estén** bien.
Le he dicho	que	no los **compre**.

↑
THIS
determines
whether the
subjunctive
will appear-----------→ HERE

Some common determiners that normally indicate a disposition of (1) mind, (2) heart, and (3) will, are:

1. **aconsejar**   to advise
   sugerir (II)   to suggest
   dudar   to doubt
   preferir (II)   to prefer
   recomendar (I)   to recommend

   no creer   not to believe
   no estar cierto   not to be certain
   no estar seguro   not to be sure
   no poder decir   not to be able to say

2. **agradecer**   to be grateful, to appreciate
   alegrarse (de)   to be glad
   celebrar   to be glad
   esperar   to hope

   sentir (II)   to be sorry, to regret
   temer   to fear, to be afraid
   tener miedo   to be scared, to be afraid

3. **autorizar**   to authorize
   consentir (II) **en**   to consent to
   decir   to tell (request)
   dejar   to let, to allow
   evitar   to avoid
   exigir   to demand
   hacer   to have (something done)

   impedir (III)   to prevent, to hinder
   insistir en   to insist
   mandar   to command, to order
   ordenar   to order
   pedir   to request, to ask
   permitir   to permit
   prohibir   to prohibit
   querer   to want
   tolerar   to tolerate

Generally, all the expressions in the three groups listed above, except **dudar** and those beginning with **no** (*group 1*), are determiners for the subjunctive, whether in the affirmative or negative. When **no creer** represents a strong conviction, the subjunctive may not be used in the dependent clause.

53. COMMANDS AND THE "LET'S/VERB" EXPRESSION

a) Habl*a*.   No hables. (*tú*)   ⎤
   Habl*ar*.   No habléis. (*vosotros*) ⎥ Speak. Don't speak.
   Hable.   No hable. (*usted*)   ⎥
   Hablen   No hablen. (*ustedes*)   ⎦

   Escríb*e*lo.   No lo escribas.   ⎤
   Escribi*r*lo.   No lo escribáis.   ⎥ Write it. Don't write it.
   Escríb*a*lo.   No lo escriba.   ⎥
   Escríb*a*nlo.   No lo escriban.   ⎦

   Hablemos.   No hablemos.   ]Let's speak. Let's not speak.

   Escribámoslo.   No lo escribamos.   ]Let's write it. Let's not write it.

LENGUA

The formation of the commands and the "let's/verb" expression:

1. ALL forms are the same as the PRESENT SUBJUNCTIVE when the construction is NEGATIVE.
2. All forms, except for **tú** and **vosotros**, are the same as the present subjunctive when the construction is affirmative.
3. The affirmative form for **tú** is the same as the 3d, singular of the present indicative.*
4. The affirmative form for **vosotros** is as a rule the infinitive.

b) Observations and additional remarks

1) With-verb pronouns come after and are attached to affirmative commands. They come before negative commands.
2) **Usted(es)** may or may not be expressed. **Tú** and **vosotros** seldom are expressed other than to indicate selection:

Recógelo tú.   You pick it up. (*i.e., not he or someone else*)

3) In popular speech, the negative **vosotros** form frequently is the same as the affirmative, that is, the infinitive—¡**No hablar**! (Don't talk!), ¡**No pegarle**! (Don't hit him!)
4) There is the old affirmative **vosotros** form—**hablad, comed, salid**, etc. This form, however, seems to be falling into disuse.
5) As an affirmative command, **vamos a/infinitive** (*Vamos a comer*) is more common than the simple form (*Comamos*).

54. SUBJUNCTIVE—PATTERN II

No es preciso que lo **hagan** hoy.	It isn't necessary that they do it today.
Es hora que te **cases**.	It's (*high*) time that you got married.
Me parece raro que no nos **hayamos** encontrado hasta ahora.	It seems strange to me that we didn't meet until now.
No le molesta que **use** la máquina de escribir, ¿verdad?	It doesn't bother you that I use the typewriter, does it?
No es que **desconfíe** de ti.	It isn't that I distrust you.

DETERMINER "IT" EXPRESSION		DEPENDENT CLAUSE
No es preciso	que	lo **hagan** hoy.
Es hora	que	te **cases**.

↑
THIS
determines
whether the
subjunctive
will appear--------------→HERE

* Refer to **Diálogo 25** for exceptions.

195

The determiners for Pattern II may be called "IT" expressions. Some common "IT" expressions (*affirmative or negative*) that are determiners for the subjunctive, are:

es absurdo		is absurd
es hora		is (high) time
es imposible		is impossible
es inútil		is useless
es lamentable		is lamentable
es lástima		is a pity, a shame
es lógico		is logical
es maravilloso		is marvelous
es mejor		is best
es natural		is natural
es necesario		is necessary
es posible	it	is possible
es preciso		is necessary
es preferible		is preferable
es probable		is probable
es ridículo		is ridiculous
apena		grieves
conviene		is desirable, is advisable, suits
extraña		is strange, seems strange
gusta		pleases (to be glad)
importa		matters
molesta		bothers
parece imposible		doesn't seem possible
parece mentira		seems incredible
parece raro		seems strange

Some "IT" expressions determine the use of the subjunctive only when they are negative:

no es		is not
no es cierto		is not certain
no es evidente	it	is not evident
no es seguro		is not sure
no es verdad		is not true

55. SUBJUNCTIVE—PATTERN III

Deseo otro que no **sea** tan caro.	I want another that isn't so expensive.
Escriban ustedes lo que **quieran**.	Write whatever you want.
Voy a hacer todo lo que **esté** en mi mano.	I'm going to do everything that is in my power.

Nadie que le **conozca** bien le admira.   No one who knows him well admires him.

No hay nada que usted **pueda** hacer.   There isn't anything that you can do.

DETERMINER UNKNOWN, INDEFINITE, OR NON-EXISTENT ITEM		DEPENDENT CLAUSE
Deseo otro	que	no **sea** tan caro.
Nadie	que	le **conozca** bien . . .

THIS determines whether the subjunctive will appear------------------→HERE

When a dependent clause refers to (*modifies*) any person or thing that is UNKNOWN, INDEFINITE or NON-EXISTENT, the verb in that clause is in the subjunctive.

In the last two example sentences, **que** refers to **nadie** and **nada**. As a rule of thumb, the verb in any clause that modifies a negative term is in the subjunctive. In the other sentences, **otro** and **lo** represent unknown or indefinite things.

No hay quien me lo **pueda** quitar.   There isn't anyone who can take it from me.

Te llevo donde me **digas**.   I'll take you wherever you say (*tell me*).

Haga usted cuanto **pueda** por ella.   Do all that you can for her.

Quien, donde, and **cuanto** frequently have the following meanings:

quien	a person who, one who
donde	a place that or where, wherever
cuanto	all that, everything that, whatever

If the person, place, or quantity is non-existent or indefinite, the conjugated verb following these terms is in the subjunctive.

56. SUBJUNCTIVE—PATTERN IVa

Tenemos que alquilar los esquís antes de que **haya** más gente.   We must rent the skis before there are more people.

Toma el desayuno antes que se **enfríe**.   Eat your breakfast before it gets cold.

Le he llamado para que nos **refiera** cierta historia.   I've called him so that he tell us a certain story.

197

Llevo el coche al garaje a que me lo **arreglen**.	I'm taking the car to the garage to have it fixed.
A menos que **sea** una corrida buenísima.	Unless it is a very good bullfight.
Voy a escribirlo en caso de que se me **olvide**.	I'm going to write it down in case I forget.

	DETERMINER CERTAIN LINKAGE EXPRESSIONS		DEPENDENT CLAUSE
Toma el desayuno	antes	que	se **enfríe**.
Le he llamado	para	que	nos **refiera** ...

↑
THIS
determines
that the
subjunctive
will appear --------------→HERE

Linkage expressions that always determine that the conjugated verb in the dependent clause will be in the subjunctive, are:

antes (de)	before	**a condición de**	on the condition
a		**en caso de**	in case
a fin de	in order, so	**dado el caso (de)**	in the event, supposing
para		**sin**	without
a menos	unless	**con tal**	provided

57. INFINITIVE OR SUBJUNCTIVE

Hágale **entrar**.	Have him come in.
¿Cómo te has hecho **conocer**?	How did you make yourself known?
¿Quién la ordenó **venir**?	Who ordered her to come?
¿Me permites **ayudar**?	Will you allow me to help?

The infinitive may follow verbs of suasion—**hacer** (to have, to make), **dejar** (to let), **mandar** (to command), **ordenar** (to order), **permitir** (to permit, to allow).

Si no haces que el público se **entere** de lo que sientes, no serás nunca un buen actor.	If you don't make the public understand what you feel, you will never be a good actor.

198

Dejen que **cuente** Remedios.	Let Remedios tell it.
Ordenó a Ernesto que **cerrara** con llave.	He ordered Ernesto to lock the door. (to close with key)
El ruido hace que no nos **enteremos** de nada.	The noise prevents our understanding anything.

When the dependent verb is negative or when its subject is expressed, it is conjugated in the subjunctive and joined to the verb of suasion by **que**.

Verbs of suasion are determiners for the subjunctive. (See paragraph 52, section 3.)

58. CONJECTURE—ANOTHER USE OF THE FUTURE

¿Dónde estarán? No los encuentro.	I wonder where they are? I don't find them.
—¿Qué hora será?	—I wonder what time it is?
—Serán las doce.	—It must be twelve.
Juzgando por las voces, habría más de veinte personas.	Judging by the voices, there probably were more than twenty persons.
Eso se lo dirá usted a todas.	You probably tell that to all the girls.
Aquí viene ahora. Habrá comprado mucho.	Here she comes now. She probably has bought a lot.

The future and retro-future are also used to express conjecture, i.e., likelihood, probability.

59. *ÍSIMO*—very, most, extremely, etc.

Es un chico **altísimo**.	He's a **very tall** boy.
Su mujer es **guapísima**.	His wife is **most beautiful**.
Los exámenes fueron **facilísimos**.	The exams were **extremely easy**.
Después de lavadas, las sábanas se quedaron **blanquísimas**.	After being washed, the sheets came out **dazzling white**.

A superlative connotation is produced by dropping the final vowel (*if there is one*) of an adjective and adding **ísimo, ísima, ísimos, ísimas**.

199

60. *MISMO*—self

Me enfadé conmigo mismo.	I got mad at myself.
Ellas se burlan de sí mismas.	They make fun of themselves.

mí mismo (misma)	myself
ti mismo (misma)	yourself
sí mismo (misma)	himself, herself, yourself, itself
nosotros (-as) mismos (mismas)	ourselves,
vosotros (-as) mismos (mismas)	yourselves,
sí mismos (mismas)	themselves, yourselves

The **mí**, **ti**, and **sí** constructions are employed *only after prepositions*. To express "I myself," "she herself," etc., the native says **yo mismo, ella misma, ellos mismos**, etc.

61. THE RELATIVE PRONOUN *QUE*—who, whom, that, which

a) **que**—*who*

Julia, **que** acababa de leer la carta, palideció.	Julia, **who** had just read the letter, became pale.
Son el capitán y los dos tenientes **que** fueron condecorados.	They are the captain and the two lieutenants **who** were decorated.
Buero es un autor de la generación actual en España **que** sabe escribir teatro. (**Autor** is the logical antecedent.)	Buero is an author of the present generation in Spain **who** knows how to write dramatic works.

b) **que**—*whom*

Esta señorita es mi prima **que** usted ya conoce.	This young lady is my cousin **whom** you already know.
Es el hombre **que** vi ayer.	He's the man (**whom**) I saw yesterday.

c) **que**—*that, which*

Entró por la puerta de la escalera, **que** había quedado abierta. (**Puerta** *is the logical antecedent*.)	He entered by the stairway door **that** had remained open.
Aceptó lo del ayuntamiento **que** le consiguió un amigo. (**Que** refers to **lo**.)	He accepted the city hall's offer **that** a friend got for him.
¿Recuerda la pulsera **que** vimos en el escaparate, y **que** a usted le gustaba?	Do you remember the bracelet (**that**) we saw in the store window and **that** you liked?
¿Logrará el puesto a **que** tiene derecho?	Will he get the position to **which** he has a right?

Hubo un tiempo, hace cinco o seis años, en **que** tus versos me divertían.	There was a time, five or six years ago, **when** (in which) your poetry amused me.
No se sabe el sitio en **que** nació.	They don't know the place **where** (in which) he was born.
Es la pintura de **que** te hablaba.	It's the painting about **which** I was telling you.

Que generally refers to a noun immediately preceding it, but may refer to a distant antecedent if it is the logical one.

Frequently **que** is directly linked to its antecedent by the prepositions **a, de, en,** or **con.** Note that **en que** not only means "in which" but sometimes "when" and "where."

62. RELATIVE PRONOUN CONSTRUCTIONS

EL (LOS, LA, LAS) QUE—whom, which

Es el ladrón **al que** busca la policía.	He's the thief (**whom**) the police are after.
Yo soy la chica con **la que** se va a casar.	I'm the girl (**whom**) he's going to marry.
La persona por **la que** iba a hacer aquello, murió.	The person for **whom** I was going to do that, died.
Tropezó contra la silla, en **la que** tuvo que apoyarse para no caerse.	He stumbled against the chair, on **which** he had to support himself in order not to fall down.
A todos nos llega un momento en la vida en **el que** hemos de dudar entre dos o más caminos.	There comes to us all a moment in our lives **when** we will doubt between two or more paths.
Había momentos en **los que** yo la creía perdida para siempre.	There were moments **when** I thought that I had lost her for good.

The definite article is used with **que** when the latter is linked by a preposition to its noun antecedent. The linkage may be direct, or there may be a pause or some form of modifier between the preposition and the noun antecedent. The definite article agrees in gender and number with the noun:

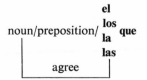

In the last example, the definite article (**los**) may be omitted. (Refer to paragraph 61c.)

63. OMISSION OF NOUNS

a) **Noun not repeated**

una cama grande y una pequeña	one large bed and one small (a large bed and a small one)
unas fotos buenas y unas malas	some good photographs and some bad (ones)
Esa chica y la que cantó son hermanas.	That girl and the one who sang are sisters.
Lleva la cuenta de los obreros, de los que entran y de los que salen.	He keeps tab on the workers, on the ones who enter and on the ones who leave.
La cifra era más elevada de la que habían marcado.	The figure was higher than the one that they had marked.
un helado de vainilla y uno de fresa	one vanilla ice cream and one strawberry

Observations:

1. A Spanish construction is not altered in any way when a noun is not repeated. The remaining words and their order are unchanged:

la cuenta de los (obreros) **que entran y de los** (obreros) **que salen**

2. **Un** means *one* and, by extension, *a* or *an*. When not followed by a noun, **un** reverts to **uno**.

3. The English equivalent for the Spanish construction may or may not require *one(s)* to replace the omitted noun.

4. Note the following equivalents:

$$\textbf{los (las) que} \begin{cases} \text{the ones who, those who} \\ \text{the ones that, those that} \end{cases}$$

b) **Noun not stated but implied**

Yo lamento ser el que tenga que abrirte los ojos.	I'm sorry to be the one who has to open your eyes.
La pobre Juanita no es ni sombra de la que era.	Poor Juanita isn't even the shadow of the person (*the one who*) she used to be.

It cannot be said just what nouns are implied in this type of sentence. The definite article before **que**, nevertheless, agrees in gender (*sex, in this case*) and number with the person to whom reference is made.

Fue ella la que empezó.	{She was the one who started it. {It was she who started it.

In constructions involving the verb **ser**, there are two possible English versions.

c) *QUIEN*—**who, he who, she who, the one who, whoever, someone who, the person who**

QUIENES—**who, those who, the ones who, whoever**

Fue él quien se lo dijo.	{It was he who told him. {He was the one who told him.
Ustedes son quienes han de disculparme.	{It's you who must pardon me. {You are the ones who must pardon me.
Nosotros perdonamos a quienes nos hacen daño.	We pardon those who do us harm.
Quien habla solo, espera hablar con Dios un día.	He who talks alone hopes to speak to God one day.

Quien(es) often alternates for **el que, la que, los que** and **las que**.

64. *QUIEN*—anyone who

No hay quien te entienda.	There isn't anyone who understands you.
Yo no sé quien me lo pueda hacer.	I don't know anyone who can do it for me.

Note that the verb in the dependent clause is in the subjunctive. **Quien** is not only the subject of the verb of this clause but its indefinite or negative antecedent. (Refer to paragraph 55.)

65. WHEN TO USE THE PRESENT OR RETRO-SUBJUNCTIVE

a) Siento que **estés** enfermo. — I am sorry that you **are** ill.

Es natural que les **parezcan** mejores. — It is natural that they **(will) seem** better to them.

—¿Va a comprar pan? — —Is she going to buy bread?

—Le he dicho que lo **compre**. — —I told her **to buy** it.

Era natural que les **parecieran** mejores. — It was natural that they **seemed (would seem)** better to them.

Siento que **estuvieras** enfermo. — I am sorry that you **were** ill.

—¿Por qué ha comprado más pan? — —Why did she buy more bread?

—Porque le dije que lo **comprara**. — Because I told her **to buy** it.

¿Por qué no has comprado pan? Te dije que lo **compraras**. — Why didn't you buy bread? I told you **to buy** it.

203

1) Use the PRESENT subjunctive if the action presently is taking place, or is to take place, as far as the speaker is concerned.

2) Use the RETRO-subjunctive if the action was then taking place, did take place, or was to take place.

b) If, instead of the simple verb, the perfect constructions are used, let yourself be guided by the English:

Dudo que lo $\left\{\begin{array}{l}\textbf{haya}\\\textbf{hubiera*}\end{array}\right\}$ hecho.

I doubt that he **has (will have)** done it.
I doubt that he **had (would have)** done it.

66. SUBJUNCTIVE—PATTERN IVb

a) Rosa tocó el piano de manera que él **pudiera** oirlo através de la puerta.

Rosa played the piano so that he could hear it through the door.

Hará lo imposible porque no os **caséis**.

She will go to all lengths to prevent your getting married. (in order that you not marry)

b) Escríbeme alguna vez cuando **tengas** tiempo.

Write me some time when you have time.

No lo hagas hasta que te **avise**.

Don't do it until I give you the word.

c) Pensaba estudiar mientras ella **estuviera** fuera.

I intended to study as long as she was away.

d) Yo voy aunque **llueva**.

I'm going even if it rains.

Haga usted como **quiera**.

Do as you like.

Como le **molestes**, te pego.

If you bother him, I'll beat you.

e) Por extraña que **sea** la explicación, la aceptaré.

However strange the explanation may be, I'll accept it.

Siempre quiere más joyas por muchas que **tenga**.

She always wants more jewelry no matter how much she may have.

f) Aunque **tuvieras** una mina de oro, no me casaría contigo.

Even if you had a gold mine, I wouldn't marry you.

Si **tomara** la medicina, se sentiría mejor.

If he took the medicine, he would feel better.

---

* **hubieron**: 3d, plural, preterit of **haber**

LENGUA

Pattern IVa (see par. 56) and IVb linkage terms differ only in that the first are *always* determiners for the subjunctive, while the second are determiners *only in special circumstances*.

IVb LINKAGE TERMS	SPECIAL CIRCUMSTANCES
a) **de manera que**⎤ ⎡so that, in **de modo que** ⎦ ⎣a manner that **porque*** so that, in order that	The principal actor directs his action to produce the result expressed in the dependent clause.
b) **cuando** when, whenever **en cuanto** as soon as **después que** after **hasta que** until **luego que** as soon as	Action in the dependent clause is or was yet to take place.
c) **mientras** while, as long as **siempre que** as long as, every time	The termination of the action of the independent clause is related to or determined by the termination of the action in the dependent clause. The action of the dependent clause is or was yet to terminate.
d) **aunque** although, even if **como** as, if	The verb of the dependent clause expresses a future or uncertain action.
e) **por**/*adjective*/**que** however, no matter how **por**/*adverb*/**que** however, no matter how **por mucho**/*noun*/**que** no matter how much (many) **por poco**/*noun*/**que** no matter how little (few)	The action in the dependent clause is uncertain. In English, *may* and *might* often are indicative of such actions.
f) **aunque** even if **si** if	When an "if" clause expresses what is considered unlikely or contrary to fact, the conjugated verb in the "if" clause IS IN THE RETRO-SUBJUNCTIVE.

---

* *Porque* differs from *para que*, in that it is used when a great or maximum effort is exerted.

67. PLACEMENT OF WITH-VERB PRONOUNS

a) **Before the Verb**

Le llevaron a la comisaría.	They took him to the police station.
No **me** he afeitado.	I haven't shaved.
No **se lo** digas.	Don't tell it to him.

With-verb pronouns come immediately before a conjugated verb, except an affirmative command.

b) **After the Verb**

Date prisa.	Hurry up.
Acercándose.	Approaching.
Me gustaría ver**os** a todos.	I would like to see all of you.
Siento no haber**lo** visto.	I regret not having seen it.
Es capaz de hacer**lo**.	He is capable of doing it.

With-verb pronouns are in post-position and appended to:

1) an affirmative command
2) a present participle not preceded by an auxiliary verb
3) an infinitive not preceded by an auxiliary verb.

c) **Before or After the Verb**

Me está doliendo esta pierna.	This leg is hurting me.
Estaba llamándo**la**.	I was calling her.
Me voy a bañar.	I'm going to bathe.
Voy a ver**la**.	I'm going to see her.
¿No **se los** quiere enviar hoy?	Don't you want to send them to her today?
¿Quieres leér**melo**?	Would you read it to me?
Lo sé hacer.	I know how to do it.
Saben preparar**lo**.	They know how to prepare it.
Lo tengo que hacer hoy.	I must do it today.
Tenemos que dejar**los** aquí.	We must leave them here.
¡Y **me** vienen a pedir a mí información acerca de todo eso!	And they come to ask me information about all that!
Papá no volverá a llevar**te** al parque a jugar.	Papa won't take you again to the park to play.
Me **lo** permitieron ver.⎫ Me permitieron ver**lo**. ⎬	They permitted me to see it.

With-verb pronouns may precede the first verb (*if not an infinitive*) or be attached to the last verb form of:

estar/*present participle*
ir a/*infinitive*   **venir a**/*infinitive*
poder/*infinitive*   **volver a**/*infinitive*
querer/*infinitive*   **dejar**/*infinitive*
saber/*infinitive*   **permitir**/*infinitive*
tener que/*infinitive*

In the last two constructions, the choice of post or pre-position of the with-verb pronouns is restricted to the objects of the infinitive, not to the objects of **dejar** and **permitir**.

68. *PONERSE, VOLVERSE, HACERSE, LLEGAR A SER*—to become

a) **Ponerse, Volverse**

Ella se puso bien. (mala, pálida, roja)	She became well. (ill, pale, red)
Se puso hecho una fiera. (de mal humor, contento, rabioso, triste)	He became like a wild beast. (ill-tempered, happy, furious, sad)
El pan se ha puesto duro.	The bread became stale (hard).
El cielo se pone nublado.	The sky becomes cloudy.

Ponerse generally is used when expressing a change of physical or mental state or condition that takes place relatively quickly.

Ella se volvió loca.	She became (*went*) crazy.
Se volvió tan sordo como una tapia.	He became stone deaf.
Cada día me volvía más débil.	I was becoming weaker day by day
El cielo se estaba volviendo pesado.	The sky was becoming overcast.
¡Qué serio se ha vuelto el niño!	How serious the child has become!

Volverse is used, generally, when expressing a change of physical or mental state or condition that takes place relatively slowly.

b) **Hacerse, Llegar a Ser**

Me hice médico.	I became a doctor.
Se hicieron ricos.	They became wealthy.
Nos hicimos novios.	We became sweethearts.
Él se hace viejo.	He is becoming old.
La discusión se hacía violenta.	The argument was becoming violent.

Hacerse is used when expressing a status attained through the actor's own doing, by agreement, or naturally. In the last example, the violent nature of the **discusión** can also be expressed with **se volvía** or **se ponía**.

Llegó a ser un escritor de fama.	He became a famous writer.
A veces su odio llegó a ser grande.	At times his hatred became intense.
El general había llegado a ser objeto de aversión.	The general had become an object of dislike.
¿Crees que podríamos llegar a ser amigos de verdad?	Do you think that we could become real friends?
Llegó a ser jefe del partido.	He became the party leader.

Llegar a ser is used, generally, to express a status or level that is gradually attained, and frequently through the reaction, recognition, or support of others.

69. *DE, QUE*—than

a) **De**

No más **de** cien kilómetros.	No more *than* 100 kilometers.
Menos **de** la mitad.	Less *than* (a) half.
Tengo más **de** lo necesario.	I have more *than* enough.
Quería más **de** los diez que le había prometido.	He wanted more *than* the ten I had promised him.
Comió más **de** una docena de empanadillas.	He ate more *than* a dozen turnovers.

De equals *than* before a quantity that concerns the same kind of item(s) implied by the **más** or **menos**.

Gastan más **de** lo que ganan.	They spend more (money) *than* (that which) they earn.
Es más fácil **de** lo que era.	It's easier *than* (what) it was.
Come más de prisa **de** lo que debe.	He eats faster *than* (what) he ought to.
Tiene menos fuerza **de** lo que te figuras.	He has less strength *than* (what) you imagine (he has).

De lo que equals *than* (*what* or *that which*) before a dependent clause that refers to (1) an unexpressed noun, implied by the **más** or **menos**, (2) an adjective or adverb modified by the **más** or **menos**, or (3) the entire statement containing the **más** or **menos**. Note that the English equivalent commonly omits the relative pronoun "what" or "that which."

208

Le dieron menos dinero **del** que necesitaba.	They gave him less money *than* (what) he needed.
Tiene más valentía **de** la que muestra.	He has more courage *than* (that which) he shows.
Cultivan más verduras **de** las que necesitan.	They cultivate more vegetables *than* (those which) they need.

Instead of **lo,** the definite article is used when the dependent clause refers solely to a noun modified by the **más** or **menos.** The article (**el, la, los, las**) shows agreement with the noun. Again note that we usually omit "what," "that which," or "those which" in the English equivalent.

b) **Que**

Comió más **que** siete.	He ate more (food) *than* seven (persons).
Esta máquina es más grande **que** la que vi ayer.	This machine is larger *than* the one I saw yesterday.
Me quiere a mí más **que** a nadie.	She loves me more *than* (she loves) anyone.
¡Qué mejor momento **que** ahora!	What better moment *than* now!
Prefiere estudiar **que** ir al cine.	He prefers to study *than* to go to the movies.

Que equals *than* in all cases not covered in the preceding section.

70. DATES

—¿A cuántos estamos?	What is the date today?
—A tres (de noviembre).	The third (of November).
Hoy es el primero de abril.	Today is the first of April.
Llegó el dos de mayo.	He arrived (on) the second of May.
¿Qué día es hoy?	What day is today?
Viernes, quince.	Friday, the fifteenth.
Comienza a primeros (mediados, últimos) del mes.	It starts around the beginning (middle, end) of the month.

To express the days of the month, the native uses **el primero** for "the first," and the cardinal numbers for all other dates.

When asking the date of an event, the expression is **¿Cuál es la fecha de . . .?** For example, **¿Cuál es la fecha de la boda?** (What is the date of the wedding?)

71. *HACER* IN TIME EXPRESSIONS

a) **For** (*so much time*)

Hace dos años que lo tengo.	I have had it for two years.
Hacía dos años que lo tenía.	I had had it for two years.
Hace un año que están casados.	They have been married for a year.
Hacía un año que estaban casados.	They had been married for a year.
Hace mucho tiempo que te están llamando.	They have been calling you for a long time.
Hacía mucho tiempo que te estaban llamando.	They had been calling you for a long time.

Note the Spanish construction:

TIME block		ACTION block
Hace **Hacía**	**dos años** **que**	**lo tengo.** **lo tenía.**

When the action *continues* into the present moment of speaking, the verb in both the TIME and ACTION blocks is in the present. If the action *continued* into a past moment of speaking, the verb in both the TIME and ACTION blocks is in the imperfect.

Lo tengo desde hace dos años. I have had it for two years.

The reverse order of the blocks is quite common. When switching the blocks, use **desde** in place of **que**.

No he podido conseguir una conferencia con Ávila desde hace una hora.	I haven't been able to get a call through to Avila for an hour.
No han probado bocado desde hace veinte y cuatro horas.	They haven't had a bite to eat for twenty-four hours.

When a negative action is not deliberate and has continued for a relatively long time, the action verb is generally in the present perfect construction.

b) **Ago**

—¿Has visto a Carlos?	Have you seen Carlos?
—Estaba aquí hace poco.	He was here a moment ago.
—¿Cuánto tiempo hace que se casaron?	How long ago did they get married?
—Hizo un mes ayer que se casaron.	They got married a month ago yesterday.
—Hace un año, yo estaba en Madrid en casa de mis suegros.	A year ago, I was in Madrid at the home of my father and mother-in-law.

210

LENGUA

There are three Spanish patterns for *ago*:

> ACTION block/TIME block
> TIME block/**que**/ACTION block
> TIME block/ACTION block

The first pattern, generally speaking, serves for all purposes. The second pattern may be used if the interest is in the TIME. The third pattern may be used if the interest is in the ACTION.

72. *LLEVAR, TOMAR*—to take

a) **Llevar**

La llevó al cine.	He took her to the movies.
Lleva tu impermeable.	Take your raincoat.
Le llevaron a la comisaría.	They took him to the police station.
¿A dónde nos llevará este camino?	Where will this road take us?

Llevar means *to take* when the actor carries, leads, or accompanies the object (thing or person) from one place to another.

b) **Tomar**

Tomo clases particulares.	I take private lessons.
Toma el que te guste más.	Take the one you like best.
Le tomó de la mano.	He took him by the hand.
Tomaron el fuerte.	They took the fortress.
Tome usted una cucharada cada cuatro horas.	Take one tablespoon every four hours.
Tomaron un taxi.	They took a taxi.
Me tomó la tensión.	He took my blood pressure.
Le tomamos por un atracador.	We took him for a holdup man.
No debes tomarlo en serio.	You ought not to take it seriously.

Tomar means *to take* if the action does not require the actor to carry, lead, or accompany the object from one place to another.

211

73. *PARA, POR*—for

By now, you are well aware of the fact that Spaniards generally do not express themselves in terms that match the English word for word. You will recall that the indirect object, at times, equals a *for* construction:

Me lo hizo mi padre.	My father made it *for me*.
Le planeamos el viaje **a Juan**.	We planned the trip *for Juan*.
¿**Te** preparo otro?	Shall I prepare another *for you*?

Also note:

Trabaja **en** una compañía de seguros.	He works *for* an insurance company.
Pagó el coche.	He paid *for* the car.
Lo estamos buscando.	We are looking *for* it.

Normally, *for* is associated with **para** and **por**. The English equivalents of these two words indicate that they are very different in basic meaning:

para—for, to, in order to, toward

por— for, by, through, across, about, during, in exchange for, in behalf of, on account of, via, by way of

Para and **por**, as all prepositions, link two items (persons, things, activities):

$$\text{item 1} \begin{Bmatrix} \textbf{PARA} \\ \textbf{POR} \end{Bmatrix} \text{item 2}$$

a) **Para**

1)

la llave para el coche	the key for the car
la llave para abrir la caja fuerte	the key for opening the strong box
Éste es para ti.	This one is for you.
Son las entradas para los toros.	They are the tickets for the bullfights.
Hazlo para mañana.	Do it for tomorrow.
¿Cuál es la lección para hoy?	What's the lesson for today?

When item 2 represents that for which item 1 is intended or designated, **para** is used.

2)

Marcha muy bien para un coche tan viejo.	It runs very well for such an old car.
Escribe mal para un niño de su edad.	He writes poorly for a boy of his age.
Es un poco alocada para mi gusto.	She's a bit scatterbrained for my liking.

When item 2 represents a norm or personal standard on which a judgment, item 1, is founded, **para** is used.

3)

Partió para Europa.	He left for Europe.
Van a embarcar para España la semana que viene.	They are embarking for Spain next week.

When item 2 represents the geographic destination that completes the meaning of item 1 (certain verbs of motion), **para** is used.

b) **Por**

1)

Por eso no van.	For that reason they aren't going.
Lucharon por la independencia.	They fought for independence.
Lo hizo por mí.	He did it for me.
Fue por la medicina.	He went for the medicine.
No lo hice por falta de tiempo.	I did not do it for lack of time.
Es importante por sus productos lácteos.	It is important for its dairy products.
Fue muy estimado por su lealtad.	He was highly esteemed for his loyalty.
Su pasión por ella es grande.	His passion for her is great.
Le dieron una paliza por haber sido malo.	They gave him a beating for having been bad.

When item 2 represents that which motivates, arouses, or gives cause for item 1, **por** is used.

2)

Votó por su sobrino.	He voted for his nephew.
Estoy por dejarlo como está.	I'm for leaving it as it is.

When item 2 represents a preference, **por** is used.

3)

Le pagué setenta mil pesetas por el coche.	I paid him seventy thousand *pesetas* for the car.
Le tomaron por un atracador.	They took him for a holdup man.

When item 2 represents what is given or taken in a real or figurative exchange for item 1, **por** is used.

4)

Le firmaron un contrato por dos años.	They signed a contract with him for two years.
Los presté por quince días.	I lent them for two weeks.

Por is also used in expressing the duration of the secondary stage of an action. The *time* factor in the last two examples do not tell how long it took to sign the contract or to lend the items, the primary actions. The time factor refers to the effective duration of the result (*secondary stage*) of the primary action. When there is only a primary stage, English *for* is optional, while in Spanish **por** is either not used or generally omitted:

Duró cinco minutos.	It lasted (*for*) five minutes.
Tuve que esperar un rato.	I had to wait (*for*) a while.
Estuvo aquí mucho tiempo.	He was here (*for*) a long time.

Por is also used in the following expressions:

por ahora	for now
por primera (última, segunda, etc.) vez	for the first (last, second, etc.) time
por el momento	for the moment

The foregoing discussion is by no means complete. The examples, nevertheless, illustrate the fundamental uses and differences of **para** and **por**, in the rôle of *for*.

74. ORDER OF ITEMS AND EVENTS

Ella pagó la cuenta.	She paid the bill.
La cuenta fue pagada por ella.	The bill was paid by her.

ORDER I		ORDER II	
item 1	**ella**	**la cuenta**	item 2
event	**pagó**	**fue pagada**	event
item 2	**la cuenta**	(*por*) **ella**	item 1

The two sentences above communicate the same information. They differ in the order of the items and the manner of expressing the event. Item 1 is the item that "acts," and item 2 is the item that "is acted upon."

ORDER I	ORDER II
item 1 — event → item 2	item 2 ← event — item 1

The event in Order II is expressed by the construction **ser**/*past participle*, the latter functioning as an adjective.

214

Las dos querían ser recibidas antes que las otras.	The two (*women*) wanted to be received before the others.
El monasterio fue construido en mil quinientos.	The monastery was built in 1500.

When item 1 is omitted in the communication, use the syntax of the first two constituents of Order II.

75. AN ALTERNATE FOR ORDER II—ANOTHER USE OF *SE*

Los papeles **se perdieron** cuando ardió el archivo.	The papers *were lost* when the archive burned.
Salvará lo que pueda **salvarse**.	He will save what can *be saved*.
¿No **se han hecho** las invitaciones?	*Have*n't the invitations *been made*?
Las muchachas ya no **se encuentran** con facilidad.	Maids no longer *are* easily *found*.

When item 2 is not a definite person, and item 1 is omitted, the Spaniard almost always uses, in lieu of Order II, the construction:

$$\text{item 2 / se / verb}$$

_____.agree____

76. SUBJUNCTIVE—MISCELLANEA

The following popular constructions, employing the subjunctive, should be carefully studied and imitated:

a) "*may*"

¡Dios te lo pague!	May God repay you!
Que usted descanse.	(May you) rest well.
Mi enhorabuena, y que sean felices.	My congratulations, and may you be happy.
Pase lo que pase.	Come what may.
No iré, sea donde sea.	I won't go, wherever it may be.

b) "*let*" *or* "*have*"

Sea lo que Dios quiera.	Let it be as God wishes.
Si quieren comer, que coman.	If they want to eat, let them eat.
Que pase.	Have him come in.
Cuando termine, que ponga la mesa.	When she finishes, have her set the table.

215

c) **Ojalá (que)**/(*present subjunctive*)—"I hope . . ."
Ojalá (que)/(*retro-subjunctive*)—"If only . . ."

Ojalá (que) no llueva.	I hope it doesn't rain.
¡Ojalá (que) fuera soltero!	If only I were single!

d) **¡Quién**/(*retro-subjunctive*)—"I wish I . . ."

¡Quién tuviera su talento!	I wish I had his talent!

e) **Quizá, tal vez, acaso**—"perhaps"

Ahora pienso que quizá hubiera sido mejor.	Now I think that perhaps it might have been better.
Acaso puedan venir.	Perhaps they may be able to come.
Tal vez esto sea la clave del asunto.	Perhaps this may be the key to the matter.

But:

Quizá allí estaba la clave del asunto.	Perhaps there was the key to the matter.

The indicative and subjunctive moods are used after **quizá**, **tal vez**, and **acaso**. A simple guide is to employ the subjunctive whenever you would use in the English construction *may* or *might* with the verb. Almost invariably, however, the indicative is used when the *perhaps* term comes after the verb:

La casa está quizá un poco abandonada.	The house is perhaps a bit run-down.

f) **Quisiera**—"I should like . . ."

Quisiera hacerle ver la necesidad de encontrar una solución.	I should like to make it clear to you the necessity of finding a solution.

A *wish* or *desire* can be toned down by putting the verb **querer** in the retro-subjunctive. If one wishes to imply *pleasure* use **gustar**:

Me gustaría que usted me acompañara.	I should like for you to accompany me.

77. *TANTO(S)* . . . *COMO*—as much (many) . . . as

Tiene **tantos** parientes **como** yo.	He has *as many* relatives *as* I.
Él gasta **tanto** dinero **como** ella.	He spends *as much* money *as* she.
No bebe **tanta** leche **como** su hermanita.	He doesn't drink *as much* milk *as* his little sister.

Nunca he visto **tantas** flores **como** las que vi allí.

I have never seen *as many* flowers *as* those I saw there.

Tiene mucha fiebre pero no **tanta como** ayer.

He has a high fever but not *as high* (much) *as* yesterday.

Ella lee **tanto como** él.

She reads *as much as* he.

Tanto shows agreement with the noun it modifies or refers to. When the referent is not specified, as in the last example, **tanto** is used as a neuter form.

78. COMPARISONS

a) ¿Cuál es el **más** caro?

Which is *more* (the most) expensive?

El **más** fuerte venció.

The strong*er* (strong*est*) won.

La camisa **más** blanca es la mía.

The whit*er* (whit*est*) shirt is mine.

Es la capital **más** hermosa del mundo.

It is the *most* beautiful capital in the world.

Ella habla **más** de prisa que nadie.

She talks fast*er* (*more* rapidly) than anyone.

Más = *more*, *most*, or *-er* and *-est*.

Note that *in*, in a superlative construction, is **de**—**del mundo**.

b) El **mejor** es éste.

The *best* (better) is this one.

Conduce **peor** de lo que yo creía.

He drives *worse* than I thought.

Mi hijo **menor** es médico.

My *younger* (youngest) son is a doctor.

Ella es la **mayor**.

She is the *older* (oldest).

There are several irregular comparative modifiers:

mejor	better, best	**menor**	younger, youngest
peor	worse, worst	**mayor**	older, oldest

79. *TAN . . . COMO, LO MÁS . . .*—as . . . as

a) **tan . . . como**

Esta flor es **tan** bonita **como** ésa.

This flower is *as* pretty *as* that one.

El árbol es **tan** alto **como** la casa.

The tree is *as* tall *as* the house.

No me parecen **tan** azules **como** los suyos.

I don't think they are *as* blue *as* his.

La lluvia no cae **tan** fuerte **como** antes.

The rain doesn't fall *as* hard *as* it did.

b) **lo más**

Sujétalo **lo más** firme posible.	Fasten it *as* firmly *as* possible.
Hazlo **lo más** pronto **que** puedas.	Do it *as* soon *as* you can.
Lo colocó **lo más** alto **que** pudo.	He placed it *as* high *as* he could.

To express the maximum of one's capacity, the construction is:

posible

lo más /*adverb* /   *or*

que /*form of* **poder**

80. THE DEFINITE ARTICLE—A REVIEW OF ITS USES

The Spanish definite article is used:

a) **With terms representing abstractions—**

La vida universitaria parece divertida.	University life seems to be fun.
Es buen ejercicio para **la** salud.	It's good exercise for one's health.

b) **With terms that represent a** whole, i.e., **class, kind, species,** etc.—

El agua fresca es mejor.	Cool water is better,
Las máquinas no me convencen.	I'm not sold on appliances.
Los deportes de nieve se practican con entusiasmo.	Snow sports are practiced with enthusiasm.
los toros	bullfights
los españoles	Spaniards
los profesores	teachers

c) **With modified proper names—**

La pobre Ana lloraba.	Poor Anne was crying.
La España de la Edad Media.	Spain of the Middle Ages.

d) **In place of the possessive adjective, when ownership is obvious—**

¿Cuándo vais a comprar **los** muebles?	When are you going to buy your furniture?
Se metió **la** mano en **el** bolsillo.	He put his hand in his pocket.
Me duelen **el** estómago, **la** garganta y **la** cabeza, y me zumban **los** oídos.	My stomach, my throat, and head hurt, and my ears are ringing.
¿No has hecho aún **la** maleta?	Haven't you packed your suitcase yet?

218

e) **With the days of the week—**

¿Es seguro que iremos **el** domingo a Segovia?

Is it certain that we shall go (on) Sunday to Segovia?

El lunes es fiesta.

Monday is a holiday.

The article is not used after **ser** if the day is unmodified; e.g., **Hoy es martes.**

f) **With nouns modified by de + proper noun—**

la familia de Elisa	Elisa's family
el Puerto de Navacerrada	Navacerrada Pass
la Calle de Serrano	Serrano Street
la Avenida de América	America Avenue
el Parque del Retiro	Retiro Park
la Plaza de Oriente	Oriente Plaza (*or* Square)
el Barrio de Argüelles	Argüelles District
la Estación del Norte	North Station

g) **With titles in indirect discourse—**

Ahora viene **el** doctor Fabra.

Here comes Dr. Fabra.

La señorita Martín no está.

Miss Martin isn't in.

h) **With names of meals—**

¿Está **el** desayuno?

Is breakfast ready?

¿A qué hora es **la** cena?

When is supper?

i) **With the hours of the day—**

Son **las** nueve menos diez.

It's ten of nine.

Estoy en la biblioteca desde **las** ocho y media.

I've been in the library since eight-thirty.

j) **With infinitives, to express the doing of whatever the stem of the infinitive symbolizes—**

El beber con exceso es malo.

Drinking excessively is bad.

The use of **a** before the **el**/*infinitive* construction, gives the notion of *at the moment of*, usually translated *when, as, on, upon, while*, or *at*—

Al levantarse el telón no hay nadie en escena.

When the curtain goes up, there is no one on stage.

Ten cuidado **al** hacerlo.

Be careful while doing it.

Cojea **al** andar.

She limps as she walks.

Encendimos la luz **al** entrar.

We turned on the light on entering.

Al llegar a casa se sintió mala.

Upon arriving home, she felt ill.

Nos marchamos **al** anochecer.

We leave at nightfall.

81. DIMINUTIVE SUFFIXES

a) **Types and connotations**

¡Compraron un coche**cito** más mono!	They bought the cutest little car.
Envié un recad**ito**.	I sent a short message.
Al herman**ito** le llaman Juan**ito**.	They call their little brother Johnny.
¡El pobre**cito**, lo mal**ito** que está!	The poor dear, how very sick he is!

The Spaniard uses numerous diminutive suffixes—**ito, illo, ico, uelo, ete,** and **ín.** In view of certain connotations in addition to and often more important than the diminutive aspect, only a person with much practical experience in Spain can effectively use them all. This section deals only with the **ito** suffix, the one most often heard in Central Spain.

TYPE OF WORD	CONNOTATIONS
NOUN (*person, animal*)	smallness of size and/or a note of sentiment
NOUN (*thing*)	smallness (*figuratively or physically*)
NOUN MODIFIER	reinforces meaning—"very," "quite," etc.

b) Formation

árbol	**arbolito**	(little tree)
igual	**igualito**	(exactly the same)
callado	**calladito**	(very quiet)
mano	**manita**	(tiny hand)
poco	**poquito**	(very little)

If the word is polysyllabic and ends in **o** or **a**, drop this vowel and add **ito** (**ita, itos, itas**). Likewise, if the word ends in **l**, add these suffixes. There are exceptions to this statement.

cajón	**cajoncito**	(small drawer)
favor	**favorcito**	(small favor)
tambor	**tamborcito**	(small drum)
madre	**madrecita**	(mother dear)

220

LENGUA

If the word is polysyllabic and ends in **n, r,** or **e,** add **cito (cita, citos, citas).** There are exceptions to this statement.

Note the diminutive forms of the following words:

flor	**florecita**	(little flower)
luz	**lucecita**	(speck of light)
pez	**pececito**	(little fish)
pie	**piececito**	(tiny foot)

ADDENDA

ADDENDUM ONE

TÚ-VOSOTROS, USTED-USTEDES—you

a) **Tú-Vosotros**—the familiar form

As a general statement, the familiar form is used when the speaker does not feel the need of formality. Specifically, the familiar form is used:

1. by young people among themselves
2. by older people when speaking to children
3. between friends
4. between relatives
5. when speaking to animals
6. when addressing God (*Dios*), Christ (*Cristo*), the Virgin Mary (*la Virgen María*), and the Saints (*los santos*).

b) **Usted-Ustedes**—the formal form

As a general statement, the formal form is used with persons we address by a title. Specifically, the formal form is used:

1. between persons of different social status or rank
2. between grown-ups who are not close friends
3. by young people when speaking to older people

When speaking to someone of lower status or rank, it is common to use the first name instead of **señor** or **señorita** plus the family name. For example, the head of **a** household may say the following to the apartment utility man:

Antonio, ¿me puede usted arreglar esta cañería?   Antonio, can you fix this pipe for me?

ADDENDUM TWO

SER AND ESTAR

Ser and estar are copulas. If what the actor is associated with, functions as a:

1. *Substantive*, the verb is **Ser**

Ellas son *mis primas.*	They are my cousins.
(*Mis primas*) Son *ellas.*	They are.
Aquí es *donde* los puse.	Here is where I put them. (*donde* = *el sitio donde*)
La fiesta es *hoy.*	The holiday is today. (*hoy* = *este día*)

2. *Verb modifier*, the verb is **Estar**

Él está *en la farmacia.*	He is at the drugstore.
La estatua va a estar *aquí.*	The statue is going to be here. (*aquí* = *en este sitio*)
Ellos están *para salir.*	They are about to leave.
Yo estoy *de vacaciones.*	I'm on vacation.
Ellos están *en camino.*	They are on their way.
Los obreros están *por más dinero y menos trabajo.*	The workers are for (in favor of) more money and less work.
Nosotros estamos *progresando.*	We are progressing.

3. *Noun modifier*, the verb is—

a) **Ser**, when expressing a *concept* or a *fixed notion*

La leche es *buena.*	Milk is good (for one).
Elena es *alegre.*	Elena is (a) gay (person).
El gato es *limpio.*	The cat is (a) clean (animal).
El Volkswagen es *pequeño.*	The Volkswagen is small.
El asunto es *para morirse de risa.*	The matter is laughable.

ADDENDUM

b) **Estar**, when expressing a non-concept or state or condition

La leche está *cortada.*	The milk is curdled.
Elena está *alegre.*	Elena is (feels) happy.
La ventana está *sucia.*	The window is dirty.
Estos zapatos me están *pequeños.*	These shoes are small for me.

The condition of milk or of a window, and one's state of mind or body are variables, and, therefore, cannot represent fixed notions or concepts. A size 13 shoe **es grande** and a size 6 **es pequeño**. **Grande** and **pequeño** in this context represent fixed notions or concepts. But a size 13 shoe **está pequeño** if fitted to a foot requiring a size 14, and a size 6 **está grande** when fitted to a foot requiring a size 5. The terms **grande** and **pequeño** in this context are non-concepts; that is, we form no concept of the size of a shoe with respect to all feet. Consequently, when comparing one shoe with another, the verb is **ser**. When fitting a shoe to a foot, it is **estar.**

ADDENDUM THREE

NUMBERS

a) The Cardinal Numbers

1	uno	24	veinticuatro*
2	dos	25	veinticinco*
3	tres	26	veintiséis*
4	cuatro	27	veintisiete*
5	cinco	28	veintiocho*
6	seis	29	veintinueve*
7	siete	30	treinta
8	ocho	31	treinta y uno
9	nueve	32	treinta y dos
10	diez		etc.
11	once	40	cuarenta
12	doce	50	cincuenta
13	trece	60	sesenta
14	catorce	70	setenta
15	quince	80	ochenta
16	dieciséis*	90	noventa
17	diecisiete*	100	ciento, cien
18	dieciocho*	101	ciento uno
19	diecinueve*	102	ciento dos
20	veinte	115	ciento quince
21	veintiuno*	116	ciento dieciséis
22	veintidós*	158	ciento cincuenta y ocho
23	veintitrés*	199	ciento noventa y nueve

* May also be written **diez y seis, diez y siete, veinte y uno**, etc.

ADDENDUM

Use **ciento** if any number from 1 to 99 immediately follows:

ciento una cartas	101 letters
ciento doce	112
ciento ochenta dólares	$180.00

All other times, use **cien**:

Tengo cien libros.	I have one hundred books.
Ella tiene cien también.	She has one hundred also.
Cien mil habitantes.	One hundred thousand inhabitants.

200	doscientos
300	trescientos
400	cuatrocientos
500	quinientos
600	seiscientos
700	setecientos
800	ochocientos
900	novecientos
1,000	mil
2,000	dos mil
7,549	siete mil quinientos cuarenta y nueve
500,000	quinientos mil
1,000,000	un millón
2,000,000	dos millones
9,431,764	nueve millones cuatrocientos treinta y un mil setecientos sesenta y cuatro

Doscientos through **novecientos** agree in gender with the nouns they limit, whether the latter are expressed or not:

Ochocientos sesenta alumnos.	860 students.
Trescientas quince páginas.	315 pages.
Tengo seiscientas pesetas y ella sólo doscientas.	I have six hundred *pesetas* and she only two hundred.

If **millón** or **millones** is not followed by a number, use **de** to link it to a noun:

un millón **de** habitantes	1,000,000 inhabitants
tres millones **de** pesetas	3,000,000 *pesetas*
seis millones cinco mil pesetas	6,005,000 *pesetas*

229

b) **The Ordinal Numbers**

primero	(*first*)	sexto	(*sixth*)
segundo	(*second*)	séptimo	(*seventh*)
tercero	(*third*)	octavo	(*eighth*)
cuarto	(*fourth*)	noveno	(*ninth*)
quinto	(*fifth*)	décimo	(*tenth*)

Primero and **tercero** become **primer** and **tercer** if followed by a singular masculine noun. From the 11th on up, use the cardinal numbers. Just as with the days of the month, use **primero** only with the 1st century and the cardinal numbers with all other centuries:

El Siglo I is orally expressed "**el siglo primero**".

El Siglo II is orally expressed "**el siglo dos**".

230

ADDENDUM FOUR

STEM-VOWEL CHANGES IN VERBS

a) **Class I verbs**

These verbs are either *A* or *E* type. The change is either an *o* or *u* to a *ue*, or an *e* to *ie*.

Present Indicative

volver (*o* → *ue*)	jugar (*u* → *ue*)	pensar (*e* → *ie*)
v*ue*lvo	j*ue*go	p*ie*nso
v*ue*lves	j*ue*gas	p*ie*nsas
v*ue*lve	j*ue*ga	p*ie*nsa
volvemos	jugamos	pensamos
volvéis	jugáis	pensáis
v*ue*lven	j*ue*gan	p*ie*nsan

Present Subjunctive

v*ue*lva	j*ue*gue	p*ie*nse
v*ue*lvas	j*ue*gues	p*ie*nses
v*ue*lva	j*ue*gue	p*ie*nse
volvamos	juguemos	pensemos
volváis	juguéis	penséis
v*ue*lvan	j*ue*guen	p*ie*nsen

b) **Class II verbs**

These verbs are only the *I* type. The change of the stem vowel is either an *o* to *ue* or *u*, or an *e* to *ie* or *i*.

Present Indicative

dormir (*o → ue, u*)   sentir (*e → ie, i*)

d*ue*rmo	dormimos	s*ie*nto	sentimos
d*ue*rmes	dormís	s*ie*ntes	sentís
d*ue*rme	d*ue*rmen	s*ie*nte	s*ie*nten

Present Subjunctive

d*ue*rma	d*u*rmamos	s*ie*nta	s*i*ntamos
d*ue*rmas	d*u*rmáis	s*ie*ntas	s*i*ntáis
d*ue*rma	d*ue*rman	s*ie*nta	s*ie*ntan

Preterit

dormí	dormimos	sentí	sentimos
dormiste	dormisteis	sentiste	sentisteis
d*u*rmió	d*u*rmieron	s*i*ntió	s*i*ntieron

Retro-Subjunctive

d*u*rmiera	d*u*rmiéramos	s*i*ntiera	s*i*ntiéramos
d*u*rmieras	d*u*rmierais	s*i*ntieras	s*i*ntierais
d*u*rmiera	d*u*rmieran	s*i*ntiera	s*i*ntieran

Present Participle

d*u*rmiendo   s*i*ntiendo

c) **Class III verbs**

These verbs are only the *I* type, and the stem vowel is an *e* that changes to an *i*.

Present Indicative

pedir (*e → i*)

p*i*do	pedimos
p*i*des	pedís
p*i*de	p*i*den

ADDENDUM

Present Subjunctive

p*i*da	p*i*damos
p*i*das	p*i*dáis
p*i*da	p*i*dan

Preterit

pedí	pedimos
pediste	pedisteis
p*i*dió	p*i*dieron

Retro-Subjunctive

p*i*diera	p*i*diéramos
p*i*dieras	p*i*dierais
p*i*diera	p*i*dieran

Present participle—p*i*diendo

SPELLING CHANGES

Two facts must be kept in mind when spelling Spanish words:

1. *Each* of four Spanish sounds is represented by *two* symbols—

SOUND	SYMBOL	(*before*)
K	**C**	**(a, o, u)**
	QU	**(e, i)**
θ (**th** *as in* **th***in*)	**Z**	**(a, o, u)**
	C	**(e, i)**
G (*velar*)	**G**	**(a, o, u)**
	GU	**(e, i)**
X (*raspy* **h**)	**J**	**(a, o, u)**
	G or J	**(e, i)**

2. Discounting irregular verbs, the *sound* of the consonant that terminates the stem of an infinitive, a noun, or an adjective does not change, whatever inflection the word may undergo.

Examples of spelling changes:

K—

blan*c*o—blan*qu*ísimo
chi*c*a—chi*qu*ita
po*c*o—po*qu*ito

ADDENDUM

sacar {
saqué, sacaste, sacó,
sacamos, sacasteis, sacaron | Preterit

saque, saques, saque,
saquemos, saquéis, saquen | Present Subjunctive
}

θ—

lazo—lacito
capataz—capatacito
lápiz—lápices

comenzar {
comencé, comenzaste, comenzó,
comenzamos, comenzasteis, comenzaron | Preterit

comience, comiences, comience,
comencemos, comencéis, comiencen | Present Subjunctive
}

torcer {
tuerzo, tuerces, tuerce,
torcemos, torcéis, tuercen | Present Indicative

tuerza, tuerzas, tuerza,
torzamos, torzáis, tuerzan | Present Subjunctive
}

G (velar)—

largo—larguísimo
manga—manguita

pagar {
pagué, pagaste, pagó,
pagamos, pagasteis, pagaron | Preterit

pague, pagues, pague,
paguemos, paguéis, paguen | Present Subjunctive
}

seguir {
sigo, sigues, sigue,
seguimos, seguís, siguen | Present Indicative

siga, sigas, siga,
sigamos, sigáis, sigan | Present Subjunctive
}

X (raspy h)

dirigir {
dirijo, diriges, dirige,
dirigimos, dirigís, dirigen | Present Indicative

dirija, dirijas, dirija,
dirijamos, dirijáis, dirijan | Present Subjunctive
}

coger {
cojo, coges, coge,
cogemos, cogéis, cogen | Present Indicative

coja, cojas, coja,
cojamos, cojáis, cojan | Present Subjunctive
}

235

ADDENDUM SIX

IRREGULAR VERBS

The seven items listed below will be given only if irregular in form, spelling, or accent mark:

1. Past Participle
2. Present Participle
3. Present Indicative
4. Imperfect
5. Preterit
6. Future
7. Present Subjunctive

Remember that the present subjunctive, if not irregular, is based on the *yo* form of the present indicative, and that the retro-subjunctive is based on the *ellos* form of the preterit.

Andar (to walk)
5. **anduve, anduviste, anduvo, anduvimos, anduvisteis, anduvieron**

Caer (to fall)
1. **caído**
2. **cayendo**
3. **caigo,** caes, cae, caemos, caéis, caen
5. caí, **caíste, cayó, caímos, caísteis, cayeron**

236

ADDENDUM

Dar (to give)

3. **doy,** das, da, damos, dais, dan
5. **di, diste, dio, dimos, disteis, dieron**
7. **dé, des, dé, demos, deis, den**

Decir (to say, tell)

1. **dicho**
2. **diciendo**
3. **digo, dices, dice,** decimos, decís, **dicen**
5. **dije, dijiste, dijo, dijimos, dijisteis, dijeron**
6. **diré, dirás, dirá, diremos, diréis, dirán**

Estar (to be)

3. **estoy, estás, está,** estamos, estáis, **están**
5. **estuve, estuviste, estuvo, estuvimos, estuvisteis, estuvieron**
7. **esté, estés, esté, estemos, estéis, estén**

Haber (to have)

3. **he, has, ha, hemos,** habéis, **han**
5. **hube, hubiste, hubo, hubimos, hubisteis, hubieron**
6. **habré, habrás, habrá, habremos, habréis, habrán**
7. **haya, hayas, haya, hayamos, hayáis, hayan**

Hacer (to make, do)

1. **hecho**
3. **hago,** haces, hace, hacemos, hacéis, hacen
5. **hice, hiciste, hizo, hicimos, hicisteis, hicieron**
6. **haré, harás, hará, haremos, haréis, harán**

Ir (to go)

2. **yendo**
3. **voy, vas, va, vamos, vais, van**
4. **iba, ibas, iba, íbamos, ibais, iban**
5. **fui, fuiste, fue, fuimos, fuisteis, fueron**
7. **vaya, vayas, vaya, vayamos, vayáis, vayan**

Oir (to hear)

1. **oído**
2. **oyendo**
3. **oigo, oyes, oye, oímos,** oís, **oyen**
5. **oí, oíste, oyó, oímos, oísteis, oyeron**

Poder (to be able, can)

2. pudiendo
5. pude, pudiste, pudo, pudimos, pudisteis, pudieron
6. podré, podrás, podrá, podremos, podréis, podrán

Poner (to put, place)

1. puesto
3. pongo, pones, pone, ponemos, ponéis, ponen
5. puse, pusiste, puso, pusimos, pusisteis, pusieron
6. pondré, pondrás, pondrá, pondremos, pondréis, pondrán

Querer (to wish, want, love)

5. quise, quisiste, quiso, quisimos, quisisteis, quisieron
6. querré, querrás, querrá, querremos, querréis, querrán

Reir (to laugh)

1. reído
2. riendo
3. río, ríes, ríe, reímos, reís, ríen
5. reí, reíste, rio, reímos, reísteis, rieron

Saber (to know, find out)

3. sé, sabes, sabe, sabemos, sabéis, saben
5. supe, supiste, supo, supimos, supisteis, supieron
6. sabré, sabrás, sabrá, sabremos, sabréis, sabrán
7. sepa, sepas, sepa, sepamos, sepáis, sepan

Salir (to leave, to go out)

3. salgo, sales, sale, salimos, salís, salen
6. saldré, saldrás, saldrá, saldremos, saldréis, saldrán

Ser (to be)

3. soy, eres, es, somos, sois, son
4. era, eras, era, éramos, erais, eran
5. fui, fuiste, fue, fuimos, fuisteis, fueron
7. sea, seas, sea, seamos, seáis, sean

Tener (to have)

3. tengo, tienes, tiene, tenemos, tenéis, tienen
5. tuve, tuviste, tuvo, tuvimos, tuvisteis, tuvieron
6. tendré, tendrás, tendrá, tendremos, tendréis, tendrán

ADDENDUM

Valer (to be worth)

3. **valgo,** vales, vale, valemos, valéis, valen
6. **valdré, valdrás, valdrá, valdremos, valdréis, valdrán**

Venir (to come)

2. **viniendo**
3. **vengo, vienes, viene,** venimos, venís, **vienen**
5. **vine, viniste, vino, vinimos, vinisteis, vinieron**
6. **vendré, vendrás, vendrá, vendremos, vendréis, vendrán**

Ver (to see)

1. **visto**
3. **veo,** ves, ve, vemos, veis, ven
4. **veía, veías, veía, veíamos, veíais, veían**

VOCABULARY

SPANISH—ENGLISH
VOCABULARY

This vocabulary contains all the Spanish words used in the text, except proper personal names, and other proper names that are spelled the same as in English. Adverbs of the **-mente** type are also excluded if the stem appears as an adjective. With regard to verbs, only infinitives and irregular past participles are listed. Radical changing verbs are indicated by I, II, or III.

Nouns, whose gender cannot be determined by meaning or ending (*see* **Lengua 1**), are denoted by the definite article in parentheses.

A dash indicates that the entry word is repeated.

A

a   to, at, by
abajo   down, downstairs
abandonar   to abandon
abierto   *past. part. of* **abrir**
abonar   to pay
abrigo   overcoat
abril   April
abrir   to open
absurdo   absurd
aburrido   boring, bored
acabar   to finish; — **de** to have just
acaso   perhaps
accidente (el)   accident
aceite (el)   oil
acelerador (el)   gas pedal

aceptar   to accept
acera   sidewalk
acerca de   about
acercarse   to approach
acompañar   to accompany
aconsejar   to advise
acordarse (I)   to remember
acostarse (I)   to go to bed
actitud (la)   attitude
acto   act; **en el** — immediately
actor   actor
actual   present
acueducto   aqueduct
adecuado   adequate
adelante   ahead, forward; **de aquí en** — from now on
además   besides

243

adicional   additional
adiós   hi, good-by, good night
admirar   to admire
adquisición   acquisition
adverbio   adverb
aerograma (el)   air letter
afeitar   to shave
afirmativo   affirmative
agosto   August
agradecer   to appreciate, to be grateful for
agua   water
aguinaldo   Christmas gift usually given to
   servants, public or private
¡Ah!   Oh!, Ah!
ahí   there
ahora   now
aire (el)   air, wind; hacer — to be windy;
   al — libre outdoor(s)
ajo   garlic
alba   dawn
alcachofa   artichoke
alcohol (el)   alcohol
alegrarse   to be glad
alegre   happy, gay
alegría   happiness
alemán   German
alfombra   rug, carpet
algo   something, anything
alguien   somebody, anybody, someone,
   any one
algun(o)   some, any; a few
alma   soul
almanaque (el)   calendar
almendra   almond
alocado   scatterbrained
alquilar   to rent
alto   tall, high
altura   height
alumno   student
allá   there, over there
allí   there, over there
amable   kind
americana   suitcoat

americano   American
amigo   friend
¡Anda!   Come on!; Well, I'll be!
andar   to walk
animal (el)   animal
anoche   last night
anochecer   to turn night; al — at night fall
anorak (el)   parka
anotar   to make a note of
antepuesto   pre-position, placed before
antes   before, beforehand
antigüedad   antique
antiguo   old
antipático   disagreeable
anular   to cancel
año   year
aparador (el)   buffet
aparato   apparatus
aparcar   to park
aparecer   to appear
aparte   aside
apenar   to grieve
aplaudir   to applaud
apoyar   to support
apreciar   to appreciate
aprender   to learn
apropiado   appropriate
aprovechar   to take advantage of
aproximado   approximate
apunte (el)   note, notation
aquel   that, those
aquél   that one, the former; that, those
aquello   that, that thing (matter, etc.)
aquí   here
árabe   Arab
árbol (el)   tree
arco   arch
archivo   archive
arder   to burn
arrancar   to start off; to yank off
arreglar   to fix
arreglo   adjustment; no tener — to be
   hopeless

244

VOCABULARY

arriba up, upstairs
arroz (el) rice
arte (el *or* **la)** art
artículo article
asar to roast
ascensor (el) elevator
así thus, so
asignatura class subject
asistir to attend
aspirina aspirin
asunto matter
asustar to scare; —**se** to become frightened, to get scared
atención attention
atracador holdup man
atraer to attract
atragantarse to choke
atrás backward
através de through
atropellar to run over
aula classroom
aumentar to increase
aún still; **aun** even
aunque although, even if
autobús (el) bus
autor author
autorizar to authorize
avenida avenue
avergonzar (I) to embarrass; —**se** to be ashamed
aversión dislike, aversion
avión (el) airplane
avisar to notify, to inform
ayer yesterday
ayudar to help
ayuntamiento city hall
azafrán (el) saffron
azul blue

B

bailar to dance
bailarina dancer
baile (el) dance
bajar to bring down; to come down, to get out of, to go down
bajo low; **piso —** ground floor; **por lo —** in a low voice
bala bullet; **tirar con —** to make a "dig"
banco bank
bañar to bathe; —**se** to take a bath
bar (el) snack bar, bar
barato cheap
barba beard
barbaridad barbarity; **¡Qué —!** Good grief!
bárbaro barbarian
barra café counter
barrendero street cleaner
barrio city district
bastante rather, enough, quite, quite a lot
bastón (el) pole, cane
basurero garbageman
batalla battle
batido (milk) shake
bebé baby
beber to drink
bebida drink
bedel beadle
Belén (el) Bethlehem, nativity scene
besugo sea bream, red gilthead
biblioteca library
bien fine, well
billete (el) bill (paper money); ticket
blanco white
boca mouth
bocado morsel of food
boda wedding
bolsillo pocket
bolso bag, purse
bonito pretty
bordillo curb
bota boot
bote: de — en — filled, crowded, jam-packed

botijo   earthern water jug
brillante   brilliant, bright
brincar   to jump
broma   practical joke
buen(o)   well; good, fine
bujía   spark plug
burlarse de   to make fun of
buscar   to look for, to get
buzón (el)   mailbox

C

caballero   gentleman, man
cabeza   head
cabizbajo   dejected
cabo   end
cacharro   pot, worthless item, jalopy
cada   each, every
caer   to fall; —**se** to fall down, to fall off
café (el)   coffee
cafetería   snack bar
caja   box, cash register; **la — fuerte** strong box, safe
cajón (el)   drawer
calcetín (el)   sock
calidad   quality
caliente   hot, warm
calma   calm, calmness
calor   heat; **hacer —** to be hot, to be warm (*temperature*)
calvo   bald
callado   quiet, silent
calle (la)   street
cama   bed
camarero   waiter
cambiar   to change
cambio   change; **— de velocidades** gear shift
camino   road, path
camión (el)   truck
camisa   shirt
campanada   stroke of a bell

campeón   champion
canción   song
candidato   candidate
cansar   to tire
cantar   to sing
caña   small glass of beer
cañería   pipe
capataz (el)   foreman
capaz   capable
capital (la)   capital city
capitán   captain
carburador (el)   carburetor
carga   load, cargo
carne (la)   meat; **— asada** roast beef
carnet (el): — de conducir driver's license
caro   expensive
carpintero   carpenter
carrera   college work leading to a degree, career, profession
carta   letter
cartaginés   Carthaginian
cartera   briefcase, wallet
cartero   mailman; **— de urgencia** special delivery mailman
casa   house, home; **— de pisos** apartment house; **— de socorro** first-aid station
casar   to marry; —**se** to get married
casi   almost
caso   case
casualidad   coincidence
catalán   Catalonian
cebolla   onion
celebrar   to celebrate, to be glad
célebre   famous
celos   jealousy; **tener —** to be jealous
cemento   cement
cena   supper
cenar   to dine, to have supper
central   central
centro   center, downtown
cerca   nearby; **— de** near
cerrar (I)   to close
certificado(s)   registered mail

certificar to register (*mail*)
cerveza beer
cesta basket
cielo sky
cien one hundred
ciento one hundred; **por —** percent
cierto sure, certain
cifra figure (*number*)
cinco five
cincuenta fifty
cine (el) movie house
cinta ribbon; **— métrica** measuring tape
ciudad city
claro clear; of course, naturally; **— que sí** of course
clase (la) class, classroom; **dar — de** to tutor, to teach
clave (la) key
clavo nail; **dar en el —** to hit the nail on the head
club (el) club
cobrar to collect
cocodrilo crocodile
coche (el) car
codazo blow with the elbow; **dar un —** to nudge
coger to pick up, to get a hold of
coincidir to coincide
cojear to limp
colección collection
colgar (I) to hang
colina hill
colocar to place
color (el) color
comedia play
comedor (el) dining room
comenzar (I) to begin
comer to eat
comida meal, noonday meal, food
comilón glutton, big eater
comisaría police station
como as, like, if
cómo how

cómoda chest of drawers
cómodo comfortable
compañero classmate, companion
compañía company
comparar to compare
completo complete
comprar to buy
comunicar to communicate; **estar comunicando** to be busy (*telephone*)
con with
concierto concert
concordar (I) to agree
condecorar to decorate, to bestow a medal on
condenar to condemn
condición condition
conducir to drive
conferencia lecture, long distance call
conmigo with me
conocer to know, to be acquainted with
conocido well-known
conseguir (III) to get, to obtain, to attain
consentir (II) to consent
construir to construct
contar (I) to tell, to relate, to count
contemporáneo contemporary
contento happy
contestación answer
contestar to answer
contigo with you (*fam. sing.*)
contra against
contrato contract
convencer to convince
convenir to suit, to be advisable or desirable
copiar to copy
coqueta vanity table
corbata tie
coronel colonel
correcto correct
corredor (el) hall
correo mail
correos: casa de — post office

247

correr to run
corresponder to be allotted to
corrida bullfight
corriente (la) current; **lo** — the usual, what is customary
cortado curdled
cortés courteous
corto short
cosa thing
coser to sew
costar (I) to cost
costumbre custom, habit
creer to believe
crisis (la) crisis
crítico critic
cruzar to cross
cuál which, what
cualquier just any
cuando when; **cuándo** when
cuanto all that, whatever; **en** — as soon as
cuánto how much; *pl.* how many
cuarto quarter, fourth, room
cuatro four
cuatrocientos four hundred
cubierta tire
cubierto *past. part. of* **cubrir**
cubiertos silverware
cubrir to cover
cucharada tablespoonful
cuenta account, bill, tab; **darse** — **de** to realize
cuento story, tale
cuidado care; **tener** — to be careful; **¡Cuidado!** Be careful!
cuidadoso careful
culpa fault; **tener la** — to be at fault
cultivar to cultivate
culto educated
cumbre top

CH

charlar to chat
chica girl
248

chico boy, young fellow
chiste (el) joke
chistoso funny
chocolate (el) cocoa, chocolate
churro a fritter in the form of a loop

D

daño harm
dar to give; — **clase** to teach, to tutor; — **un codazo** to nudge; —**se prisa** to hurry
de of, from, than, about, by
deber must, ought, have to, to owe; — **de** probably
débil weak
decente worthwhile
decidir to decide
décimo tenth; lottery ticket
decir to say, to tell
definido definite
dejar to leave behind, to let, to allow; — **de** to stop
delante in front
delgado thin
demasiado too, too much
demora delay
dentro within, inside
dependiente dependent; (el) — clerk
deporte (el) sport
deportivo *adj.* sport
derecho *adj.* right; (el) — right; **a la derecha** to the right
desaparecer disappear
desayunarse to have breakfast
desayuno breakfast
descansar to rest
desconfiar de to distrust
desconocido unknown person
descortés discourteous
descubrir to find out, to discover
descuidado careless
desde since, from

desear to want, to wish, to desire
desenlace (el) conclusion, dénouement
desinflar to deflate
despacio slowly
después afterwards; — **de** after
destruir to destroy
devolver (I) to give back, to return
día (el) day
diablo devil
diálogo dialog
dibujar to draw
diciembre December
dicho *past. part. of* **decir**
diez ten
diferencia difference
diferente different
difícil difficult, hard
dinero money
Dios God
diplomacia diplomacy
dirigir to direct, to drive
disco record
disculpar to excuse
discusión argument
discutir to argue
disfrutar de to enjoy
dislocar to sprain
disparar to shoot
disparate (el) nonsense
distancia distance
distinto different
divertido amusing
divertir (II) to amuse; —**se** to have a good time
doblar to fold
doble double
docena dozen
doctor doctor (*title*)
dólar (el) dollar
doler (I) to hurt, to pain
dolor (el) pain
domingo Sunday
don Don (a title used before Christian names)

doña Doña (feminine counterpart of Don)
doncella maid
donde where, wherever, in which
dónde where
dormir (II) to sleep; —**se** to fall asleep
dormitorio bedroom, dorm room, bedroom set
dos two
doscientos two hundred
dudar to doubt
durar to last

E

echar to throw; — **de menos** to miss; —**se** to take a nap; —**(se) la siesta** to take an afternoon nap
edad age
educar to bring up
ejemplo example
ejercicio exercise, homework
el the
él he, him
elegante elegant
elegir (III) to choose, to pick out, to select, to elect
elevado high
ella she, her
ellas they, them
ellos they, them
embarcar to embark
embrague (el) clutch
emoción emotion
emocionante thrilling
empanadilla turnover
empezar (I) to begin
empleado employee, attendant
emplear to use, to employ
empujar to push
en in, on, at, into
encantado delighted, charmed, pleased to meet you
encantador charming

249

encender (I)   to light, to start (*a motor*)
encendido   ignition
encima   on top
encontrar (I)   to meet, to find
encuentro   meeting, encounter
enemigo   enemy
enero   January
enfadarse (con)   to get mad or angry (at)
enfático   emphatic
enfermera   nurse
enfermo   sick
enfrente (de)   opposite, in front, across the street
enfriarse   to get cold
engordar   to put on weight
engrasador   greaser
enhorabuena   congratulations
ensalada   salad
enseñar   to teach, to show
entender (I)   to understand
enterarse (de)   to find out, to understand
entonación   intonation
entonces   then
entrada   ticket
entrar   to enter, to come in
entre   among, between
entresuelo   mezzanine
entretener   to amuse, to entertain; —se to dally
entusiasmo   enthusiasm
enviar   to send
equipo   equipment
esbelto   slender
escalera   stairway
escapar   to escape; —se to flee
escaparate (el)   store or shop window
escena   scene
escribir   to write
escrito   *past. part. of* escribir
escritor   writer
escuchar   to listen
escuela   school
ese   that, those

ése   that one, that fellow
esfera   face of watch, sphere
eso   that
España   Spain
español   Spanish
especie   species
espectáculo   spectacle, show
espejo   mirror
esperanza   hope
esperar   to hope, to wait for
esquí (el)   ski
esquiador   skier
esquiar   to ski
esquina   corner
estación   station, season
estado   state, federal government
Estados Unidos   United States
estar   to be
estatua   statue
este   this, these
éste   this one, the latter, this fellow
estimar   to esteem
estómago   stomach
estrella   star
estrenar   to put on for the first time
estreno   first performance
estropear   to ruin
estudiante   student
estudiar   to study
estupendo   wonderful
evidente   evident
evitar   to avoid, to prevent
exacto   exact, right
examen (el)   test, exam
examinar   to examine
exceso   excess
excitar   to excite
exclamación   exclamation
exclamativo   exclamatory
excusa   excuse
exigir   to demand
experiencia   experiment
explicación   explanation

explicar to explain
explosión explosion
expresar to express
extranjero foreigner; **al —** to a foreign country, abroad
extrañar to seem strange
extraño strange

F

fácil easy
facilidad ease; **con —** easily
falda skirt
falta lack, need
faltar to be missing, to miss, to be lacking
fama fame
familia family
famoso famous
fantasía fantasy
farmacia drugstore
favor (el) favor; **por —** please
febrero February
fecha date
felicitar to greet, to congratulate
feliz happy
fenicio Phoenician
feo ugly
fiebre (la) fever
fiera wild beast
fiesta fiesta, party; **día de —** holiday
figura figure
figurarse to imagine
fijar to fix, to fasten; **—se en** to notice
Filosofía y Letras Liberal Arts
fin (el) end; **a — de** in order to
final (el) end
fino fine, refined, thin
firmar to sign
flaco skinny
flamenco Flemish, Spanish song and dance
flan (el) custard
flor (la) flower

fontanero plumber
forma form
foto (la) picture
fracaso failure
francés French
franqueo postage
frase (la) sentence
frecuencia frequency; **con —** frequently
freno brake
fresa strawberry
fresco cool
frigorífico refrigerator, freezer
frío cold
frito *past. part. of* **freir** (to fry)
fuego fire
fuera away, outside
fuerte strong; **(el) —** fortress
fuerza force, strength; **a la —** by force
fumar to smoke
funcionar to function, to work, to run
fusilar to execute by shooting
fútbol (el) soccer
futuro future

G

gafas glasses
galante gallant
galería gallery; **— de antigüedades** antique shop
gallina chicken, hen
gamba shrimp
ganar to earn, to win
ganga bargain
garaje (el) garage
garganta throat
gasolina gasoline
gastar to spend, to wear out
gasto expense
gato cat, jack (*car*)
generación generation
general general

gente (la)   people
gerundio   present participle
gesto   grimace
gimnasio   gym
gordo   fat, stout; premio — first prize (*lottery*)
gorro   cap
grabar   to engrave
gracia   grace, humor; hacer — to be funny
gracias   thanks
gracioso   funny
gramática   grammar
gran   great
grande   great, big, large
gratis   free
grave   grave, serious
griego   Greek
gris   gray
gritar   to shout
grito   shout, shouting
grúa   tow truck
grupo   group
guapo   good-looking
guerra   war
guión (el)   hyphen
guisado   stew
guisante   pea
guisar   to cook
guitarra   guitar
gustar   to like, to please, to appeal to
gusto   taste, pleasure, flavor, liking

habla: al — speaking (*on the phone*); poner al — to connect
hablar   to speak, to talk
hacer   to make, to do; —se to become
hacia   toward
hambre (la)   hunger; tener — to be hungry
hasta   up to, till, until; — luego *or* la vista so long, until later
hay   there is, there are
hecho   *past. part. of* hacer
helado   ice cream
hermano   brother
hermoso   beautiful
hierba   grass
hijo   son, child
historia   story, history
histórico   historical
hojear   to page (leaf) through
hola   hi, hello
hombre   man
honrado   honest
hora   hour, time
horario   schedule (*time*)
horchata   a milk drink made from chufa tubers
hoy   today
hueso   bone
huevo   egg
huir   to flee
humor (el)   humor; mal — temper

I

idea   idea
identificar   to identify
idioma (el)   language, foreign language
igual   equal
imaginación   imagination
imaginarse   to imagine
imitar   to imitate
impedir (I)   to prevent, to hinder
impermeable (el)   raincoat

H

haber   to have; — de to have to, to be to, must
hábil   skillful
habitación   room; — de servicio service quarters
habitante (el)   inhabitant

VOCABULARY

importante important
importar to matter, to be important
imposible impossible
impresión impression
impuesto tax
inculto uneducated
independencia independence
indicar to indicate, to tell, to show, to point out
industria industry
infinitivo infinitive
inflarse to puff up, to blow up
información information
informar to inform
ingeniero engineer
Inglaterra England
inglés English
ingreso revenue
inicial (la) initial
inmediatamente immediately
inquilino tenant
insistir (en) to insist
Instituto public secondary school
insultar to insult
inteligente intelligent
intención intention
interés (el) interest
interesante interesting
interesar to interest
internacional international
interponer to interpose; —se to get in between
interrumpir to interrupt
inútil useless
invasión invasion
inventor inventor
invierno winter
invitación invitation
invitado invited guest
invitar to invite
ir to go; —se to leave, to go away, to depart, to go
italiano Italian

J

jactancioso braggart
jamón (el) ham
jardín (el) garden
jefe chief, leader
jersey (el) sweater
joven young; young person
joyas jewelry
judías verdes string beans
juego game; hacer — to match
juerguista carouser
jueves Thursday
jugar (I) to play
jugo juice
julio July
junio June
junto a next to, near
juntos together
justamente right, exactly
juzgar to judge

K

kilo kilo = 2.2 pounds
kilómetro kilometer = about 5/8 of a mile

L

la the; her, it
lácteo adj. dairy
lado side; al — de next to
ladrón robber, thief
lamentar to lament
lámpara lamp
lana wool
lápiz (el) pencil
largo long
las the; them, you
lástima pity; qué — what a pity
latín (el) Latin

lavar   to wash
lazo   bow
le   (to, for, from) him, her, you, it
lealtad   loyalty
lección   lesson
leche (la)   milk
leer   to read
lejos   far
lengua   language, tongue
lento   slow
les   (to, for, from) them, you
letra   letter of the alphabet; words of a song
levantar   to lift, to raise; —se to get up, to rise
leyenda   legend
libre   free
libro   book
licenciado   person holding a Master's degree
ligadura   binding
limón (el)   lemon; — natural lemonade
limosna   alms
limpio   clean
lindo   pretty
línea   line
Lisboa   Lisbon
listo   ready, alert, clever
literatura   literature
litro   liter = *about 1.057 quarts*
lo   it; — que that which, what
loco   crazy
locutor   announcer
locutorio   booth (*telephone*)
lógico   logical
lograr   to get, to attain
Londres   London
los   the; them, you
lotería   lottery
luchar   to fight
luego   then; — que as soon as
lugar   place; tener — to take place
luna   moon

lunes   Monday
luz (la)   light

LL

llama   flame
llamar   to call; — a la puerta to knock at the door; — la atención to attract attention; se llama his (her, your) name is
llave (la)   key
llegar   to arrive
lleno   full
llevar   to take, to carry, to wear; —se to carry off; — la cuenta to keep tab; — (tiempo) for (*time*)
llorar   to cry
llorón   crybaby; weeping
llover (I)   to rain
lluvia   rain

M

macarrones (los)   macaroni
madre   mother
madrugada   early morning
mal   badly; bad; tomar a — to mind
maleta   suitcase
malo   bad, sick
mamá   mama, mom
mancha   spot, stain
mandar   to command
manecilla   hand of a clock or watch
manera   manner
manga   sleeve
maniquí (el)   fashion model, mannequin
mano (la)   hand
manopla   mitt, mitten
mantequilla   butter
mañana   tomorrow; morning

máquina machine, appliance; **— de escribir** typewriter; **— fotográfica** camera
maravilloso marvelous
marcar to mark
marcha: en — in motion; **ponerse en —** to start up; **— atrás** reverse, backup
marchar to run, to march; **—se** to leave, to go away
marisco shellfish
marrón brown
martes Tuesday
marzo March
más more, most
masticar to chew
matar to kill
materia material
máximo maximum
mayo May
mayor bigger, biggest, older, oldest
mazapán (el) marchpane
me me, myself, to (for, from) me
mediado: a —s de around the middle of
medicina medicine
médico doctor
medida measurement; **a la —** to one's measurements
medio half
mediodía (el) noon, noontime; **al —** at noontime
medir (III) to measure
Méjico Mexico
mejor better, best
mejorar to better, to get better
menor younger, youngest
menos minus, less
mente (la) mind
mentira lie; **parecer —** to seem incredible
menudo: a — often
merecer to deserve
merendar (I) to have a snack or tea around 6 p.m.
mermelada preserves, marmalade

mes (el) month
mesa table
meter to put into
metro meter = *about 39 inches*; subway
mi my
mí me
miedo fear; **tener —** to be scared
miembro member
mientras while, as long as
miércoles Wednesday
mil thousand
militar military
millón (el) million
mina mine (*ore*)
ministro minister
minuto minute
mirar to look, to look at
misa mass (*church*); **M— del Gallo** Christmas Eve Midnight Mass
mismo same, self
mitad (la) (a) half
moderno modern
modificar to modify
modismo idiom, expression
modo mode, manner
molestar to bother, to annoy
molesto annoying
momento moment
monasterio monastery
monedero coin purse
mono cute
moreno dark complexioned
morir (II) to die; **es para —se de risa** it is very funny *or* laughable
mostrar (I) to show
motor (el) motor
mover (I) to move
muchacho boy
mucho much, a lot, many
muebles (los) furniture
mujer woman
multa fine
mundo world

musarañas: pensar en las — to daydream
museo museum
muy very

N

nacer to be born
nacimiento birth, Bethlehem scene
nada nothing; **de** — you are welcome
nadie no one, nobody, anyone
naranja orange
nariz (la) nose
natural natural
náusea nausea
Navidad Nativity, Christmas
necesario necessary
necesidad necessity
necesitar to need
negativo negative
nervioso nervous
ni nor, neither, or, either
nieve (la) snow
ningun(o) no, any; no one, none
niña girl
niñera nursemaid
niño boy
no no, not
noche (la) night
Nochebuena Christmas Eve
nogal (el) walnut
nombre (el) name
nominal nominal
nos (to, for, from) us
nosotros we, us
noticia news
novecientos nine hundred
novela novel
noventa ninety
novia sweetheart, fiancée, bride
noviembre November

novio fiancé, groom
nublado cloudy
nuestro our
nueve nine
nuevo new
número number
nunca never

O

o or, either
objeto object
obra work
obrero worker
ocasión occasion, opportunity
octavo eighth
octubre October
ocupado busy
ocurrir to occur, to happen
ocho eight
ochocientos eight hundred
odio hatred
oído inner ear
oir to hear
ojalá *exclamation (See par. 76.)*
ojo eye
olor (el) odor
olvidar to forget; **—se de** to forget to; **—se (a uno)** to slip one's mind
omitir to omit
oportunidad opportunity
oposición competitive exam
oración sentence, clause, expression
oral oral
ordenar to command, to order
oro gold
os (to, for, from) you
oscuro dark
otoño fall
otro other, another

VOCABULARY

P

paciencia patience
padre father; —s parents
paella *See footnote in* **Diálogo 11.**
pagar to pay
página page
país (el) country (*nation*)
palabra word
palidecer to become pale
pálido pale
paliza beating
palma palm of the hand; **hacer —s** to clap
pan (el) bread; — **tostado** toast
pantalón de sierra (el) ski pants
pantalones (los) trousers, pants
papá papa, dad, daddy, pop
papel (el) paper
paquete (el) package
par (el) pair, couple
para to, for, in order to
parada stop
parar to stop; —se to stop, to come to a stop
parecer to seem, to look like; — **mentira** to seem incredible
pariente (el) relative
parque (el) park
parte (la) part
participio participle; — **pasivo** past participle
particular private, particular
partido party
partir to leave, to depart
pasado last, past; past
pasar to come in, to pass, to happen; ¿**Qué pasa?** What's the matter?
pascua church holiday; **Felices Pascuas** Merry Christmas
paseo walk, stroll; **dar un** — to take a stroll
pasillo hall, corridor

pasión passion
pasivo: participio — past participle
paso pass, step; — **para peatones** pedestrian crossing
pastel (el) cake
patata potato; —**s fritas** French fried potatoes
patriótico patriotic
pavo turkey
peatón (el) pedestrian
pedir (III) to ask, to ask for; — **hora** to make an appointment
pegar to beat
peinar to comb
película film, movie
pelo hair; **tomar el** — to pull one's leg
pelota ball
peluquería barber shop, beauty parlor
pena pity
pensar (I) to think, to intend
peor worse, worst
pequeño small
perder (I) to lose; — **el tiempo** to waste time
perdón (el) pardon
perdonar to pardon
permitir to permit
pero but
perro dog
persona person
personaje (el) character
perspectiva perspective
pesado heavy, overcast
pesar to weigh; **a** — **de** in spite of
pescado (caught) fish
peseta *basic Spanish coin worth about 1.7 cents*
pez (el) fish
piano piano
pie (el) foot
piedra rock, stone
piel (la) skin
pierna leg
píldora pill

pillar   to run over
pimiento   green pepper
pinchazo   puncture, flat tire
pintar   to paint
pintor   painter
pintura   painting
pipa   pipe; **fumar en —** to smoke a pipe
pirulí (el)   lollipop
pisar   to step on
piso   floor, apartment; **— bajo** ground
   floor; **casa de pisos** apartment building
pista   trail, track
pistola   gun
pizarra   blackboard
plan (el)   plan
planchar   to iron
planear   to plan
plano   plane
playa   beach
plaza   plaza, square; **— de toros** bullring
pluma   pen
plural (el)   plural
pobre   poor
poco   few, little; **por —** almost
poder (I)   to be able, can
policía (el)   policeman; **(la) —** police
político   political
polvo   dust
poner   to put, to place, to set, to turn on;
   —se to put on, to become
popular   popular
por   by, on account of, as, because of, in,
   at, for, through, along; **— la calle** down
   the street; **— poco** almost
porque   because, so that, in order that
portal (el)   entrance
posesivo   possessive
posibilidad   possibility
posible   possible
postre (el)   dessert
practicar   to practice
precio   price
precioso   precious, pretty, beautiful

preciso   necessary, precise
preferible   preferable
preferir (II)   to prefer
pregunta   question
preguntar   to question, to ask, to inquire
premio   prize, reward; **— gordo** first prize
   (*lottery*)
prenda   item, article of clothing
prensa   newspaper press
preocupar   to preoccupy, to worry
preparar   to prepare, to fix
preposición   preposition
presentar   to introduce, to present
presente (el)   present (*time or tense*)
presidente   president
prestar   to lend
pretérito   preterit
primavera   spring
primer(o)   first
primo   cousin; **materia prima** raw material
principal   main, principal
prisa   haste, rush; **de —** rapidly, quickly,
   fast; **darse —** to hurry
privado   private
probable   probable
probar (I)   to try, to taste
producto   product
profesor   teacher, professor
progresar   to progress
prohibir   to prohibit
pronombre (el)   pronoun
pronominal   pronominal
pronto   early, soon
propiedad: un profesor en —   a full professor
propina   tip
propio   own
propósito: a —   speaking of (matter already
   mentioned)
próspero   prosperous
próximo   next
público   public
pueblo   people, nation, town
puerta   door

puerto pass (mountain), port
pues then, well, for, since
puesto (el) position, job; stall, stand
puesto *past. part. of* **poner**
pulsera bracelet
pulso pulse
puntilla: de —s on tiptoes
punto point, dot
puntual on time, punctual
pupitre (el) desk
purgante (el) laxative, purgative
puro pure, just, only

Q

que that, who, which, than
qué what, which
quedar to remain, to be left; **—se** to stay behind
quejarse (de) to complain
querer (I) to want, to wish, to love
quien who, he who, she who, the one who, whoever, someone who, the person who
quién who
quince fifteen
quinientos five hundred
quinto fifth
quitar to take away; **—se** to take off
quizá perhaps

R

rabioso furious
radio (la) radio
rápido rapid; rapidly
raro strange
rato while, short while
raya line, mark
razón (la) reason; **tener —** to be right
realidad reality

rebajar to reduce, to lower
recado message
receta prescription
recibir to receive
recoger to pick up
recomendar (I) to recommend
reconocer to examine, to recognize, to acknowledge, to admit
recordar (I) to remember
Redentor Redeemer
referir (II) to tell, to refer
regalar to give (*as a gift*)
regalo gift
reina queen
reir (III) to laugh
relativo relative
religión religion
reloj (el) clock, watch
rellenar to fill out, to stuff
reparación repair; **taller de —** repair garage
repartir to distribute
repetir (III) to repeat
representar to put on
repuesto: de — spare (*tire*)
reservar to reserve
respeto respect
restorán (el) restaurant
resultado result
reunión gathering, reunion
reunirse to meet
reverso back, reverse
rey (el) king
rico rich, delicious
ridículo ridiculous
rincón (el) corner
río river
risa laugh
rival rival
robar to rob, to steal
rojo red
romance (el) ballad
romano Roman

romanticismo Romanticism (a type of literature that appeared in the first half of the 19th century)
romper to break
ropa clothes
roto *past. part. of* **romper**
rubio blond; — **jaro** red head
rueda wheel
ruido noise

S

sábado Saturday
sábana sheet (*bedding*)
saber to know
sacar to take out, to stick out
sala living room, gallery
saldo sale
salida departure, exit
salir to go out, to leave
salto jump, hop
salud (la) health
saludar to greet
salvar to save
se *equals* **le** *or* **les** *as indirect object;* (*to, for*) himself, herself, yourself, etc.; each other, to each other, one another
secreto secret
sed (la) thirst; **tener —** to be thirsty
segoviano Segovian
seguida: en — immediately
seguido straight, consecutive
seguir (III) to continue, to follow, to go on
según according to
segundo second
seguramente undoubtedly
seguro sure; **estar —** to be sure
seguros insurance
seis six

seiscientos six hundred
sello stamp
semana week
sentar (I) to seat, to fit, to suit; —**se** to sit down
sentido sense, meaning
sentir (II) to feel, to regret, to hear
señas address
señor mister, sir, gentleman
señora Mrs., lady, wife, madam
señorita Miss, young lady
septiembre September
séptimo seventh
ser to be
sereno night watchman
serio serious; **tomar en —** to take seriously
servir (III) to serve
sesenta sixty
setecientos seven hundred
setenta seventy
sexto sixth
si if, whether
sí yes; her, him, your, it, them (*when used with* **mismo**)
siempre always
sierra mountain range; **pantalón de —** ski pants
siesta afternoon nap (usually right after the noon meal)
siete seven
siglo century
siguiente following
silencioso silent
silla chair
sillón (el) armchair
símbolo symbol
simpático nice
sin without
sindicato union
singular singular
sino but, but on the contrary, but rather
sitio place, spot, space, room
sobra: de — plenty

sobrar to be more than enough
sobre on top of, about, on, around, upon, concerning; — **todo** especially
sobrepuesto placed on top of
sobrino nephew
socorro aid, help; **Casa de** — First Aid Station
sofá (el) sofa
sol (el) sun; **hacer** — to be sunny; **tomar el** — to sit in the sun, to sun oneself
solamente only
solo alone; **café** — black coffee
sólo only
soltero single, bachelor
sombra shadow
sombrero hat
sonar (I) to sound
sonrisa smile
sopa soup; — **boba** handout
sordo deaf
sorteo drawing
sospechoso suspicious
su his, her, its, your, their
subir to go up, to come up; — **a** to get on *or* in
subjuntivo subjunctive
substantivo substantive
substituir to substitute
sucio dirty
suegra mother-in-law
suegro father-in-law
suelo floor
suelto loose; **dormir a pierna suelta** to sleep like a log
sueño dream; **tener** — to be sleepy
suerte (la) luck; **tener** — to be lucky
sugerir (II) to suggest
sujetar to fasten, to hold
sujeto subject
supuesto: por — of course
surtidor (el): — **de gasolina** gas pump
sustantivo substantive
susto fright, scare

suyo your, his, her, its, their, of his, of hers, of theirs

T

tacañería stinginess
tal such; **¿Qué** —? How are you?
tal vez perhaps
talento talent
taller (el) workshop; — **de reparaciones** repair garage
también also, too
tambor (el) drum
tampoco either, neither, also
tan so, as
tanto as much, so much, as many, so many
tapia wall, fence; **sordo como una** — stone deaf
tardanza delay, tardiness
tardar to delay, to take (time)
tarde (la) afternoon
tarde late
tarjeta card
taxi cab, taxi
taxista cabdriver
taza cup
te (to, for, from) you
teatro theater; **escribir** — to write dramatic works
tejano Texan
Tejas Texas
tela cloth
telediario television newscast
telefonear to telephone
Telefónica Telephone Building
telefonista telephone operator
teléfono telephone
telegrama (el) telegram
telesilla (el) cablechair
televisión television
televisor (el) television set

telón (el)   stage curtain
tema (el)   theme, topic, matter
temblar (I)   to tremble
temer(se)   to fear, to be afraid
tener   to have; — que to have to, must
teniente   lieutenant
tenis (el)   tennis
tensión   blood pressure
tercer(o)   third
terminar   to finish
termómetro   thermometer
terreno   terrain, land
ti   you
tiempo   time, tense, weather; a — on time
tienda   store
timbre (el)   bell
tinte (el)   cleaners
tirano   tyrant
tirar   to throw, to throw away, to shoot,
   to spill; — de to pull
tirón (el): de un — in a row or stretch
tobillo   ankle
tocadiscos (el)   record player, phonograph
tocar   to play (an instrument), to ring (a
   bell), to blow (a horn); — a uno to win
todo   all, every
tolerar   to tolerate
tomar   to take
tomate (el)   tomato
tontería   foolish remark or act
tonto   foolish, stupid, silly; fool
torcer (I)   to twist
torear   to fight bulls
torero   bullfighter
toro   bull; los —s bulls, bullfights
torpe   clumsy
trabajar   to work
trabajo   work
traducir   to translate
traer   to bring
trágico   tragic
traje (el)   suit, gown
tranquilo   quiet, tranquil

tranvía (el)   streetcar
trapero   ragman
tratar   to treat; — de to try
trece   thirteen
treinta   thirty
tren (el)   train
tres   three
trescientos   three hundred
triste   sad
trolebús (el)   trolley bus
tropezar (I)   to stumble
tú   you
turista   tourist
turrón (el)   almond nougat
tuyo   your, of you

U

último   last (*in a series*)
un(o)   a, an, one
único   only, sole, unique
unir   to unite; —se to join
universidad   university
universitario   *adj.* university
unos   some, several, a few
urgencia: cartero de — special delivery
   mailman
usar   to use
usted   you
útil   useful
uva   grape

V

vaca   cow
vacación   one day of vacation
vacaciones (las)   vacation
vacante (la)   vacancy, vacant position or
   job
vacío   empty
valentía   courage
valer   to be worth
valiente   courageous

VOCABULARY

valioso valuable
variar to change, to vary
varios various, several
vaso drinking glass
vecindad neighborhood
vecino neighbor
veinte twenty
velocidad speed
vencer to conquer, to win
vendar to bandage
vender to sell
¡Venga! Come on!
venir to come; — **bien** to be suitable, to do
ventaja advantage
ventana window
ventanilla ticket window
ver to see
verano summer
verbal verbal
verbo verb
verdad truth; **¿De** —? Really?
verdadero true, real
verde green
verdura vegetable
verso verse
vestido dress
vestir (III) to dress; —**se** to get dressed
vez (la) time (*occasion*)
viajar to travel
viaje (el) trip
vida life
viejo old; **de** — used, secondhand
viento wind
viernes Friday
villancico Christmas carol

vino wine
violento violent
visitar to visit
vista sight, view
visto *past. part. of* **ver**
¡Viva! Hurrah!
vivir to live, to dwell
vocabulario vocabulary
volante (el) steering wheel
voluntario voluntary
volver (I) to come back, to return; —**se** to become
vosotros you
votar to vote
voz (la) voice
vuelta turn, change (*money*); **dar la** — to turn
vuelto *past. part. of* **volver**
vuestro yours

Y

y and
ya already, now; — **no** no longer, any more
yo I

Z

zapato shoe
Zulú Zulu
zumbar to ring, buzz
zumo juice

INDEX

Spanish words are in boldface, and English translations are in italics. The key to the reference numbers is illustrated by these three examples:

25 (Section 25 in **LENGUA**)
D-6 (**Diálogo 6**, reference **Modismos y Vocabulario Adicional**)
A-2 (**Addendum**, section 2)